The Laughter Is on My Side

The Laughter Is on My Side

An Imaginative Introduction
to Kierkegaard

edited by

Roger Poole and Henrik Stangerup

Preface and headnotes by Roger Poole

Princeton University Press · Princeton, New Jersey

First published in the United Kingdom by Fourth Estate
Published by Princeton University Press,
41 William Street, Princeton, New Jersey 08540

Library of Congress Cataloging-in-Publication Data

Kierkegaard, Søren, 1813-1855.
   [Dansemesteren. English]
   The laughter is on my side: an imaginative introduction to
Kierkegaard/edited by Roger Poole and Henrik Stangerup: preface
and headnotes by Roger Poole
      p.   cm.
   Translation of: Dansemesteren.
   Bibliography: p.
   ISBN 0-691-07361-9   ISBN 0-691-02058-2 (pbk.)
   1. Meditations. I. Poole, Roger, 1939- .
   II. Stangerup. Henrik, 1937- .
   III. Title.
BV4836.K4813   1989
198' .9-dc20   83-3943

There is a man whom it is impossible to omit in any account of Denmark, but whose place it might be more difficult to fix; I mean Søren Kierkegaard. But as his works have, at all events for the most part, a religious tendency, he may find a place among the theologians. He is a philosophical Christian writer, evermore dwelling, one might almost say harping, on the theme of the human heart. There is no Danish writer more in earnest than he, yet there is no one in whose way stand more things to prevent his becoming popular. He writes at times with an unearthly beauty, but too often with an exaggerated display of logic that disgusts the public. All very well, if he were not a popular author, but it is for this he intends himself.

I have received the highest delight from some of his books. But no one of them could I read with pleasure all through. His "Works of Love" has, I suppose, been the most popular, or, perhaps, his Either/Or, a very singular book. A little thing published during my stay, gave me much pleasure, Sickness unto Death.

Kierkegaard's habits of life are singular enough to lend a (perhaps false) interest to his proceedings. He goes into no company, and sees nobody in his own house, which answers all the ends of an invisible dwelling; I could never learn that anyone had been inside of it. Yet his one great study is human nature; no one knows more people than he. The fact is he walks about town all day, and generally in some person's company; only in the evening does he write and read. When walking, he is very communicative, and at the same time manages to draw everything out of his companion that is likely to be profitable to himself.

I do not know him. I saw him almost daily in the streets, and when he was alone I often felt much inclined to accost him, but never put it into execution. I was told his 'talk' was very fine. Could I have enjoyed it, without the feeling that I was myself being mercilessly pumped and sifted, I should have liked very much.

Andrew Hamilton, *Sixteen Months in the Danish Isles* (1852)

Table of Contents

Preface

On the Danish island of Møn, at the cultural centre called Marienborg, with Mozart and Monteverdi on the record player, Henrik Stangerup and I put together the following selection of texts from the great Danish writer Søren Kierkegaard. It was the summer of 1983.

Marienborg is a country estate, comprising large grounds planted with trees from all over the world, and a farm. The estate surrounds a magnificent château in the Italian style, which dates from the early nineteenth century. The château, painted in Italian tints of ochre and sienna, was empty. But the estate had been left by Count Peter Moltke, its last owner, to the nation as a centre for artistic work, work that might demand silence, solitude and concentration. The vast grounds around the house were deserted all through the summer days; the empty château stared down over them. In various cottages and outhouses on the estate, however, work went on. In the cool of the evening, people would gather from various quarters of the estate for drinks and conversation.

Apart from a small lake, the most attractive feature of the estate was its enormous range of trees. These trees had been repatriated from all over the world by various travelling Moltkes. One, in particular, stood out. It was a huge balsam poplar which, in the late part of August, produced an immense and unusual quantity of sweet-smelling blossom. The bees, buzzing round it for pollen all through the hot summer days, miscalculated what they could gather. They fell in their thousands to the ground, where they lay helpless while they were eviscerated by wasps. It was an uncanny event, which seemed to symbolize the sense of a 'last summer'. Indeed, the wasps were but too prophetic. In the spring following that last summer, Peter Moltke's château was knocked flat by lead ball and bulldozer, and shovelled into a vast hole in the ground. Because of some legal technicality, and in spite of four appeals for a reprieve, Danish bureaucracy struck. The demolition men moved in. This enclave of culture disappeared for ever.

But it was there at Marienborg, that last summer of 1983, that Henrik Stangerup and I put together a text that had, as its first aim, to introduce the work of Kierkegaard to his countrymen in a new and pleasurable guise. In this beautiful and spacious setting of

Marienborg, surrounded by music, we cut and spliced this work together, and it is in the hope that something of this mood can be passed on to English and American readers that this volume is now offered.

This selection, then, was originally constructed with a Danish readership in mind, and it duly appeared in Danish in 1985. It is strange, but even today the Danes will not read Kierkegaard. They still nurse their old resentment against a man who, although he died in 1855, irritates them almost as much dead as alive. Alive, Kierkegaard emphasized everything the Danes most mistrust, and then attacked every form of State and Church institution. And now, all through the twentieth century, the Danes have to put up with an uninterrupted string of foreigners, all of whom have come on a pilgrimage to the land of Søren Kierkegaard. Americans, Japanese, Germans, Italians, Britons; scholars, researchers, writers, students – and still they come, raking around in the bookshops, asking questions about Søren Kierkegaard, endlessly interested in *him*. For a people which deeply disapproves of Kierkegaard and all his works, this is really too much.

The picture the Danes retain of Kierkegaard is one built up not on a first-hand knowledge of the texts, but aggregated from the cartoons of the 1850s, and from a general tradition of dislike and disapproval. The Danes are (they will cheerfully assert it themselves) materialists. Kierkegaard was an idealist, a believer in matters of the spirit. The Danes are law-abiding, they respect their authorities and their political institutions. Kierkegaard treated them as shams, with contempt. The Danes like a peaceful, quiet life, with things agreed, understood and traditional. Kierkegaard argued, in book after book, for the exceptional, the individual and the personally authentic. The Danes enjoy the pleasures of the flesh. Kierkegaard renounced all these pleasures of what he called 'the universal' for the austere world of self-denial and celibacy. The Danes, although they have a State Church, and confirm all their children, do not on the whole believe in God, and their confirmation is the last time they see a church until they arrive there feet-first for their funeral. Kierkegaard believed in God, and indeed believed with a passion and inwardness that the Danes find alienating.

The Danes are democrats, left of centre, socialists and believers in the welfare state. Kierkegaard was Conservative by temperament (even though he had scant respect for the King himself) and regarded the uprisings of 1848 with horror, seeing in the manifestations of popular solidarity the onset of a 'blood-dimmed tide'. The Danes believe in public correctness, form, style and attitude – all of which could be said to add up to consistent conformism. Kierkegaard threw all social pacts and agreements to the winds, and emphasized the absolute priority of the category of 'the individual'. The Danes see themselves as constrained by law. Kierkegaard affirmed that 'there are exceptions' to the law, there are individuals whose inner convictions mean they have to transcend or disregard the law. The Danes believe in academic prestige. Kierkegaard poured contempt on what he called *Privat Docents* – that is, university lecturers, whom he saw simply as failed 'individuals'. The Danes always follow European fashion in ideas, and hence in the 1840s they were trying to keep up with Hegelianism. Kierkegaard thought Hegel a charlatan and the Danish Hegelians, such as J.L. Heiberg and Bishop Martensen, ridiculous or contemptible, or both.

Not much common ground, then, between Kierkegaard and the Danes, either then or now. It therefore follows that, with so many *a priori* ideas about what Kierkegaard is like, the Danes somehow rarely get around to reading him. Like a few passages of the Bible, certain 'famous' texts of Kierkegaard (like the famous 'eulogy of the Danish language' which is in fact a bitter expostulation about linguistic provincialism) get read in school, and then, like the Bible, are never read again. A cheap edition in twenty volumes was published by Gyldendal in the early 1960s, and this can often be seen remaindered on the back shelves of the second-hand bookstores in Fiolstraede. The typical bookshelf of a Danish home will contain a long row of Danish classics, all in identical plastic bindings, and this will, of course, include a token volume or two of Kierkegaard; but these volumes are never read, any more than the Holberg and Oehlenschläger which rub shoulders with them. 'The Golden Age' in literature is something every Dane is proud of, but the texts of which he never consults. Kierkegaard, and all his works, is in effect an unread author in Denmark.

It was against this situation that Henrik Stangerup and I set our faces in 1983. Why not put together a collection of some of the best texts of Kierkegaard – not the heavy, 'Hegelianized', incomprehensible texts, but the early, lighter, witty ones of the early 1840s, when Kierkegaard was a rich young man about town, with a new doctorate under his arm, and engaged to a lovely girl called Regine Olsen? Might not Danes take to their great writer if he were presented to them anew? What if we even modernized the spelling (for nineteenth-century Danish is far more antique to the eye than nineteenth-century English is)? It was worth a try.

Henrik and I shared two basic motives. These had begun to form as long ago as 1978, when Henrik Stangerup was working as a journalist in Paris, and we used to go for long walks around that city discussing literature and politics. I had written a research thesis on Kierkegaard's 'indirect communication' years before, at a time when Kierkegaard was little more than a name in England. But the remorselessly positivist climate of philosophical discussion in England had led me to pursue other themes, and the fact that we recurred again and again to Kierkegaard in our Paris walks came as something of a surprise to both of us. Henrik, though a novelist, had just returned from making a film in Brazil based on Holberg's *Erasmus Montanus*. The contact with Brazil had started in his mind that chain of reflection which was to culminate in his immensely successful novel *The Road to Lagoa Santa* (1981).

The Road to Lagoa Santa tells the story of Peter Wilhelm Lund, to whom Kierkegaard was related by marriage, a naturalist and paleontologist whose discoveries in Brazil in the first half of the nineteenth century had anticipated some of Darwin's. The young Søren Kierkegaard had been so awed by the scientific reputation of P.W. Lund that he even briefly considered taking up a scientific career (see Part III, Text 3 in the present volume). Shattered by what he had discovered, P.W. Lund retired to a remote area of Brazil, and lived as a recluse. His presence and reputation were wrapped in mystery. Lund and Kierkegaard, separated by the Atlantic Ocean, swapped roles in intellectual space. Whereas Lund nearly tempted the young Kierkegaard into a scientific career, the elder Lund discontinued his, influenced (amongst other things) by the philosophy of Søren Kierkegaard.

The first basic motive Henrik and I began to share, then, was a desire to present Kierkegaard as a writer. Did the Danes know just how well Kierkegaard could actually write? And the second basic motive sprang from the first. In our walks around Paris, it was

Kierkegaard the writer of genius on matters political who began to intrigue us. The Danes have always believed that Kierkegaard had nothing to say on politics. But we began to recur to certain texts of Kierkegaard which proved the opposite, especially the text called *The Present Age* (Part IV, Text 5). Henrik's flat was in the rue Bassano, and our walks led us again and again past the building used by the Gestapo as a headquarters during the occupation of Paris. But Kierkegaard had foreseen all this. He had seen forward, through some strange intersection of the time-tunnels, to the totalitarianisms of our twentieth century – indeed, the very title *The Present Age* (*Nutiden* in Danish) had, it seemed to us, a quite uncanny doubled valency. From what premises and assumptions, then, had Kierkegaard been able to make such accurate predictions?

Once again, Kierkegaard took his place in a literary nexus: George Orwell's *1984*, of course; but what about Pasternak and Akhmatova? What about Solzhenitsyn's *Gulag Archipelago* (subtitled as it is *An Experiment in Literary Investigation*)? Yet didn't Kierkegaard also have something of the panache of Henry Miller? Didn't he operate his textual subterfuges in ways which Derrida had only recently begun to present and to analyse? Our two basic motives – to present Kierkegaard first as a writer, and then as a writer who had something to say on politics – began to come together. Obviously we had to present Kierkegaard anew.

Søren Kierkegaard is a late arrival upon the literary and philosophical scene in England, and relatively recent in America. When he died in 1855, he descended into an obscurity that was only partly lessened by borrowings from him by Karl Jaspers, Martin Heidegger, Dietrich Bonhoeffer, Jean-Paul Sartre and others. The fact of the language barrier was important, and it is amazing that a man who read German easily, and whose culture was in every sense international, never learnt to speak or write in French, German or English. It would have lessened his tremendous sense of linguistic and philosophical isolation. But he wrote on ceaselessly in Danish, a language with (then) only some 1.3 million speakers, of whom very few indeed were willing to read Kierkegaard sympathetically.

Søren Aabye Kierkegaard was born in 1813, the seventh and last child of a rich hosier from the heaths of Jutland. Michael Pedersen Kierkegaard had not always, however, been a rich man. As a child, he was miserably poor and is always remembered for having cursed God on the heaths of Jutland because he was so hungry and so cold. The fear that he had actually incensed God against him on this occasion never left him.

Michael Pedersen Kierkegaard married Søren's mother, Ane Lund, rather rapidly after the death of his first wife, Kirstine Røyen. One of the curious facts about Søren Kierkegaard's huge Journal, which runs to twenty-five printed volumes, is that in it he never once mentions his mother. This must surely, in a man who loved to consider every aspect of his own relationship with his father, reflect to some extent the way his mother was treated by his father.

A precocious child, dry, arrogant and witty, Søren Kierkegaard went to a distinguished Copenhagen school. Miserable and contemptuous of his fellows, he was a solitary youngster. His best friend was – perhaps – his father. They used to go on long walks together, and talk about everything they saw – but the curious fact about these walks was that the pair never left the sitting-room of the house in Nytorv. Everything they discussed was imaginary.

Søren's father was a perverse thinker. Ever since the stock exchange crash of 1813 (the very same year that Søren was born) when he became a rich man, he had never ceased to believe that God was planning an evil revenge for that childish curse from the heath. The richer and more prosperous he grew, the more suspicious Michael Pedersen Kierkegaard became of God's intentions. He was sure that the Ancient of Days was going to get his revenge, somehow.

And in 1832, God struck. The old man had been quite right. His daughter Nicoline Christine died in childbirth at the age of thirty-three. In 1833, his son Niels Andreas died, at the age of twenty-four. In 1834, Ane Lund, his second wife and mother of all his children, also died. Only six months later, in December 1834, his daughter Petrea Severine died in childbirth at the age of thirty-three, just as her sister had done two years before.

After these two calamitous years, there were only two children left: Peter Christian and Søren. The house must have been desolate. Everyone was convinced that Michael Pedersen had been right all along: God had indeed finally punished him for his sin in cursing Him upon the heath.

When his mother died, Søren Kierkegaard was twenty-one. His relationship with his father had always been very intense. In 1835, Søren took a holiday at a seaside resort in northern Sjælland, at Gilleleje. Here he ruminated on what sort of career he wanted for himself. He wrote a long and detailed letter to Peter Wilhelm Lund, in which, as he debated inwardly the choices which confronted him, the major categories of his existential philosophy can be clearly seen emerging.

Then there occurs a famous event about which we can tell nothing for sure. In a Journal entry dating from 1838, Kierkegaard, looking back to a period somewhat earlier, refers to 'the great earthquake': 'Then it was that the great earthquake occurred, the terrible revolution which suddenly forced upon me a new and infallible law of interpretation of all the facts. Then I suspected that my father's great age was not a divine blessing but rather a curse . . . There must be a guilt upon the whole family, the punishment of God must be upon it; it was to disappear, wiped out by the powerful hand of God.' Speculation has never ceased as to what this shattering event was, but certainly Kierkegaard was never the same again. He began to suspect an evil destiny, an evil inheritance in the family strain. Michael Pedersen Kierkegaard himself died in August 1838, and, urged on by bad conscience, Søren wrote up and submitted his thesis for the Magister Artium degree, which was published as *The Concept of Irony, with constant reference to Socrates* in September 1841. He had found a theme, and a mentor, sufficient for the whole course of his writing. Nothing in the published books, and indeed nothing in the privacy of the Journal, can be read without an eye to the possibility of irony. Irony was his mask and his rapier. The 'constant reference to Socrates' lasted a lifetime.

The only event in his life which he himself did not take ironically but with highest seriousness was his engagement to Regine Olsen, an engagement that was doomed to be broken off with great suffering on both sides. Why Søren, knowing himself and suspecting what he did about the evil inheritance of the family, ever allowed himself to actually get into the situation is quite unclear. It seems, from his own accounts in the Journal, to have been an impulse which, within a day or two, he bitterly regretted. Nevertheless, in September 1840 he asked Regine to marry him; and in

October 1841 he broke off the engagement and fled to Berlin. Although he took a great quantity of manuscripts with him, it was there that he put together, at high speed and under immense strain, the book we know as *Either/Or*. It was published in February 1843, and must rate as the longest love letter on record. Nevertheless, Regine could not – or did not – understand it, and got engaged to someone else. From the moment of these two catastrophic shocks to his love affair, Kierkegaard became a walking mystery in the streets of Copenhagen.

Who was he? Why had he broken his engagement? What was this massive book *about*? The questions began to pullulate. Loving the sensation he had caused in what he always regarded as a boring provincial town, he lived the part with a vengeance. He loved increasing mysteries and hated solving them. So he put himself seriously to the task of creating the mystery of the peripatetic philosopher.

He began to publish book after book, all written in the same high-flown vein, clotted with Hegelian terminology and Socratic jokes, and all under pseudonyms. Over the years, the pseudonyms grew into quite a crew. After Victor Eremita, who was the official 'editor' of *Either/Or*, Johannes de Silentio published *Fear and Trembling* and Constantine Constantius brought out *Repetition*. This was in 1843, the same year as the massive *Either/Or*, and just to make sure that no one missed the point these two books were published on the same day, 16 October. Not only that, but on the same day again appeared *Three Edifying Discourses*, published in his own name. Three books on a single day, and each by a different 'author', and all by Søren Kierkegaard.

In 1844, Johannes Climacus published *Philosophical Fragments*, and only four days later – not to be outdone – Vigilius Haufniensis brought out *The Concept of Dread*. Not to be outdone by *him*, Nicolas Notabene brought out, on the same day, 17 June, *Prefaces*. In April 1845, Hilarius Bookbinder published his *Stages on Life's Way*. In February 1846, Johannes Climacus silenced them by crushing them all under an enormous *Concluding Unscientific Postscript to the Philosophical Fragments*. Much longer than the work to which it purported to be a Postscript, this book was also in no sense unscientific and far from concluding.

There was in fact a doubled pair of dialectics going on during this first period of literary production. Side by side with the pseudonymous books, Kierkegaard was publishing volume after volume of *Edifying Discourses*, all dedicated to the memory of his father. The contrast between the books published pseudonymously and those published under his own name was arranged to be as glaring as possible. The pseudonyms write with curious erudition and vastly academic humour, as if they were all present at some sort of intellectual beheading, while the *Edifying Discourses* are written in a kind of pietistic underfelt. The pseudonyms attack abstract problems at the abstract level, while the *Discourses* are simple, practical and applied. The pseudonyms seem to have no other pressures on their time, while the *Discourses* are conscious of each passing minute. The pseudonyms adopt an adversarial stance, while the writer of the *Discourses* seems positively eager to be helpful.

This dialectic between the two sorts of writing was itself counterpointed by a dialectic between the works as such, and the existential text of the philosopher's walks and presence in the town. It is hardly an extension of the Kierkegaardian meaning to suggest that the books were the written text, while the promenades were the existential or fleshly text set over against them. The books were in a sense the thesis, the body the antithesis. The ramparts round the town at this period were still the old circumvallations which had once defended Copenhagen from the sea, and, lined with trees and visited always by a fresh wind, they provided an ideal stroll for the peripatetic philosopher. Copenhagen was made into a new Academy. The narrow streets and squares, the cobbled quays of the old canals, the restaurants and the theatre too, were all ideal settings for an existential theatre which aimed to bring a wandering and dispersed public consciousness to bear on the published work. It was, no doubt, an innocent enough ploy, though crafty. The public was certainly aware of a super-tensile relationship between the published and the 'lived' texts, even if they could not give an exact value to the relationship itself.

Never was this technique of setting text against text more useful than when Kierkegaard was having to negotiate those passages in his life in which he was not in complete control of the overall effect. One such instance was his relationship with Regine Olsen after the breaking of the engagement and the return to Copenhagen from Berlin.

As part of his intention – misguided no doubt in principle and hopeless of success in practice – to convince Regine Olsen that she was better off without him, and that he was, in breaking off so brutally, little better than his own 'Seducer', he brought out *Either/Or*, containing its famous 'Seducer's Diary'. Nevertheless, on hearing of Regine's new engagement in July 1843, he could not restrain himself from bitterly upbraiding her for her faithlessness in sections of *Repetition* and *Fear and Trembling*. To offset this effect of doubled faithlessness, he began to publish the *Edifying Discourses*, all dedicated to the memory of his tyrannical old father, and thus creating an impression of filial devotion and fundamental reliability.

Although the two sets of books now began to appear in an uninterrupted succession, Kierkegaard was still careful to keep up his daily extended walks round the town and to maintain the impression that he had time on his hands and was not doing any strenuous work. He delighted to speak to all and sundry as he circulated – his 'people-bath' as he called it – while at the same time keeping himself unknowably apart. As the visiting Scotsman Andrew Hamilton observed, Kierkegaard was known as the best conversationalist in town, and yet no one was ever admitted to his private apartments. His faithful manservant Anders had instructions to turn everyone away. By the play of absence and presence, then, a further dialectic was brought into being – over against the dialectic between written and 'lived' texts. The entire ensemble of dialectics adds up to a very complex notion of communication, and to what might be called a 'super-existential text' itself.

The philosophical work, strictly so conceived, ended up in the massive *Concluding Unscientific Postscript to the Philosophical Fragments*. In it, the central structures of a philosophy of subjectivity are beautifully and economically laid out. The book brings to a satisfying conclusion the various debates that the pseudonyms had been having among themselves, and in 'A First and Last Declaration' at the end of the book, Kierkegaard acknowledges authorship of all the books he had published pseudonymously. The authorship was complete.

But then disaster struck. P.L. Møller, thought to be the model for Johannes the Seducer in *Stages on Life's Way*, published an extremely penetrating and also hurtful account of Kierkegaard's book in *Gaea* in December 1845. His critique was so well directed that Kierkegaard, stung, exposed P.L. Møller as the editor of a low political rag called *The Corsair*. By doing so, he torpedoed Møller's chances of an academic chair that he particularly wanted. Møller and his friend Meier Goldschmidt riposted by employing a carica-turist, Klaestrup, to portray Kierkegaard as he least wanted to see himself: in terms of his clothes, his hat, his umbrella, and above all his slightly curved spine. Kierkegaard was infuriated. But relent-lessly the caricatures kept on appearing in *The Corsair* for a year and more. Kierkegaard was forced to give up the walks round town which he so much enjoyed; his easy contact with ordinary people in the street was cut off; and even trips into the country were not without danger – even of physical molestation (see Epigraph to Part IV in the present volume).

In this moment of exposure and loneliness, Kierkegaard expected some support from those who knew him; a bit of help from the influential Heiberg circle would not have come amiss. But absolutely no one stepped into the breach on Kierkegaard's behalf. He discovered what it really cost to be 'that individual' – the central category of his own philosophy. But, forced back against the wall as he was, he developed category after category of analysis of what we can now see is a typically 'modern' situation: when the press attacks, yet no one in particular seems to be responsible for the attack.

Kierkegaard was forced to analyse the phenomenon of 'the public' as such, and how the press was the impersonal tool of the public, responsible to no one but keen on sales and profits. This led him to explore the profit motive – which itself overrides ethical considerations altogether. Above all, he saw how the press, repre-senting the public, is impersonal: there is no one doing the hurting, therefore no one is getting hurt.

Into a text of 1847, a review of a novel of Fru Gyllembourg called *Two Ages*, Kierkegaard poured all the new insight gathered from bitter personal experience (see Part IV, Text 5). His analysis of 'The Present Age' is faultless, and focuses on forms of conscious-ness, publicity and oppression that would not become apparent, so clearly as he saw them, for another century. The actual debate had to go underground. Kierkegaard's own reactions to the struggle with press and public went into his Journal. Volume XIII in the Princeton edition of *Kierkegaard's Writings*, entitled *The Corsair Affair* (1982), is a precious source-book for a battle that was fought mainly in private.

Philosophically, however, the authorship was over. Various works in the other manner appeared – *Works of Love* in 1847; *The Sickness unto Death* in 1849; *Training in Christianity* in 1850. The only exception was a little tribute to the actress Johanne Luise Heiberg, *The Crisis and a Crisis in the Life of an Actress* (see Part II, Text 8) which appeared serially in a newspaper in July 1848. It contained all the intelligence and the longing for an affectionate response which had characterised his earlier books, but it was like that one final catherine wheel which goes off by chance after the main display is over, and it was succeeded by darkness.

'The silent years' they are called in the literature – the years 1850–54. The walks had been made impossible, the loneliness was entire. But on 30 January 1854, Bishop Mynster died. He had been a personal friend and ally of Kierkegaard's father, and it was out of respect for his father's memory that Kierkegaard had never given expression to what he thought of the old bishop – namely that he was a time-serving, self-interested, shuffling servant of the State.

It fell to Kierkegaard's old lecturer on Hegel, Professor Martensen, to give one of the public addresses, 'a speech of remembrance it might be called for the reason that it brought to Professor Martensen's remembrance the vacant Episcopal See'. According to Martensen, Mynster had been 'one of the genuine witnesses to the truth' and was introduced 'into the holy chain of witnesses to the truth which stretches through the ages from the days of the Apostles'.

This was all it needed. Kierkegaard threw himself into a final onslaught on official hypocrisy and humbug, and even founded his own journal, *The Instant*, to carry on his campaign. Martensen was the perfect target: he represented the Establishment, the *status quo*, the State Church, and something very like the complete Flaubertian Encyclopaedia of Received Ideas.

But the Copenhagen public had learnt a decade earlier that it could win by taking no action at all. A second time, that public decided to adopt this tactic. It was silent, unresponsive. It did not see the issues, and it would not have felt moved to self-defence even if it had. Kierkegaard was defeated only because there was no enemy to fight.

'The Instant', according to Kierkegaard's late categorization, is the moment when eternity crosses time, the moment of vital decision, the moment when one has finally to decide which side to fight on. Never had Kierkegaard written so well as he did in *The Instant*. With all the brilliance and panache of a past master in the art of symbol, allegory, metaphor and parable, he castigated the poverty of an age of public mediocrity, passionlessness, received opinion leading to herd behaviour. Hostility was thick in the air. But there was, of course, no reasoned reply.

What reply could there be? Kierkegaard was obviously right in a way that Copenhagen was not prepared to recognize, and Copenhagen was also obviously right in a way which Kierkegaard was not prepared to parley with. It was a battle of losers. Kierkegaard collapsed in the street as the last number of *The Instant* lay on his desk ready for publication, and he was carried off to the hospital in Bredgade to die. Copenhagen, out of all patience with the critique it had had to endure, lost its greatest citizen and son, and never realized the quality of its loss. It does not to this day.

Kierkegaard as writer, then, and Kierkegaard as political thinker: the selection of texts to show Kierkegaard at his aesthetic best was not hard, once all didactic purpose had been dropped. This selection of texts is not meant to propose some coherent line of thought, since the texts have been disposed to give maximum contrast. However, each text could be used to lead the curious reader into the labyrinth of Kierkegaardian reflection. A first move could take the form of reading through one of the most remarkable works of synthesis and empathetic reconstruction ever created, Alexander Dru's *The Journals of Kierkegaard 1834–1854* (Oxford University Press, 1938). Anyone who can resist the mysteries of that volume can resist Kierkegaard.

The first part of this volume is entitled 'The Fork' after a nickname Søren had at school – something sharp, pointed and pronged which can be used for vigorous prodding. Even at school, Søren Kierkegaard had the ability to impose Socratic self-questioning upon his unwilling small colleagues, and they returned the compliment by also calling him Søren Sock, a reference to the trade of his father – lucrative but undistinguished. This dialectic between fork and sock, between the sharp and the woolly, might stand as a small metonymy for the whole of Kierkegaard's effort to bring his countrymen to 'awareness'. It proved a task beyond his powers.

'The Fork' contains texts which reflect Kierkegaard's early search for an idea 'for which I can live and die', the beginnings of the search for existential authenticity which was to prove so powerful a concept in his later writing, and in his European influence in the twentieth century. It contains references to his semi-hilarious engagement with the ruling Hegelianism of the time, an engagement which took the form of continuing to insist that outer appearance and inner reality were *not* one and the same. It was semi-hilarious because Kierkegaard could never quite take Hegel seriously. He suffered under the lecturing technique at the university of one Hans Lassen Martensen, who later rose to be Bishop of Sealand. Martensen had the infuriating habit of saying in lectures that Hegelian thought was about to 'go further'. To the young Kierkegaard, it seemed as if the prime necessity was to go back and start again from some premises that one could understand. But for the Hegelianism of the time, this was an unnecessary and over-punctilious exercise.

The second part, 'Women', has a double valency. What were 'women' for Kierkegaard? From the fact that he never once mentions his mother in all his writing, much can be deduced. His mother must be the presiding presence, the central lack, the origin. But she functions as an absence in the writing, the text which never gets written. Regine Olsen obsessed him from the moment he first saw her. His relation to her, erotic yet coldly intellectual, passionate yet withdrawn, is the existential point around which the huge dialectical web of texts is slowly gathered. P.L. Møller, the authentic 'Don Juan' who doubtless provided material for the Seducer in *Either/Or* and *Stages on Life's Way* and who forms the central figure in Henrik Stangerup's novel *The Seducer: It is hard to die in Dieppe*, formed a kind of possibility which Kierkegaard examines in depth again and again. But *The Seducer's Diary* is actually a masterwork of sadism, crueller than de Sade because the infliction of pain takes place in virtual space only. Where Møller went, Kierkegaard could not follow. The phenomenology of the body in Kierkegaard's case is quite fascinating.

So the three speeches selected from *The Banquet* represent outer points of reference, not existential realities. None of the three speeches reproduces authentic Kierkegaardian traces; but then, all are pseudonymous anyway. Kierkegaard was writing under the influence of the German Romantic Ironists. Where Friedrich Schlegel's *Lucinde* is, there is Kierkegaard.

But with the text on Judge Wilhelm, sitting having breakfast in the garden in the freshness of the early morning, we can trace one point of desire in Kierkegaard: the ethical stability of a happy marriage. And with the text on Johanne Luise Heiberg, we can trace the other: the possibility, ever more unlikely in fact but ever more delicious in interiority, of a 'repetition' with one wife in particular, Regine Olsen/Schlegel. (The literary joke of the naming is complex, yet not entirely without its own ironic significance.)

The third part, 'The Midnight Hour', gathers together the existential texts. Here the keynote is authenticity – authenticity for which one is personally responsible, and which no one else can either relieve or remove. This authenticity is arrived at through suffering, and at the hour when all must unmask. Later writers like Heidegger and Sartre have cunningly drained off much of Kierkegaard's theory, for the greater part without acknowledgement, and through their re-writings, *Either/Or*, *Fear and Trembling* and *The Concept of Anxiety* have become twentieth-century texts. Even the idea of the Absurd, so central to the twentieth century, is Kierkegaard's. Like Flaubert, with whom he has much in common, Kierkegaard has had more influence in the twentieth than in his own century.

In the fourth part, '1848:1984', which operates an uneasy oscillation between the date of European revolution and a date towards which we are in many senses still tending, Kierkegaard emerges again as a thinker whose wisdom is ahead of us, not behind. The nightmare of total bureaucratic control, and the impersonal and ruthless manipulation of vast international financial forces, are only the updated forms of those forces which Kierkegaard knew and named. The rights of 'that individual' have never been more imperilled, not only in those countries where 'human rights' are daily put in doubt, but also in developed countries where rights scarcely exist without the economic power to enforce their recognition. It may often seem as if there is no contemporary thinker who can help oppose the malign drift towards '1984'. But the Kierkegaardian texts are rich in modes of resistance.

Roger Poole, 1989

PART ONE

The Fork

1836

I have just returned from a party of which I was the life and soul; wit poured from my lips, everyone laughed and admired me – but I went away – and the dash should be as long as the earth's orbit ――――――――――
――――――――――――――――――
―――――――――――― and wanted to shoot myself.

1. Creating difficulties everywhere

It is now about four years ago that I got the notion of wanting to try my luck as an author. I remember it quite clearly; it was on a Sunday, yes, that's it, a Sunday afternoon. I was seated as usual, out-of-doors at the café in the Frederiksberg Garden, that wonderful garden which for the child was fairyland, where the King dwelt with his Queen, that delightful garden which for the youth was his happy diversion in the joyful merriment of the people, where now for the man of riper years there is such a homely feeling of sad exaltation above the world and all that is of the world, where even the envied glory of the royal dignity has faded to what it is indeed out there, a queen's remembrance of her deceased lord. There I sat as usual and smoked my cigar. Unfortunately, the only resemblance I have been able to discover between the beginning of my bit of philosophic effort and the miraculous beginning of that poetical hero is the fact that it was in a public resort. For the rest there is no resemblance whatever, and notwithstanding I am the author of the *Fragments*, I am so insignificant that I stand outside of literature, have not even contributed to increase literature on the subscription plan, nor can with truth affirm that I occupy an important place in it.

  I had been a student for half a score of years. Although never lazy, all my activity nevertheless was like a glittering inactivity, a kind of occupation for which I still have a great partiality, and for which perhaps I even have a little genius. I read much, spent the remainder of the day idling and thinking, or thinking and idling, but that was all it came to; the earliest sproutings of my productivity barely sufficed for my daily use and were consumed in their first greening. An inexplicable persuasive power constantly held me back, by strength as well as by artifice. This power was my indolence. It is not like the impetuous inspiration of love, nor like the strong prompting of enthusiasm, it is rather like a housekeeper who holds one back, with whom one is very well off, so well off that it never occurs to one to get married. So much at least is certain, that although I am not unacquainted with the comforts and conveniences of life, of all conveniences indolence is the most comfortable.

So there I sat and smoked my cigar until I lapsed into thought. Among other thoughts I remember these: 'You are going on,' I said to myself, 'to become an old man, without being anything, and without really undertaking to do anything. On the other hand, wherever you look about you, in literature and in life, you see the celebrated names and figures, the precious and much heralded men who are coming into prominence and are much talked about, the many benefactors of the age who know how to benefit mankind by making life easier and easier, some by railways, others by omnibuses and steamboats, others by the telegraph, others by easily apprehended compendiums and short recitals of everything worth knowing, and finally the true benefactors of the age who make spiritual existence in virtue of thought easier and easier, yet more and more significant. And what are you doing?' Here my soliloquy was interrupted, for my cigar was smoked out and a new one had to be lit. So I smoked again, and then suddenly this thought flashed through my mind: 'You must do something, but inasmuch as with your limited capacities it will be impossible to make anything easier than it has become, you must, with the same humanitarian enthusiasm as the others, undertake to make something harder.' This notion pleased me immensely, and at the same time it flattered me to think that I, like the rest of them, would be loved and esteemed by the whole community. For when all combine in every way to make everything easier, there remains only one possible danger, namely, that the ease becomes so great that it becomes altogether too great; then there is only one want left, though it is not yet a felt want, when people will want difficulty. Out of love for mankind, and out of despair at my embarrassing situation, seeing that I had accomplished nothing and was unable to make anything easier than it had already been made, and moved by a genuine interest in those who make everything easy, I conceived it as my task to create difficulties everywhere. I was struck also with the strange reflection, whether it was not really my indolence I had to thank for the fact that this task became mine. For far from having found it, as Aladdin did the lamp, I must rather suppose that my indolence, by hindering me from intervening at an opportune time to make things easy, has forced upon me the only task that was left over.

2. One walks and walks

A walk on the heath. (The wooded area near Hald. The woman and the little boy who hid in the thicket when I came along, and although unwilling to look at me, answered my question.) I lost my way; in the distance loomed a dark mass which restlessly undulated to and fro. I thought it was a wood. I was utterly amazed, since I knew there was no wood in the vicinity except the one I had just left. Alone on the burning heath, surrounded on all sides by sheer sameness except for the undulating sea straight ahead of me. I became positively seasick and desperate over not being able to get closer to the wood in spite of all my vigorous walking. I never reached it, either, for when I came out on the main road to Viborg it was still visible; but now that I had the white road as a starting point, I saw that it was the heathered hills on the other side of Viborg Lake. Simply because a person has such a wide vista out on the heath he has nothing at all to measure with; he walks and walks, objects do not change since there actually is no *ob*-ject [*G j e n-stand*] (an object always requires the *other* by virtue of which it becomes an *ob*-ject [*G j e n-stand*]. But this [other] is not the eye; the eye is the associating factor).

3. A waterspout

'A man should never lose his courage; when misfortunes tower most fearfully about him, there appears in the sky a helping hand.' Thus spoke the Reverend Jesper Morten last evensong. Now I am in the habit of travelling much under the open sky, but I had never seen anything of the kind. A few days ago, however, while on a walking tour, some such phenomenon took place. It was not exactly a hand, but something like an arm which stretched out of the sky. I began to ponder: it occurred to me that if only Jesper Morten were here, he might be able to decide whether this was the phenomenon he referred to. As I stood there in the midst of my thoughts, I was addressed by a wayfarer. Pointing up to the sky, he said: 'Do you see that waterspout? They are very rare in these parts; sometimes they carry whole houses away with them.' 'The Lord preserve us,' thought I, 'is that a waterspout?' and took to my heels as fast as I could. I wonder what the Reverend Jesper Morten would have done in my place?

4. That Archimedean point

July 29. As one goes from the inn through Sortebro across the bare fields that run along the coast, about a mile and a quarter to the north one comes to the highest point in the district, to Gilbjerg. It has always been one of my favourite places. And as I stood there one quiet evening as the sea struck up its song with a deep and calm solemnity, whilst my eye met not a single sail on the vast expanse of water, and the sea set bounds to the heavens, and the heavens to the sea; whilst on the other side the busy noise of life subsided and the birds sang their evening prayer – the few that are dear to me came forth from their graves, or rather it seemed to me as though they had not died. I felt so content in their midst, I rested in their embrace, and it was as though I were out of the body, wafted with them into the ether above – and the hoarse screech of the gulls reminded me that I stood alone and everything vanished before my eyes, and I turned back with a heavy heart to mix in the busy world, yet without forgetting such blessed moments. – I have often stood there and looked out upon my past life and upon the different surroundings which have exercised their power upon me; and the pettiness which so often gives offence in life, the numerous mis-understandings too often separating minds which if they properly understood one another would be bound together by indissoluble ties, vanished before my gaze. Seen thus in perspective only the broad and powerful outline showed, and I did not as so frequently happens to me lose myself in the moment, but saw everything as a whole and was strengthened to understand things differently, to admit how often I had blundered, and to forgive others.

As I stood there, without that feeling of dejection and despondency which makes me look upon myself as the enclitic of the men who usually surround me, and without that feeling of pride which makes me into the formative principle of a small circle – as I stood there alone and forsaken, and the power of the sea and the battle of the elements reminded me of my own nothingness, and on the other hand the sure flight of the birds recalled the words spoken by Christ: Not a sparrow shall fall on the ground without your Father: then all at once I felt how great and how small I was; then did those two mighty forces, pride and humility, happily unite in friendship. Lucky is the man to whom *that* is possible at every moment of his life; in whose breast those two factors have not only come to an agreement but have joined hands and been wedded – a marriage which is neither a *mariage de convenance* nor a *mésalliance* but a tranquil marriage of love held in the most secret chamber of man's heart, in the holy of holies, where there are few witnesses but where everything proceeds before the eyes of Him who alone witnessed the marriage in the Garden of Eden – a marriage, which will not remain unfruitful but bears blessed fruits, as may be seen in the world by an experienced observer; for like cryptograms among plants, they withdraw from the notice of the masses and only the solitary inquirer discovers them and rejoices over his find. His life will flow on peacefully and quietly and he will neither drain the intoxicating cup of pride nor the bitter chalice of despair. He has found what the great philosopher – who by his calculations was able to destroy the enemy's engines of war – desired, but did not find: that Archimedean point from which he could lift the whole world, the point which for that very reason must lie outside the world, outside the limitations of time and space.

5. The flight to Berlin

The brilliant short book Repetition *(1843), written under the pseudonym Constantine Constantius, proposes itself a series of insoluble problems to solve. Does the young man want to marry the girl, or does he dread that more than anything? Does he want to go into a future with her, or re-live an endless past? Can wonderful moments be repeated, or are they always a disappointment?*

Without letting anybody know about it (lest all the gossip might render me inept for the experiment and create a disgust for repetition), I went by steamer to Stralsund, and there took a seat in a diligence for Berlin. Among the learned there are various opinions as to which seat in a diligence is the most comfortable. My *Ansicht* is that it is misery for the whole crowd. On my previous journey I had the end seat inside the carriage near the front (some consider this a great prize), and then for thirty-six hours was so shaken together with my nearest neighbors, all too near, that upon reaching Hamburg I had not merely lost my mind but lost my legs too. We six persons who sat inside the carriage were kneaded into one body, and I had a lively sense of what had happened to the people of Mol, who after they had been sitting together for a long time could not distinguish their own legs. In order at least to be a member of a smaller body I chose a seat in the coupé. It was a change. Nevertheless everything was repeated. The postillion blew his horn, I closed my eyes, resigned myself to despair, and thought, as I am accustomed to do on such occasions, 'God knows whether thou wilt ever reach Berlin, and in that case whether thou wilt ever become a man again, capable of emancipating thyself in the individuality of isolation, or whether thou wilt retain the memory that thou art a member of a greater body.'

I arrived in Berlin after all, and hastened at once to my old lodging in order to convince myself how far a repetition might be possible. I can assure every sympathetic reader that on my first visit I succeeded in getting one of the most agreeable apartments in Berlin, and this I can now affirm with the more confidence because I have seen many. Gendarmes Square is surely the most beautiful in Berlin. The theater and the two churches make a fine appearance, especially as viewed from a window by moonlight. The recollection of it contributed much to hasten my steps. One ascends a flight of stairs in a house illuminated by gas, one opens a small door, one stands in the vestibule. On the left is a glass door leading to a cabinet. One goes straight ahead, one finds oneself in an antechamber. Beyond this are two rooms entirely alike and furnished entirely alike, with the effect of seeing one room doubled in a mirror. The inner room is tastefully lighted. A branch candlestick stands on the writing table, beside which stands a handsome armchair covered with red velvet. The first room is not illuminated. Here the pale light of the room is blended with the stronger illumination from the inner room. One sits down upon a chair by the window, one looks out upon the great square, one sees the shadows of pedestrians hasten along the walls. Everything is transformed into a theatrical decoration. A dreamy reality looms up in the background of the soul. One feels a desire to throw on a cloak and slink quietly along the walls with a searching glance, attentive to every sound. One does not do it, one merely sees oneself doing it in a renewed youth. One has smoked one's cigar, one retires to the inner room and begins to work. Midnight is past. One extinguishes the candles, one lights a small night lamp. The moonlight triumphs unalloyed. A single shadow appears still darker, a single footstep takes a long time to disappear. The cloudless vault of heaven seems sad and meditative, as though the end of the world were past and heaven undisturbed were concerned only with itself. One goes out again into the antechamber, into the vestibule, into that little cabinet, one goes to sleep – if one is of that fortunate number that can sleep.

But, alas, here no repetition was possible. My host, materialist that he was, *hatte sich verändret*, in the pregnant sense in which the Germans use this word, and as it is used in some quarters of Copenhagen, if I am correctly informed, in the sense of getting married. I wanted to wish him good fortune; but as I have not sufficient command of the German language to be able to turn a sharp corner, nor had promptly at my disposition the phrases appropriate to such an occasion, I confined myself to pantomimic motions. I laid my hand upon my heart and looked at him, while tender sympathy was legibly depicted upon my countenance. He pressed my hand. After we had thus come to an understanding with one another he proceeded to prove the aesthetic validity of marriage. In this he was extraordinarily successful – just as he was formerly in proving the perfection of the bachelor life. When I am talking German I am the most compliant person in the world.

My former host was eager to serve me, and I was eager to lodge with him; so I took one chamber and the vestibule. When I came home the first evening and had lit the candles, I thought to myself, 'Alas, alack, is this repetition?' I was in a sadly depressed mood, or if you prefer to say so, I was in a mood precisely appropriate to the day; for fate had strangely contrived that I arrived in Berlin on the first day of Lent, a day of universal fasting and penitence. It is true they did not cast dust in one's eyes, with the words *Memento, o homo, quod cines est et in cinerem rivertaris*, but nevertheless the whole city was one cloud of dust. I thought at first that it was all arranged by the government, but later I was convinced that the wind had made itself responsible for this and without respect of persons was following its whim or its evil habit; for in Berlin at least every other day is Ash Wednesday. But the dust has little relevance to my subject. This discovery had nothing to do with 'repetition,' for on my previous visit I had not observed this phenomenon, presumably because it was winter.

When one has got comfortably and snugly settled in one's dwelling, when one has thus a fixed point from which to dart out, a safe hiding-place where one can retire to devour one's prey in solitude (something I prize in particular, because like certain beasts of prey I cannot eat when anybody is looking on) – then one makes oneself acquainted with the sights of the city. If one is a traveller *ex professo*, a globetrotter who travels on the scent of everything others have scented out, or in order to write the names of the principal sights in his diary, or his own name in the register of guests, then one engages a *Lohndiener* and buys *Das ganze Berlin* for 4 *Groschen*. By my method one remains an impartial observer whose declaration ought to be taken on faith in every police protocol. On the other hand, if one is travelling without any pressing pretext, one may do as one pleases, see once in a while something which others have not seen, overlook the important things, and get a casual impression which has significance only for oneself. Such a carefree vagabond generally has not much to recount to others, and if he does it he readily runs the risk of impairing the good opinion good people have formed of his virtuousness and morality. If a man had journeyed abroad for a long time and had never been *auf der Eisenbahn*, ought he not to be expelled from all good society? What if a man had been in London and had never taken a ride in the Tunnel! What if a man were to come to Rome, fall in love with a small corner of the town which offered him inexhaustible material for delight, and were to leave Rome without having seen one single sight!

6. Letters home

Having escaped to Berlin from the pain of his broken engagement, Kierkegaard spent the loneliest winter of his life. All day he sat and wrote draft after draft of Either/Or, *intended to explain everything to Regine Olsen. In the evening he went to a German restaurant to eat, always alone. The letters home to his nephew Karl (11 years old) and to his niece Henriette (12 years old) show the depth of his homesickness, and a loving avuncular side to his nature which few suspected. He adored Henriette, whom he called Jette, and the emotion was richly returned. Henriette understood Kierkegaard better than any other woman in his life, as her autobiography,* Memories from My Home *(1909), amply demonstrates.*

Berlin   December 8, '41

MY DEAR CARL,

It probably cost you a certain effort before you could make up your mind to write to me, because you were afraid that you had nothing to write about, or did not write well enough, or did not spell correctly. You must not worry about all that, just write. Indeed, you write very well, and with the exception of one word, everything is so grammatically and calligraphically sound that a *magister artium* [Master of Arts] would be pleased to sign his name to it. But it is precisely because you may have more obstacles to contend with that you should also be allowed to see a spur to continue in the pleasure with which I receive your epistle.

Time changes everything, and as I see from your postscript in which you have noted what is most important, it has also changed you: *Carl* in a shirt and pants! When all is said and done, you may be the one who has changed most by the time I hope to be home. I may not even be able to recognize you, for by then you will probably have begun wearing a vest. From this you may also gather how pleased I am that despite this total change, this metamorphosis (a word you may have learned in natural science), you remain unchanged in your relationship with me. If I stay abroad long enough, you may even have tails on your coat. Alas! Alas! Alas! If you should refuse to acknowledge me, how shall I then recognize you?

But before I proceed to this or that little item of news, I want once and for all to ask you and the others to let me know whether the letters I write have in fact reached those for whom they were intended. I have written both Henrich and Michael, but have not learned whether these letters have arrived safe and sound in Copenhagen.

What shall I now tell *tuis auribus dignum* [worthy of your ears]? Shall I tell you that the dogs here in Berlin perform a very different role from that in Copenhagen? They are used to pull carriages. One, two, or sometimes three big dogs are hitched up to one of the little carriages used for transporting milk to the capital from the country. When there is only one dog, the man or his wife usually join in pulling, but when there are two, the driver usually walks calmly along on the pavement, with his dogs and the cart in the middle of the street. But one day I saw a little boy employed as a driver for such a cart, and he sat in it and drove along at full speed with his milk. The dogs are harnessed just like horses, but usually somewhat more loosely so that when they stop they may sit and rest. Usually these dogs are very steady and sedate, and one seldom sees a dog determined to go in a direction other than that which his driver chooses.

In the Thiergarten great numbers of squirrels with their noise and racket make it very entertaining to roam about, especially in the remoter parts. Like the Frederiksberg Gardens, the Thiergarten is intersected by a canal, but the water is cleaner than at home. In the water are innumerable goldfish. I am sure you know them; if not, you can see them at any rate in the grocer's window in Nørregade diagonally opposite my old apartment. When the sun shines and the water is clear and quiet, it looks very pretty.

Now I have no more space to write, for the last page belongs to Sophie. As I said, it was good of you to write, my dear Carl. Please accept my greetings with this, as well as greetings that you must give Henrich, Michael, Sophie, Jette, Wilhelm. Please give my regards to your father. Please give my regards to the housekeeper.

YOUR UNCLE K.

Berlin　　　　　　　　　　　　　　　　　　　　December 13

MY DEAR JETTE,

Your letter of November 25 has arrived safely and I see by its date that it was finished long ago. This pleases me very much, my dear Jette, and if as a result of my letter to her, Sophie should in any way admonish you about writing to me, you know – just as I know – that in a good sense it comes after the fact.

Just as your letter pleased me in its own right, I am also pleased that it is written so neatly and prettily that it almost encourages me to take pains with my own handwriting.

I am writing this letter on an unusual kind of paper – not, however, because I want to make amends for my handwriting but because I know that you have had a birthday while I have been absent from Copenhagen. Had I been in town that day, in all likelihood I would have brought you a little gift. But I cannot do that now. This very day I walked about in Königstrasse and looked at all the beautiful things the merchants display in their windows, but it is always a precarious matter to send such things by post if one really wants them to reach Copenhagen safe and sound. Hence I have given up that plan. Therefore you will please accept my congratulations on a special kind of paper. And is it not true, little Jette, that getting a letter like this from Berlin is quite a remarkable thing for you, one which you at least have never before experienced? I imagine you playing in your living room at home, now, and suddenly the doorbell rings, and in steps a man in a red coat with a silver badge on his chest and takes out a lot of letters, and among them there is also one for Jette Lund, and he adds that it costs three *sks.*, whereupon your father kindly advances the three *sks.*; and now you get the letter, and now you are allowed to break the sealing wax yourself, and now you are diligently and carefully trying to read what I am writing to you.

The border around this letter represents three large buildings in Berlin about which you know almost as much as I do. In Berlin there is a place, Unter den Linden, where one may travel at bargain rates in all three parts of the world. With these pictures you will get an even better bargain in your own living room at home and be able to travel in Berlin. From the drawing you will see that in front of the museum there are some trees. It is a rather poor little park. But close by the door of the museum there is a gigantic stone basin, much larger than the one you see every day at the fountain in Gammel Torv. It is made of stone but is as smooth as a mirror and very beautiful.

You tell me, as I have already learned from all the letters from the little correspondence club, that Troels Lund has become engaged. I have been waiting for your letter in order to give you the opportunity to congratulate him on my behalf.

Dear Jette, please accept my greetings, and also accept my greetings to Henrich, Michael, Carl, Sophie, Wilhelm,

FROM YOUR UNCLE S.K.

7. Repetition is not possible

Constantine Constantius flees to Berlin to see whether he can enjoy again what he once so much delighted in. He finds he cannot. There is a constant play upon the possibility of repetition. This play is achieved because there are two directions in time, two senses of the word, and two opposed emotions constantly running into relation with each other. The author never ceases to endorse one by impoverishing the other term in every pair. A description of Berlin's three theatres, and the difference between high cultural enjoyment and the relief obtained through slapstick and farce may invent a new metaphor for impersonality, and even sketch out a geography of amusement, but even the most determined effort to feel amused can fail, when one is seeking above all for repetition and also determined that it shall be impossible. In this willed diremption of the self, life loses all savour.

'The Talisman' was to be performed at the Königstäter Theater. The memory of it awoke in my soul, it all stood as vividly before me as when I left the theater the last time. I hastened to the theater. There was no box to be had for me alone, not even in those numbered 5 and 6 on the left. I had to go to the right. There I encountered a society which didn't know definitely whether it should enjoy itself or be bored. Such a company one can definitely regard as boring. There were hardly any empty boxes. The young girl was not to be seen, or else she was there and I could not recognize her because she was in company. Beckmann was unable to make me laugh. I held out for half an hour and then left the theater. 'There is no such thing as repetition,' I thought. This made a profound impression upon me. I am not so very young, nor altogether unacquainted with life, and already long before I came to Berlin the last time I had weaned myself from the habit of counting upon uncertainties. Nevertheless I still believed that the enjoyment I once had in that theater ought to be of a more durable kind, precisely for the reason that before one could really get a sense of what life is one must have learnt to put up with being disappointed by existence in many ways, and still be able to get along – but surely with this modest expectation life must be the more secure. Might existence be even more fraudulent than a bankrupt? After all, he pays back 50 per cent or 30 per cent, at least he pays something. The comical is after all the least one can demand – cannot even that be repeated?

With these thoughts in my mind I went home. My writing-table was in the accustomed place. The velvet armchair still existed. But when I saw it I was so exasperated that I was near breaking it to bits – all the more because everybody in the house had gone to bed, and there was no one to take it away. What is the good of a velvet armchair when the rest of the environment doesn't correspond with it? It is as if a man were to walk naked wearing a cocked hat. When I had gone to bed without having had a single rational thought it was so light in the room that I constantly saw the velvet armchair, whether awake or in my dreams, so when I got up next morning I carried into effect my resolution and had it thrown into a storeroom.

My home had become cheerless, precisely because it was the reverse of a repetition, my mind was unfruitful, my troubled imagination was engaged in transmuting into the delights of Tantalus the memory of how richly the thoughts presented themselves on the former occasion, and this rank weed of memory strangled every thought at birth.

I went out to the coffee-house, where on the previous visit I went every day to enjoy the drink which according to the words of the poet, if it is 'pure and warm and strong and not abused,' can be placed alongside of that with which the poet compares it, namely, 'friendship.' I insist at least upon good coffee. Perhaps the coffee was just as good as before, one might almost suppose so, but I didn't like it. The sun blazed hotly upon the window of the shop, the place was stuffy, pretty much like the air in a casserole, fit to stew in. A draft like a small trade-wind penetrated everywhere and forbade me to think of any repetition, even if an opportunity had presented itself.

That evening I went to the restaurant where I used to go on my former visit, and where, presumably by force of habit, the food agreed with me. When I went there every evening I was acquainted with it most accurately; I knew how the early guests when they were on the point of leaving greeted the fraternity they parted from, whether they put on their hats in the inner room, or in the last room, or only when they opened the door, or not till they were outside. Nothing escaped my observation. Like Proserpine I plucked a hair from every head, even the bald ones. – It was always the same, the same jokes, the same courtesies, the same expressions of comradeship; the locality in all respects the same, in short, 'the same in the same.' Solomon says that 'the contentions of a wife are like a continual dropping,' which would apply to this still-life. Dreadful thought! Here a repetition was possible!

The next night I was at the Königstäter Theater. The only thing repeated was the impossibility of repetition. In the Unter den Linden the dust was insupportable, and every attempt to press in among the people and wash off the dust with a human bath was discouraging in the highest degree. However I turned and twisted, it was in vain. The little *danseuse* who had formerly enchanted me by her grace, which consisted so to say in a leap, had taken the leap. The blind man outside the Brandenburger Thor, my harpist (for I was surely the only one who was concerned about him) was wearing a coat of mixed gray, instead of light green which corresponded with my sad longing, for it made him look like a weeping willow. He was lost for me and won for the universal human. The beadle's much admired nose had turned pale. Professor A.A. wore a new pair of trousers which imparted to him an almost military air . . .

When this experience had been repeated for several days I became so exasperated, so tired of repetition, that I resolved to make my way home again. My discovery was of no importance, and yet it was a strange one, for I discovered that there is no such thing as repetition and I had convinced myself of this by trying in every possible way to get it repeated.

My hope was set upon my home. Justinus Kerner tells somewhere of a man who was tired of his home, that he had his horse saddled in order to ride forth into the wide world. When he had gone a little distance his horse threw him. This turn of events was decisive for him, for when he turned to mount his horse his eye lit again upon the home he wished to leave, and he looked, and behold! it was so beautiful that he at once turned back. In my home I could reckon with tolerable certainty upon finding everything ready for repetition. I have always had a great distrust of upheavals, indeed I go so far that for this reason I even hate any sort of cleaning, and above all household scrubbing. So I had left the severest instructions to have my conservative principles maintained even in my absence. But what happens! My faithful servant held a different opinion. He reckoned that if he commenced the commotion soon after my departure, it surely would have ceased before my return, and he was surely man enough to put everything back punctiliously in its place. I arrive, I ring the doorbell, my servant opens. That was a momentous moment. My servant became as white as a corpse, and through the half-opened door I saw the most dreadful sight: everything was turned upside down. I was petrified. My servant in his consternation did not know what to do, his evil conscience smote him, and he slammed the door in my face. That was too much, my distress had reached its climax, I might expect the worst, to be taken for a ghost, like Commerzienrat Grünmeyer. I perceived that there is no such thing as repetition, and my earlier view of life triumphed.

8. The Writing Cabinet

In a parable of genius, Victor Eremita, the editor of Either/Or, *tells how he discovered the manuscript of the book he is now publishing.*

DEAR READER: I wonder if you may not sometimes have felt inclined to doubt a little the correctness of the familiar philosophic maxim that the external is the internal, and the internal the external. Perhaps you have cherished in your heart a secret which you felt in all its joy or pain was too precious for you to share with another. Perhaps your life has brought you in contact with some person of whom you suspected something of the kind was true, although you were never able to wrest his secret from him either by force or cunning. Perhaps neither of these presuppositions applies to you and your life, and yet you are not a stranger to this doubt; it flits across your mind now and then like a passing shadow. Such a doubt comes and goes, and no one knows whence it comes, nor whither it goes. For my part I have always been heretically-minded on this point in philosophy, and have therefore early accustomed myself, as far as possible, to institute observations and inquiries concerning it. I have sought guidance from those authors whose views I shared on this matter; in short, I have done everything in my power to remedy the deficiency in the philosophical works.

Gradually the sense of hearing came to be my favorite sense; for just as the voice is the revelation of an inwardness incommensurable with the outer, so the ear is the instrument by which this inwardness is apprehended, hearing the sense by which it is appropriated. Whenever, then, I found a contradiction between what I saw and what I heard, then I found my doubt confirmed, and my enthusiasm for the investigation stimulated. In the confessional the priest is separated from the penitent by a screen; he does not see, he only hears. Gradually as he listens, he constructs an outward appearance which corresponds to the voice he hears. Consequently, he experiences no contradiction. It is otherwise, however, when you hear and see at the same time, and yet perceive a screen between yourself and the speaker. My researches in this direction have met with varying degrees of success. Sometimes I have been favored by fortune, sometimes not, and one needs good fortune to win results along this road. However, I have never lost my desire to continue my investigations. Whenever I have been at the point of regretting my perseverance, an unexpected success has crowned my efforts. It was such an unexpected bit of luck which in a very curious manner put me in possession of the papers which I now have the honor of offering to the reading public. These papers have afforded me an insight into the lives of two men, which has confirmed my hunch that the external is not the internal. This was especially true about one of them. His external mode of life has been in complete contradiction to his inner life. The same was true to a certain extent with the other also, inasmuch as he concealed a more significant inwardness under a somewhat commonplace exterior.

Still, I had best proceed in order and explain how I came into possession of these papers. It is now about seven years since I first noticed at a merchant's shop here in town a secretary which from the very first moment I saw it attracted my attention. It was not of modern workmanship, had been used a good deal, and yet it fascinated me. It is impossible for me to explain the reason for this impression, but most people in the course of their lives have had some similar experience. My daily path took me by this shop, and I never failed a single day to pause and feast my eyes upon it. I gradually made up a history about it; it became a daily necessity for me to see it, and so I did not hesitate to go out of my way for the sake of seeing it, when an unaccustomed route made this necessary. And the more I looked at it, the more I wanted to own it. I realized very well that it was a peculiar desire, since I had no use for such a piece of furniture, and it would be an extravagance for me to buy it. But desire is a very sophisticated passion. I made an excuse for going into the shop, asked about other things, and as I was leaving, I casually made the shopkeeper a very low offer for the secretary. I thought possibly he might accept it; then chance would have played into my hands. It was certainly not for the sake of the money I behaved thus, but to salve my conscience. The plan miscarried, the dealer was uncommonly firm. I continued to pass the place daily, and to look at the secretary with loving eyes. 'You must make up your mind,' I thought, 'for suppose it is sold, then it will be too late. Even if you were lucky enough to get hold of it again, you would never have the same feeling about it.' My heart beat violently; then I went into the shop. I bought it and paid for it. 'This must be the last time,' thought I, 'that you are so extravagant; it is really lucky that you bought it, for now every time you look at it, you will reflect on how extravagant you were; a new period of your life must begin with the acquisition of the secretary.' Alas, desire is very eloquent, and good resolutions are always at hand.

The secretary was duly set up in my apartment, and as in the first period of my enamorment I had taken pleasure in gazing at it from the street, so now I walked back and forth in front of it at home.

Little by little I familiarized myself with its rich economy, its many drawers and recesses, and I was thoroughly pleased with my secretary. Still, things could not continue thus. In the summer of 1836 I arranged my affairs so that I could take a week's trip to the country. The postilion was engaged for five o'clock in the morning. The necessary baggage had been packed the evening before, and everything was in readiness. I awakened at four, but the vision of the beautiful country I was to visit so enchanted me that I again fell asleep, or into a dream. My servant evidently thought he would let me sleep as long as possible, for he did not call me until half-past six. The postilion was already blowing his horn, and although I am not usually inclined to obey the mandates of others, I have always made an exception in the case of the postboy and his musical theme. I was speedily dressed and already at the door, when it occurred to me, Have you enough money in your pocket? There was not much there. I opened the secretary to get at the money drawer to take what money there was. Of course the drawer would not move. Every attempt to open it failed. It was all as bad as it could possibly be. Just at this moment, while my ears were ringing with the postboy's alluring notes, to meet such difficulties! The blood rushed to my head, I became angry. As Xerxes ordered the sea to be lashed, so I resolved to take a terrible revenge. A hatchet was fetched. With it I dealt the secretary a shattering blow, shocking to see. Whether in my anger I struck the wrong place, or the drawer was as stubborn as myself, the result of the blow was not as anticipated. The drawer was closed, and the drawer remained closed. But something else happened. Whether my blow had struck exactly the right spot, or whether the shock to the whole framework of the secretary was responsible, I do not know, but I do know that a secret door sprang open, one which I had never before noticed. This opened a pigeonhole that I naturally had never discovered. Here to my great surprise I found a mass of papers, the papers which form the content of the present work. My intention as to the journey remained unchanged. At the first station we came to I would negotiate a loan. A mahogany case in which I usually kept a pair of pistols was hastily emptied and the papers were placed in it. Pleasure had triumphed, and had become even greater. In my heart I begged the secretary for forgiveness for the harsh treatment,while my mind found its doubt strengthened, that the external is not the internal, as well as my empirical generalization confirmed, that luck is necessary to make such discoveries possible.

I reached Hillerød in the middle of the forenoon, set my finances in order, and got a general impression of the magnificent scenery. The following morning I at once began my excursions, which now took on a very different character from that which I had originally intended. My servant followed me with the mahogany case. I sought out a romantic spot in the forest where I should be as free as possible from surprise, and then took out the documents. Mine host, who noticed these frequent excursions in company with the mahogany case, ventured the remark that I must be trying to improve my marksmanship. For this conjecture I was duly grateful, and left him undisturbed in his belief.

A hasty glance at the papers showed me that they were made up of two collections whose external differences were strongly marked. One of them was written on a kind of vellum in quarto, with a fairly wide margin. The handwriting was legible, sometimes even a little elegant, in a single place, careless. The other was written on full sheets of foolscap with ruled columns, such as is ordinarily used for legal documents and the like. The handwriting was clear, somewhat spreading, uniform and even, apparently that of a business man. The contents also proved to be very dissimilar. One part consisted of a number of aesthetic essays of varying length, the other was composed of two long inquiries and one shorter one, all with an ethical content, as it seemed, and in the form of letters. This dissimilarity was completely confirmed by a closer examination. The second series consists of letters written to the author of the first series.

9. The Rotation Method

The first half of Either/Or *is an account of the world seen from the 'aesthetic' point of view, and one of the most resourceful of the essays is also one of the most perverse. The absurd, boredom, the tediousness of life can all be overcome by an act of arbitrary intelligence. But one does*

> *not see much if one travels: one has to stay at home and*
> *bore oneself into inventiveness.*

Starting from a principle is affirmed by people of experience to be a
very reasonable procedure; I am willing to humor them, and so
begin with the principle that all men are bores. Surely no one will
prove himself so great a bore as to contradict me in this. This
principle possesses the quality of being in the highest degree
repellent, an essential requirement in the case of negative principles, which are in the last analysis the principles of all motion. It is
not merely repellent, but infinitely forbidding; and whoever has
this principle back of him cannot but receive an infinite impetus
forward, to help him make new discoveries. For if my principle is
true, one need only consider how ruinous boredom is for humanity,
and by properly adjusting the intensity of one's concentration upon
this fundamental truth, attain any desired degree of momentum.
Should one wish to attain the maximum momentum, even to the
point of almost endangering the driving power, one need only say
to oneself: Boredom is the root of all evil. Strange that boredom, in
itself so staid and stolid, should have such power to set in motion.
The influence it exerts is altogether magical, except that it is not the
influence of attraction, but of repulsion.

In the case of children, the ruinous character of boredom is
universally acknowledged. Children are always well-behaved as
long as they are enjoying themselves. This is true in the strictest
sense; for if they sometimes become unruly in their play, it is
because they are already beginning to be bored – boredom is
already approaching, though from a different direction. In choosing a governess one, therefore, takes into account not only her
sobriety, her faithfulness, and her competence, but also her aesthetic qualifications for amusing the children; and there would be no
hesitancy in dismissing a governess who was lacking in this respect,
even if she had all the other desirable virtues. Here, then, the
principle is clearly acknowledged; but so strange is the way of the
world, so pervasive the influence of habit and boredom, that this is
practically the only case in which the science of aesthetics receives
its just dues. If one were to ask for a divorce because his wife was
tiresome, or demand the abdication of a king because he was boring
to look at, or the banishment of a preacher because he was tiresome
to listen to, or the dismissal of a prime minister, or the execution of

a journalist, because he was terribly tiresome, one would find it impossible to force it through. What wonder, then, that the world goes from bad to worse, and that its evils increase more and more, as boredom increases, and boredom is the root of all evil.

The history of this can be traced from the very beginning of the world. The gods were bored, and so they created man. Adam was bored because he was alone, and so Eve was created. Thus boredom entered the world, and increased in proportion to the increase of population. Adam was bored alone; then Adam and Eve were bored together; then Adam and Eve and Cain and Abel were bored *en famille*; then the population of the world increased, and the peoples were bored *en masse*. To divert themselves they conceived the idea of constructing a tower high enough to reach the heavens. This idea is itself as boring as the tower was high, and constitutes a terrible proof of how boredom gained the upper hand. The nations were scattered over the earth, just as people now travel abroad, but they continued to be bored. Consider the consequences of this boredom. Humanity fell from its lofty height, first because of Eve, and then from the Tower of Babel. What was it, on the other hand, that delayed the fall of Rome, was it not *panis* and *circenses*? And is anything being done now? Is anyone concerned about planning some means of diversion? Quite the contrary, the impending ruin is being accelerated. It is proposed to call a constitutional assembly. Can anything more tiresome be imagined, both for the participants themselves, and for those who have to hear and read about it? It is proposed to improve the financial condition of the state by practicing economy. What could be more tiresome? Instead of increasing the national debt, it is proposed to pay it off. As I understand the political situation, it would be an easy matter for Denmark to negotiate a loan of fifteen million dollars. Why not consider this plan? Every once in a while we hear of a man who is a genius, and therefore neglects to pay his debts – why should not a nation do the same, if we were all agreed? Let us then borrow fifteen millions, and let us use the proceeds, not to pay our debts, but for public entertainment. Let us celebrate the millennium in a riot of merriment. Let us place boxes everywhere, not, as at present, for the deposit of money, but for the free distribution of money. Everything would become gratis; theaters gratis, women of easy virtue gratis, one would drive to the park gratis; be buried gratis, one's eulogy would be gratis; I say gratis, for when one always has money at hand, everything is in a certain sense free. No one should be permitted to own any property. Only in my own case would there be an exception. I reserve to myself securities in the Bank of London to the value of one hundred dollars a day, partly because I cannot do with less, partly because the idea is mine, and finally because I may not be able to hit upon a new idea when the fifteen millions are gone.

What would be the consequences of all this prosperity? Everything great would gravitate toward Copenhagen, the greatest artists, the greatest dancers, the greatest actors. Copenhagen would become a second Athens. What then? All rich men would establish their homes in this city. Among others would come the Shah of Persia, and the King of England would also come. Here is my second idea. Let us kidnap the Shah of Persia. Perhaps you say an insurrection might take place in Persia and a new ruler be placed on the throne, as has often happened before, the consequence being a fall in price for the old Shah. Very well then, I propose that we sell him to the Turks; they will doubtless know how to turn him into money. Then there is another circumstance which our politicians seem entirely to have overlooked. Denmark holds the balance of power in Europe. It is impossible to imagine a more fortunate lot. I know that from my own experience; I once held the balance of power in a family and could do as I pleased; the blame never fell on me, but always on the others. O that my words might reach your ears, all you who sit in high places to advise and rule, you king's men and men of the people, wise and understanding citizens of all classes! Consider the crisis! Old Denmark is on the brink of ruin; what a calamity! It will be destroyed by boredom. Of all calamities the most calamitous! In ancient times they made him king who extolled most beautifully the praises of the deceased king; in our times we ought to make him king who utters the best witticism, and make him crown prince who gives occasion for the utterance of the best witticism.

O beautiful, emotional sentimentality, how you carry me away! Should I trouble to speak to my contemporaries, to initiate them into my wisdom! By no means. My wisdom is not exactly *zum Gebrauch für Jedermann*, and it is always more prudent to keep one's maxims of prudence to oneself. I desire no disciples; but if there happened to be someone present at my deathbed, and I was sure that the end had come, then I might, in an attack of philanthropic delirium, whisper my theory in his ear, uncertain whether I had done him a service or not. People talk so much about man being a social animal; at bottom, he is a beast of prey, and the evidence for this is not confined to the shape of his teeth. All this talk about society and the social is partly inherited hypocrisy, partly calculated cunning.

All men are bores. The word itself suggests the possibility of a subdivision. It may just as well indicate a man who bores others as one who bores himself. Those who bore others are the mob, the crowd, the infinite multitude of men in general. Those who bore themselves are the elect, the aristocracy; and it is a curious fact that those who do not bore themselves usually bore others, while those who bore themselves entertain others. Those who do not bore themselves are generally people who, in one way or another, keep themselves extremely busy; these people are precisely on this account the most tiresome, the most utterly unendurable. This species of animal life is surely not the fruit of man's desire and woman's lust. Like all lower forms of life, it is marked by a high degree of fertility, and multiplies endlessly. It is inconceivable that nature should require nine months to produce such beings; they ought rather to be turned out by the score. The second class, the aristocrats, are those who bore themselves. As noted above, they generally entertain others – in a certain external sense sometimes the mob, in a deeper sense only their fellow initiates. The more profoundly they bore themselves, the more powerfully do they serve to divert these latter, even when their boredom reaches its zenith, as when they either die of boredom (the passive form) or shoot themselves out of curiosity (the active form).

It is usual to say that idleness is a root of all evil. To prevent this evil one is advised to work. However, it is easy to see, both from the nature of the evil that is feared and the remedy proposed, that this entire view is of a very plebeian extraction. Idleness is by no means as such a root of evil; on the contrary, it is a truly divine life, provided one is not himself bored. Idleness may indeed cause the loss of one's fortune, and so on, but the high-minded man does not fear such dangers; he fears only boredom. The Olympian gods were not bored, they lived happily in happy idleness. A beautiful woman, who neither sews nor spins nor bakes nor reads nor plays the piano, is happy in her idleness, for she is not bored. So far from idleness being the root of all evil, it is rather the only true good.

Boredom is the root of all evil, and it is this which must be kept at a distance. Idleness is not an evil; indeed one may say that every human being who lacks a sense for idleness proves that his consciousness has not yet been elevated to the level of the humane. There is a restless activity which excludes a man from the world of the spirit, setting him in a class with the brutes, whose instincts impel them always to be on the move. There are men who have an extraordinary talent for transforming everything into a matter of business, whose whole life is business, who fall in love, marry, listen to a joke, and admire a picture with the same industrious zeal with which they labor during business hours. The Latin proverb, *otium est pulvinar diaboli*, is true enough, but the devil gets no time to lay his head on this pillow when one is not bored. But since some people believe that the end and aim of life is work, the disjunction, idleness/work, is quite correct. I assume that it is the end and aim of every man to enjoy himself, and hence my disjunction is no less correct.

Boredom is the daemonic side of pantheism. If we remain in boredom as such, it becomes the evil principle; if we annul it, we posit it in its truth; but we can only annul boredom by enjoying ourselves – *ergo*, it is our duty to enjoy ourselves. To say that boredom is annulled by work betrays a confusion of thought; for idleness can certainly be annulled by work, since it is its opposite, but not boredom, and experience shows that the busiest workers, whose constant buzzing most resembles an insect's hum, are the most tiresome of creatures; if they do not bore themselves, it is because they have no conception of what boredom is; but then it can scarcely be said that they have overcome boredom.

Boredom is partly an inborn talent, partly an acquired immediacy. The English are in general the paradigmatic nation. A true talent for indolence is very rare; it is never met with in nature, but belongs to the world of the spirit. Occasionally, however, you meet a travelling Englishman who is, as it were, the incarnation of this talent – a heavy, immovable animal, whose entire language exhausts its riches in a single word of one syllable, an interjection by which he signifies his deepest admiration and his supreme indifference, admiration and indifference having been neutralized in the unity of boredom. No other nation produces such miracles of nature; every other national will always show himself a little more vivacious, not so absolutely stillborn. The only analogy I know of is the apostle of the empty enthusiasm, who also makes his way through life on an interjection. This is the man who everywhere makes a profession of enthusiasm, who cries Ah! or Oh! whether the event be significant or insignificant, the difference having been lost for him in the emptiness of a blind and noisy enthusiasm. The second form of boredom is usually the result of a mistaken effort to find diversion. The fact that the remedy against boredom may also serve to produce boredom, might appear to be a suspicious circumstance; but it has this effect only in so far as it is incorrectly employed. A misdirected search for diversion, one which is eccentric in its direction, conceals boredom within its own depths and gradually works it out toward the surface, thus revealing itself as that which it immediately is. In the case of horses, we distinguish between blind staggers and sleepy staggers, but call both staggers; and so we can also make a distinction between two kinds of boredom, though uniting both under the common designation of being tiresome.

Pantheism is, in general, characterized by fullness; in the case of boredom we find the precise opposite, since it is characterized by emptiness; but it is just this which makes boredom a pantheistic conception. Boredom depends on the nothingness which pervades reality; it causes a dizziness like that produced by looking down into a yawning chasm, and this dizziness is infinite. The eccentric form of diversion noted above sounds forth without producing an echo, which proves it to be based on boredom; for in nothingness not even an echo can be produced.

Now since boredom as shown above is the root of all evil, what can be more natural than the effort to overcome it? Here, as everywhere, however, it is necessary to give the problem calm consideration; otherwise one may find oneself driven by the daemonic spirit of boredom deeper and deeper into the mire in the very effort to escape. Everyone who feels bored cries out for change. With this demand I am in complete sympathy, but it is necessary to act in accordance with some settled principle.

My own dissent from the ordinary view is sufficiently expressed in the use I make of the word, 'rotation.' This word might seem to conceal an ambiguity, and if I wished to use it so as to find room in it for the ordinary method, I should have to define it as a change of field. But the farmer does not use the word in this sense. I shall, however, adopt this meaning for a moment, in order to speak of the rotation which depends on change in its boundless infinity, its extensive dimension, so to speak.

This is the vulgar and inartistic method, and needs to be supported by illusion. One tires of living in the country, and moves to the city; one tires of one's native land, and travels abroad; one is *europamüde*, and goes to America, and so on; finally one indulges in a sentimental hope of endless journeyings from star to star. Or the movement is different but still extensive. One tires of porcelain dishes and eats on silver; one tires of silver and turns to gold; one burns half of Rome to get an idea of the burning of Troy. This method defeats itself; it is plain endlessness. And what did Nero gain by it? Antonine was wiser; he says: 'It is in your power to review your life, to look at things you saw before, from another point of view.'

My method does not consist in change of field, but resembles the true rotation method in changing the crop and the mode of cultivation. Here we have at once the principle of limitation, the only saving principle in the world. The more you limit yourself, the more fertile you become in invention. A prisoner in solitary confinement for life becomes very inventive, and a spider may furnish him with much entertainment. One need only hark back to one's schooldays. We were at an age when aesthetic considerations were ignored in the choice of one's instructors, most of whom were for that reason very tiresome; how fertile in invention one then proved to be! How entertaining to catch a fly and hold it imprisoned under a nut shell and to watch how it pushed the shell around; what pleasure from cutting a hole in the desk, putting a fly in it, and then peeping down at it through a piece of paper! How entertaining sometimes to listen to the monotonous drip of water from the roof! How close an observer one becomes under such circumstances, when not the least noise nor movement escapes one's attention! Here we have the extreme application of the method which seeks to achieve results intensively, not extensively.

The more resourceful in changing the mode of cultivation one can be, the better; but every particular change will always come under the general categories of *remembering* and *forgetting*. Life in its entirety moves in these two currents, and hence it is essential to have them under control. It is impossible to live artistically before one has made up one's mind to abandon hope; for hope precludes self-limitation. It is a very beautiful sight to see a man put out to sea with the fair wind of hope, and one may even use the opportunity to be taken in tow; but one should never permit hope to be taken aboard one's own ship, least of all as a pilot; for hope is a faithless shipmaster. Hope was one of the dubious gifts of Prometheus; instead of giving men the foreknowledge of the immortals, he gave them hope.

To forget – all men wish to forget, and when something unpleasant happens, they always say: Oh, that one might forget! But forgetting is an art that must be practiced beforehand. The ability to forget is conditioned upon the method of remembering, but this again depends upon the mode of experiencing reality. Whoever plunges into his experiences with the momentum of hope will remember in such wise that he is unable to forget. *Nil admirari* is therefore the real philosophy. No moment must be permitted so great a significance that it cannot be forgotten when convenient; each moment ought, however, to have so much significance that it can be recollected at will. Childhood, which is the age which remembers best, is at the same time most forgetful. The more poetically one remembers, the more easily one forgets; for remembering poetically is really only another expression for forgetting. In a poetic memory the experience has undergone a transformation, by which it has lost all its painful aspects. To remember in this manner, one must be careful how one lives, how one enjoys. Enjoying an experience to its full intensity to the last minute will make it impossible either to remember or to forget. For there is then nothing to remember except a certain satiety, which one desires to forget, but which now comes back to plague the mind with an involuntary remembrance. Hence, when you begin to notice that a certain pleasure or experience is acquiring too strong a hold upon the mind, you stop a moment for the purpose of remembering. No other method can better create a distaste for continuing the experience too long. From the beginning one should keep the enjoyment under control, never spreading every sail to the wind in any resolve; one ought to devote oneself to pleasure with a certain suspicion, a certain wariness, if one desires to give the lie to the proverb which says that no one can have his cake and eat it too. The carrying of concealed weapons is usually forbidden, but no weapon is so dangerous as the art of remembering. It gives one a very peculiar feeling in the midst of one's enjoyment to look back upon it for the purpose of remembering it.

One who has perfected himself in the twin arts of remembering and forgetting is in a position to play at battledore and shuttlecock with the whole of existence.

The extent of one's power to forget is the final measure of one's elasticity of spirit. If a man cannot forget he will never amount to much. Whether there be somewhere a Lethe gushing forth, I do not know; but this I know, that the art of forgetting can be developed. However, this art does not consist in permitting the impressions to vanish completely; forgetfulness is one thing, and the art of forgetting is something quite different. It is easy to see that most people have a very meager understanding of this art, for they ordinarily wish to forget only what is unpleasant, not what is pleasant. This betrays a complete one-sidedness. Forgetting is the true expression for an ideal process of assimilation by which the experience is reduced to a sounding-board for the soul's own music. Nature is great because it has forgotten that it was chaos; but this thought is subject to revival at any time. As a result of attempting to forget only what is unpleasant, most people have a conception of oblivion as an untamable force which drowns out the past. But forgetting is really a tranquil and quiet occupation, and one which should be exercised quite as much in connection with the pleasant as with the unpleasant. A pleasant experience has as past something unpleasant about it, by which it stirs a sense of privation; this unpleasantness is taken away by an act of forgetfulness. The unpleasant has a sting, as all admit. This, too, can be removed by the art of forgetting. But if one attempts to dismiss the unpleasant absolutely from mind, as many do who dabble in the art of forgetting, one soon learns how little that helps. In an unguarded moment it pays a surprise visit, and it is then invested with all the forcibleness of the unexpected. This is absolutely contrary to every orderly arrangement in a reasonable mind. No misfortune or difficulty is so devoid of affability, so deaf to all appeals, but that it may be flattered a little; even Cerberus accepted bribes of honey-cakes, and it is not only the lassies who are beguiled. The art in dealing with such experiences consists in talking them over, thereby depriving them of their bitterness; not forgetting them absolutely, but forgetting them for the sake of remembering them. Even in the case of memories such that one might suppose an eternal oblivion to be the only safeguard, one need permit oneself only a little trickery, and the deception will succeed for the skillful. Forgetting is the shears with which you cut away what you cannot use, doing it under the supreme direction of memory. Forgetting and remembering are thus identical arts, and the artistic achievement of this identity is the Archimedean point from which one lifts the whole world. When we say that we *consign* something to oblivion, we suggest simultaneously that it is to be forgotten and yet also remembered.

The art of remembering and forgetting will also insure against sticking fast in some relationship of life, and make possible the realization of a complete freedom.

One must guard against *friendship*. How is a friend defined? He is not what philosophy calls the necessary other, but the superfluous third. What are friendship's ceremonies? You drink each other's health, you open an artery and mingle your blood with that of the friend. It is difficult to say when the proper moment for this arrives, but it announces itself mysteriously; you feel some way that you can no longer address one another formally. When once you have had this feeling, then it can never appear that you have made a mistake, like Geert Vestphaler, who discovered that he had been drinking to friendship with the public hangman. What are the infallible marks of friendship? Let antiquity answer: *idem velle, idem nolle, ea demum firma amicitia*, and also extremely tiresome. What are the infallible marks of friendship? Mutual assistance in word and deed. Two friends form a close association in order to be everything to one another, and that although it is impossible for one human being to be anything to another human being except to be in his way. To be sure one may help him with money, assist him in and out of his coat, be his humble servant, and tender him congratulations on New Year's Day, on the day of his wedding, on the birth of a child, on the occasion of a funeral.

But because you abstain from friendship it does not follow that you abstain from social contacts. On the contrary, these social relationships may at times be permitted to take on a deeper character, provided you always have so much more momentum in yourself that you can sheer off at will, in spite of sharing for a time in the momentum of the common movement. It is believed that such conduct leaves unpleasant memories, the unpleasantness being due to the fact that a relationship which has meant something now vanishes and becomes as nothing. But this is a misunderstanding. The unpleasant is merely a piquant ingredient in the sullenness of life. Besides, it is possible for the same relationship again to play a significant role, though in another manner. The essential thing is never to stick fast, and for this it is necessary to have oblivion back of one. The experienced farmer lets his land lie fallow now and then, and the theory of social prudence recommends the same. Everything will doubtless return, though in a different form; that which has once been present in the rotation will remain in it, but the mode of cultivation will be varied. You therefore quite consistently hope to meet your friends and acquaintances in a better world, but you do not share the fear of the crowd that they will be altered so that you cannot recognize them; your fear is rather lest they be wholly unaltered. It is remarkable how much significance even the most insignificant person can gain from a rational mode of cultivation.

One must never enter into the relation of *marriage*. Husband and wife promise to love one another for eternity. This is all very fine, but it does not mean very much; for if their love comes to an end in time, it will surely be ended in eternity. If, instead of promising forever, the parties would say: until Easter, or until May-day comes, there might be some meaning in what they say; for then they would have said something definite, and also something that they might be able to keep. And how does a marriage usually work out? In a little while one party begins to perceive that there is something wrong, then the other party complains, and cries to heaven: faithless! faithless! A little later the second party reaches the same standpoint, and a neutrality is established in which the mutual faithlessness is mutually canceled, to the satisfaction and content-ment of both parties. But it is now too late, for there are great difficulties connected with divorce.

Such being the case with marriage, it is not surprising that the attempt should be made in so many ways to bolster it up with moral supports. When a man seeks separation from his wife, the cry is at once raised that he is depraved, a scoundrel, etc. How silly, and what an indirect attack upon marriage! If marriage has reality, then he is sufficiently punished by forfeiting this happiness; if it has no reality, it is absurd to abuse him because he is wiser than the rest. When a man grows tired of his money and throws it out of the window, we do not call him a scoundrel; for either money has reality, and so he is sufficiently punished by depriving himself of it, or it has none, and then he is, of course, a wise man.

One must always take care not to enter into any relationship in which there is a possibility of many members. For this reason friendship is dangerous, to say nothing of marriage. Husband and wife are indeed said to become one, but this is a very dark and mystic saying. When you are one of several, then you have lost your freedom; you cannot send for your traveling boots whenever you wish, you cannot move aimlessly about in the world. If you have a wife it is difficult; if you have a wife and perhaps a child, it is troublesome; if you have a wife and children, it is impossible. True, it has happened that a gypsy woman has carried her husband through life on her back, but for one thing this is very rare, and for another, it is likely to be tiresome in the long run – for the husband. Marriage brings one into fatal connection with custom and tradition, and traditions and customs are like the wind and weather, altogether incalculable. In Japan, I have been told, it is the custom for husbands to lie in childbed. Who knows but the time will come when the customs of foreign countries will obtain a foothold in Europe?

Friendship is dangerous, marriage still more so; for woman is and ever will be the ruin of a man, as soon as he contracts a permanent relation with her. Take a young man who is fiery as an Arabian courser, let him marry, he is lost. Woman is first proud, then is she weak, then she swoons, then he swoons, then the whole family swoons. A woman's love is nothing but dissimulation and weakness.

But because a man does not marry, it does not follow that his life need be wholly deprived of the erotic element. And the erotic ought also to have infinitude; but poetic infinitude, which can just as well be limited to an hour as to a month. When two beings fall in love with one another and begin to suspect that they were made for each other, it is time to have the courage to break it off; for by going on they have everything to lose and nothing to gain. This seems a paradox, and it is so for the feeling, but not for the understanding. In this sphere it is particularly necessary that one should make use of one's moods; through them one may realize an inexhaustible variety of combinations.

One should never accept appointment to an official position. If you do, you will become a mere Richard Roe, a tiny little cog in the machinery of the body politic; you even cease to be master of your own conduct, and in that case your theories are of little help. You receive a title, and this brings in its train every sin and evil. The law under which you have become a slave is equally tiresome, whether your advancement is fast or slow. A title can never be got rid of except by the commission of some crime which draws down on you a public whipping; even then you are not certain, for you may have it restored to you by royal pardon.

Even if one abstains from involvement in official business, one ought not to be inactive, but should pursue such occupations as are compatible with a sort of leisure; one should engage in all sorts of breadless arts. In this connection the self-development should be intensive rather than extensive, and one should, in spite of mature years, be able to prove the truth of the proverb that children are pleased with a rattle and tickled with a straw.

If one now, according to the theory of social jurisprudence, varies the soil – for if he had contact with one person only, the rotation method would fail as badly as if a farmer had only one acre of land, which would make it impossible for him to fallow, something which is of extreme importance – then one must also constantly vary himself, and this is the essential secret. For this purpose one must necessarily have control over one's moods. To control them in the sense of producing them at will is impossible, but prudence teaches how to utilize the moment. As an experienced sailor always looks out over the water and sees a squall coming from far away, so one ought always to see the mood a little in advance. One should know how the mood affects one's own mind and the mind of others, before putting it on. You first strike a note or two to evoke pure tones, and see what there is in a man; the intermediate tones follow later. The more experience you have, the more readily you will be convinced that there is often much in a man which is not suspected. When sentimental people, who as such are extremely tiresome, become angry, they are often very entertaining. Badgering a man is a particularly effective method of exploration.

The whole secret lies in arbitrariness. People usually think it easy to be arbitrary, but it requires much study to succeed in being arbitrary so as not to lose oneself in it, but so as to derive satisfaction from it. One does not enjoy the immediate but something quite different which he arbitrarily imports into it. You go to see the middle of a play, you read the third part of a book. By this means you insure yourself a very different kind of enjoyment from that which the author has been so kind as to plan for you. You enjoy something entirely accidental; you consider the whole of existence from this standpoint; let its reality be stranded thereon. I will cite an example. There was a man whose chatter certain circumstances made it necessary for me to listen to. At every opportunity he was ready with a little philosophical lecture, a very tiresome harangue. Almost in despair, I suddenly discovered that he perspired copiously when talking. I saw the pearls of sweat gather on his brow, unite to form a stream, glide down his nose, and hang at the extreme point of his nose in a drop-shaped body. From the moment of making this discovery, all was changed. I even took pleasure in inciting him to begin his philosophical instruction, merely to observe the perspiration on his brow and at the end of his nose.

The poet Baggesen says somewhere of someone that he was doubtless a good man, but that there was one insuperable objection against him, that there was no word that rhymed with his name. It is extremely wholesome thus to let the realities of life split upon an arbitrary interest. You transform something accidental into the absolute, and, as such, into the object of your admiration. This has an excellent effect, especially when one is excited. This method is an excellent stimulus for many persons. You look at everything in life from the standpoint of a wager, and so forth. The more rigidly consistent you are in holding fast to your arbitrariness, the more amusing the ensuing combinations will be. The degree of consistency shows whether you are an artist or a bungler; for to a certain extent all men do the same. The eye with which you look at reality must constantly be changed. The Neo-Platonists assumed that human beings who had been less perfect on earth became after death more or less perfect animals, all according to their deserts. For example, those who had exercised the civic virtues on a lower scale (retail dealers) were transformed into busy animals, like bees. Such a view of life, which here in this world sees all men transformed into animals or plants (Plotinus also thought that some would become plants), suggests rich and varied possibilities. The painter Tischbein sought to idealize every human being into an animal. His method has the fault of being too serious, in that it endeavours to discover a real resemblance.

The arbitrariness in oneself corresponds to the accidental in the external world. One should therefore always have an eye open for the accidental, always be *expeditus*, if anything should offer. The so-called social pleasures for which we prepare a week or two in advance amount to so little; on the other hand, even the most insignificant thing may accidentally offer rich material for amusement. It is impossible here to go into detail, for no theory can adequately embrace the concrete. Even the most completely developed theory is poverty-stricken compared with the fullness which the man of genius easily discovers in his ubiquity.

10. I study myself

One ought to be a mystery, not only to others, but also to one's self. I study myself; when I am weary of this, then for a pastime I light a cigar and think: the Lord only knows what He meant by me, or what He would make out of me.

11. 'A good cut . . . and not too fat'

One must be very naïve to believe that it will do any good to cry out and shout in the world, as if that would change one's fate. Better take things as they come, and make no fuss. When I was young and went into a restaurant, I would say to the waiter, 'A good cut, a very good cut, from the loin, and not too fat.' Perhaps the waiter did not even hear me, to say nothing of paying any attention to my request, and still less was it likely that my voice should reach the kitchen and influence the cook, and even if it did, there was perhaps not a good cut on the entire roast. Now I never shout any more.

12. Our earthly existence is a kind of illness . . .

As a humorist exists, he also expresses himself; and in life one may sometimes hear a humorist speak, in books his remarks are most frequently distorted. Now let a humorist express himself, and he will speak for example as follows: 'What is the meaning of life? Aye, tell me that; how should I know, we are born yesterday and know nothing. But one thing I do know, namely, that it is most comfortable to stride unknown through the world, without being known to His Majesty the King, Her Majesty the Queen, Her Majesty the Queen Mother, His Royal Highness, Prince Ferdinand; for such aristocratic acquaintanceships only make life troublesome and painful, just as it must be troublesome for a prince who lives in straitened circumstances in a country town to be recognized by his royal family.' And so it also seems to me that to be known by God in time makes life so acutely strenuous. Wherever He is, there every half hour is of tremendous importance. But to live in that manner is not endurable for sixty years; it is scarcely possible to endure even for three years the severe study required for the professional examinations which is however not nearly so strenuous as such a half hour.

Everything resolves itself into contradiction. Now it is preached into us that we should live with the entire passion of the infinite, and buy the eternal. Very well, one takes hold of the task and puts the best foot of the infinite forward, one comes rushing in the most extreme and passionate haste, so that no man in a bombardment could hurry faster, not the Jew who fell down from the gallery could come more completely head over heels. What happens? Why then comes the announcement that the auction is postponed, that the hammer will not fall today, but perhaps only sixty years hence. So one begins to pack for departure; what happens then? In the same second the speaker comes rushing up and says: 'But it is still possible that all will be decided, perhaps this very moment, by the judgment of death.'

What does this mean? In the last analysis all men get equally far. It is with existence as it was with my doctor. I complained of feeling ill. He replied: 'You are probably drinking too much coffee and not taking enough exercise.' Three weeks later I again consult him and say I am really not feeling well, but this time it cannot be the coffee for I do not touch it, nor the lack of exercise for I walk all day. He replies: 'Well then, the reason must be that you do not drink coffee and take too much exercise.' There we have it; the lack of well-being was and remained the same, but when I drink coffee it comes from the fact that I drink it, and when I do not drink coffee it comes from the fact that I do not drink it. And so with us human beings in general. Our whole earthly existence is a kind of illness. If anyone inquires about the reason, one first asks him how he has arranged his life; as soon as he has given an account of it you answer: 'That is it, there is the reason.' And then one walks away with an air of great importance, as if one had explained everything, until one has turned the corner, when one sticks one's tail between one's legs and skulks away. If one were to offer me ten dollars I would not undertake to explain the riddle of existence. And why should I? If life is a riddle, in the end the author of the riddle will doubtless explain it. I have not invented the temporal life, but I have noticed that in the periodicals which make a custom of printing riddles, the solution is generally offered in the next number. To be sure, it does happen that some old maid or pensioner is mentioned with honor as having solved the riddle, i.e. has known the solution a day in advance – that difference is certainly not very considerable.

13. Blind violinists

These two familiar strains of the violin! These two familiar strains here at this moment, in the middle of the street. Have I lost my senses? Does my ear, which from love of Mozart's music has ceased to hear, create these sounds; have the gods given me, unhappy beggar at the door of the temple – have they given me an ear that makes the sounds it hears? Only two strains, now I hear nothing more. Just as they burst forth from the deep choral tones of the immortal overture, so here they extricate themselves from the noise and confusion of the street, with all the surprise of a revelation. – It must be here in the neighborhood, for now I hear the lighter tones of the dance music. – And so it is to you, unhappy artist pair, I owe this joy. – One of them was about seventeen, he wore a coat of green kalmuck, with large bone buttons. The coat was much too large for him. He held the violin close up under his chin, his hat was pressed down over his eyes, his hand was hidden in a glove without fingers, his fingers were red and blue from cold. The other man was older; he wore a chenille shawl. Both were blind. A little girl, presumably their guide, stood in front of them, her hands tucked under her neckerchief. We gradually gathered around them, some admirers of this music: a letter carrier with his mailbag, a little boy, a servant girl, a couple of roustabouts. The well-appointed carriages rolled noisily by, the heavy wagons drowned out the strains, which by snatches flashed forth. Unhappy artist pair, do you know that these tones are an epitome of all the glories of the world? – How like a tryst it was!

14. Trying to find a seat for *Don Giovanni*

If we apply this explanation to the opera *Don Juan*, we shall have an opportunity to see it in its true classic validity. Don Juan is the hero of the opera, the chief interest centers in him; not only so, but he lends interest to all the other characters. This must not be understood, however, in a merely superficial sense, for this constitutes the mysterious in this opera, that the hero is also the animating force in the other characters. Don Juan's life is the life-principle within them. His passion sets the passion of all the others in motion; his passion resounds everywhere; it sounds in and sustains the earnestness of the Commandant, Elvira's anger, and Anna's hate, Ottavio's conceit, Zerlina's anxiety, Mazetto's exasperation, and Leporello's confusion. As hero in the play, he gives it his name, as is generally true in the case of the hero, but he is more than a name, he is, so to speak, the common denominator. The existence of all the others is, compared with his, only a derived existence. If we now require of an opera that its unity provide the keynote, then we shall easily see that one could not imagine a more perfect subject for an opera than Don Juan. The keynote can really be, in relation to the forces in the play, a third force which sustains these. As an illustration of such an opera, I might mention *The White Lady*, but such a unity is, with relation to the opera, a more external determination of the lyric. In *Don Juan* the keynote is nothing other than the primitive power in the opera itself; this is Don Juan, but again – just because he is not character but essentially life – he is absolutely musical. Nor are the other persons in the opera characters, but essentially passions, who are posited with Don Juan, and thereby become musical. That is, as Don Juan encircles them all, so do they in turn encircle Don Juan; they are the external consequences his life constantly posits. It is this musical life of Don Juan, absolutely centralized in the opera, which enables it to create a power of illusion such as no other is able to do, so that its life transports one into the life of the play. Because the musical is omnipresent in this music, one may enjoy any snatch of it, and immediately be transported by it. One may enter in the middle of the play and instantly be in the center of it, because this center, which is Don Juan's life, is everywhere.

We know from experience that it is not pleasant to strain two senses at the same time, and it is often very confusing if we have to use our eyes hard when our ears are already occupied. Therefore we have a tendency to close our eyes when hearing music. This is true of all music more or less, and of *Don Juan* in *sensu eminentiori*. As soon as the eyes are engaged, the impression becomes confused; for the dramatic unity which presents itself to the eye is always subordinate and imperfect in comparison with the musical unity which is heard at the same time. This, at least, has been my own experience. I have sat close up, I have sat farther and farther back, I have tried a corner in the theater where I could completely lose myself in the music. The better I understood it, or believed that I understood it, the farther I was away from it, not from coldness, but from love, for it is better understood at a distance. This has had for my life something strangely mysterious in it. There have been times when I would have given anything for a ticket. Now I need no longer spend a single penny for one. I stand outside in the corridor; I lean up against the partition which divides me from the auditorium, and then the impression is most powerful; it is a world by itself, separated from me; I can see nothing, but I am near enough to hear, and yet so infinitely far away.

15. You will regret it!

EITHER/OR

An ecstatic lecture

If you marry, you will regret it; if you do not marry, you will also regret it; if you marry or do not marry, you will regret both; whether you marry or do not marry, you will regret both. Laugh at the world's follies, you will regret it; weep over them, you will also regret that; laugh at the world's follies or weep over them, you will regret both; whether you laugh at the world's follies or weep over them, you will regret both. Believe a woman, you will regret it, believe her not, you will also regret that; believe a woman, or believe her not, you will regret both; whether you believe a woman or believe her not, you will regret both. Hang yourself, you will regret it; do not hang yourself, and you will also regret that; hang yourself or do not hang yourself, you will regret both; whether you hang yourself or do not hang yourself, you will regret both. This, gentlemen, is the sum and substance of all philosophy. It is not only at certain moments that I view everything *aeterno modo*, as Spinoza says, but I live constantly *aeterno modo*. There are many who think that they live thus, because after having done the one or the other, they combine or mediate the opposites. But this is a misunderstanding; for the true eternity does not lie behind either/or, but before it. Hence, their eternity will be a painful succession of temporal moments, for they will be consumed by a twofold regret. My philosophy is at least easy to understand, for I have only one principle, and I do not even proceed from that. It is necessary to distinguish between the successive dialectic in either/or, and the eternal dialectic here set forth. Thus, when I say that I do not proceed from my principle, this must not be understood in opposition to a proceeding forth from it, but is rather a negative expression for the principle itself, through which it is apprehended in equal opposition to a proceeding or a non- proceeding from it. I do not proceed from my principle; for if I did, I would regret it, and if I did not, I would also regret that. If it seems, therefore, to one or another of my respected hearers that there is anything in what I say, it only proves that he has no talent for philosophy; if my argument seems to have any forward movement, this also proves the same. But for those who can follow me, although I do not make any progress, I shall now unfold the eternal truth, by virtue of which this philosophy remains within itself, and admits of no higher philosophy. For if I proceeded from my principle, I should find it impossible to stop; for if I stopped, I should regret it, and if I did not stop, I should also regret that, and so forth. But since I never start, so can I never stop; my eternal departure is identical with my eternal cessation. Experience has shown that it is by no means difficult for philosophy to begin. Far from it. It begins with nothing, and consequently can always begin. But the difficulty, both for philosophy and for philosophers, is to stop. This difficulty is obviated in my philosophy; for if anyone believes that when I stop now, I really stop, he proves himself lacking in the speculative insight. For I do not stop now, I stopped at the time when I began. Hence my philosophy has the advantage of brevity, and it is also impossible to refute; for if anyone were to contradict me, I should undoubtedly have the right to call him mad. Thus it is seen that the philosopher lives continuously *aeterno modo*, and has not, like Sintenis of blessed memory, only certain hours which are lived for eternity.

16. The demoniacal

In The Concept of Anxiety *(1844) Vigilius Haufniensis (The Watchman of Copenhagen) develops a theory to the effect that 'the demoniacal' is the dread of the good. The forms of 'the demoniacal' are various, 'Shut-up-ness'; 'the Sudden'; 'the Vacuous, the Tedious'. The first two forms are represented here. 'Shut-up-ness' deals with the relations of torturer and victim, and the unexpected corollary to that ('No man who has a bad conscience can endure silence'). The second, which presents 'the demoniacal' as 'The Sudden' takes, as its example, a much talked-of phenomenon from the world of the theatre. The great ballet dancer Bournonville could leap straight on to the stage from the wings and remain immobile in the pose in which he landed. This feat was the talk of all Copenhagen.*

I: Shut-up-ness

The demoniacal is *shut-upness* [*det Indesluttede,* or *Indesluttedhed*] *unfreely revealed*. These two traits denote, as they should, the same thing; for the shut-up is precisely the mute, and if it has to express itself, this must come about against its will when the freedom lying prone in unfreedom revolts upon coming into communication with freedom outside and now betrays unfreedom in such a way that it is the individual who betrays himself against his will in dread. The word 'shut-up' must therefore be taken here in a perfectly definite sense, for in the sense of reserve, in which it is commonly used, it may denote the highest freedom Brutus, Henry V of England as Prince of Wales, etc., were in this sense shut-up until the time came when it was evident that their shut-upness was a pact with the good. Such a shut-upness was therefore identical with expansion, and never is there an individuality which in the finer and nobler sense of the word is more expanded than he who is shut-up within the womb of a great idea. Freedom is precisely the expansive. It is in opposition to this I would employ the word 'shut-up,' 'in an eminent sense', for 'unfreedom.' Commonly a more metaphysical term is used for the evil. It is called 'negating.' The ethical term precisely corresponding to that, when one contemplates the effect thereof upon the individual, is shut-upness. The demoniacal does not shut itself up *with* something, but shuts *itself* up; and in this lies the mystery of existence, the fact that unfreedom makes a prisoner precisely of itself. Freedom is constantly communicating (it will do no harm to take into account even the religious significance of this word); unfreedom becomes more and more shut-up and wants no communication. This can be observed in all spheres. It shows itself in hypochondriacs, in crotcheteers, it shows itself in the highest passions when by a profound misunderstanding they introduce silence as a system. When freedom then comes in contact with shut-upness it becomes afraid [*angest*]. In common speech we have an expression which is exceedingly suggestive. We say of a person that he will not come out with it. The shut-up is precisely the mute; the spoken word is precisely the saving thing, that which delivers from the mute abstraction of the shut-up. Let the demoniacal here mean *x*; freedom's relation to it from without, *x*: the law for the revelation of the demoniacal is that against its will it comes out with it. For by speech is implied a communication. A demoniac in the New Testament says therefore to Christ, 'What have I to do with you'; he goes on to say that Christ has come to destroy him (dread of the good). Or a demoniac beseeches Christ to go another way. (When dread is dread of the evil, cf. §I, the individual seeks refuge in salvation.)

Life presents examples of this abundantly in all possible spheres and in all possible degrees. A hardened criminal will not go to confession (the demoniacal consists precisely in this, that the man is not willing to communicate with the good through the chastisement of suffering). There is a method applicable to such a case which perhaps is rarely used: it is silence and the power of the eye. If an inquisitor has the requisite physical strength and spiritual elasticity to hold out, though it were for sixteen hours, he will at last be rewarded by the admission breaking out involuntarily. No man who has a bad conscience can endure silence. Put him in solitary confinement, and he will become apathetic. But this silence, while the judge is present, and the clerk waiting to inscribe the confession in the record, is the most searching interrogation and the most terrible torture, and yet lawful; but it is by no means so easy to bring this about as one may suppose. The only power which can compel shut-upness to speak is either a higher demon (for every devil has his turn to reign) or the good which is absolutely able to be silent. And if here in this examination by silence any artfulness would put the man in embarrassment, the inquisitor himself will become ashamed, and it will prove that he at last becomes afraid of himself and must break the silence. Confronted with a subordinate demon, or with subordinate human beings whose God-consciousness is not strongly developed, shut-upness triumphs absolutely, because the former is not able to hold out, and the latter, in all innocence, are accustomed to live from hand to mouth and keep the heart on the tongue. It is incredible what power resolute reserve is capable of exercising over such men, how they end by begging and imploring for merely one word to break the stillness, but it is also shocking to crush the weak under foot in this fashion. It may be thought perhaps that such things occur only among princes and Jesuits, that to get a clear notion of it one must think of Domitian, Cromwell, the Duke of Alba, or a general of the Jesuit Order, which is almost an appellative term for this. Not at all, it occurs much more frequently. However, one must be cautious in passing judgment upon the phenomenon; for, although the phenomenon is the same, the reason for it may be exactly the opposite, since the individual who subjects others to the despotism and torture of shut-upness might himself wish to speak, might himself we waiting for a higher demon who could bring the revelation forth. But the torturer may also be selfishly related to his shut-upness.

However, I will indicate one collision, the contradiction of which is as terrible as is shut-upness itself. What the shut-up keeps hidden in his close reserve may be so terrible that he dare not utter it even in his own hearing, because it seems to him as though by this very utterance he were committing a new sin, or as though it would tempt him again. In order that this phenomenon may occur the individual must be such a blending of purity and impurity as seldom is encountered. It is therefore most likely to occur when the individual at the time of accomplishing the terrible act was not master of himself. For example, a man in a state of intoxication may have done what he remembers only obscurely, yet knows that it was so wild a thing that it is almost impossible for him to recognize himself. The same may also be the case with a man who once was insane and has retained a memory of that previous state. What decides whether the phenomenon is demoniacal is the attitude of the individual towards revelation, whether he is willing to permeate that fact with freedom, assume the responsibility of it in freedom. If he is not willing to do that, then the phenomenon is demoniacal. This distinction must be held sharply, for even the man who merely wishes revelation is nevertheless essentially demoniacal. He has in fact two wills, one of them subordinate, impotent, which wills revelation, and a stronger will which wills to be shut up; but the fact that this is the stronger shows that essentially he is demoniacal. Close reserve is involuntary revelation. The weaker the individuality originally is, or in proportion as the elasticity of freedom is consumed in the service of close reserve, the more certainly will the secret break out at last. The most trivial contact, a glance in passing, etc., is sufficient to start that terrible monologue; or it may be comical, depending upon the content of the close reserve. The ventriloquism may be plainly declarative, or it may be indirect, as when an insane man points to another person and says, 'He is very objectionable to me, he's probably insane.' Revelation may declare itself in words when the unfortunate man ends by intruding upon everyone his hidden secret. It may declare itself by a look, by a glance; for there is a glance of the eye by which a man involuntarily reveals what is hidden. There is an accusing glance which reveals what one almost dreads to understand; a contrite, imploring glance which hardly tempts curiosity to peer into this involuntary telegraphy. Depending upon the content of close reserve, all this in turn may be almost comical, when what dread reveals against its will are ludicrous incidents, pettiness, vanity, pranks, petty envy, little crotchets about medicine and health, etc.

II: The sudden

The demoniacal is the sudden. The sudden is a new expression for close reserve seen in another aspect. The demoniacal is character- ized as the shut-up when one reflects upon the content, it is characterized as the sudden when one reflects upon time. Close reserve was the effect of the negating retrenchment of the ego in the individuality. Reservedness closed itself constantly more and more against communication. But communication is in turn the expres- sion for continuity, and the negation of continuity is the sudden. One might suppose that close reserve would have an extraordinary continuity. But exactly the opposite is the case, although in com- parison with the soft and vapid dispersion of oneself which ends with the sense impression, this has an appearance of continuity. The continuity which close reserve may have can be compared with the vertigo we may suppose a top must feel as it revolves perpe- tually upon its pivot. In case this close reserve does not carry the thing so far as to become completely insane, insanity being the pitiful *perpetuum mobile* of monotonous indifference, the indivi- duality will still retain a certain continuity with the rest of human life. Against the foil of this continuity, that apparent continuity of close reserve will display itself as the sudden. One instant it is there, the next it is gone, and no sooner is it gone than it is there again as large as life. It cannot be embroidered upon any continuity, nor woven into it, but what expresses itself thus is precisely the sudden.

In case the demoniacal were something somatic, there never would be the sudden. When a fever, insanity, etc., comes back again, one discovers at last a law, and this law in some degree annuls the sudden. But the sudden recognizes no law. It does not properly belong among natural phenomena but is psychic, is the expression of unfreedom.

Like the demoniacal, the sudden is dread of the good. The good in this context means continuity, for the first expression of salvation is continuity. While the life of the individual goes on in a certain degree in continuity with the rest of human life, close reserve maintains itself in him as continuity's abracadabra which communi- cates only with itself and therefore does not cease to be the sudden.

Depending upon the content of close reserve, the sudden may

signify the terrible, but also, for the observer, the effect may appear comic. In this connection we must note that every individual has a little of this suddenness, just as every individual has a little bit of *l'idée fixe*.

I will not follow this out further, but to uphold my category I will recall the fact that the sudden is always due to dread of the good, because there is something which freedom is not willing to permeate. Among the formations which lie in dread of the evil it is weakness which corresponds to what we here call 'the sudden.'

If in a different way we would make clear to ourselves how it is the demoniacal is the sudden, we may from a purely aesthetic point of view consider the question how the demoniacal can best be represented on the stage. If one would present Mephistopheles, it is well enough to give him lines to recite, if one wishes to use him as an efficient force in the dramatic action, rather than depict his character properly. In that case Mephistopheles is not really represented but is vaguely indicated as a malicious, witty, intriguing pate. This is a volatilization which a popular legend has already improved upon. It recounts that the devil sat and speculated for 3000 years how to overthrow man – then finally he found it out. Here the accent is placed upon the 3000 years, and the picture this produces in the mind is precisely that of the brooding shut-upness of the demoniacal. If one would not volatilize Mephistopheles in the way above indicated, one may choose another mode of representation. In this it will appear that Mephistopheles is essentially mimic. Even the terrible words which rise out of the abyss of malice are incapable of producing such an effect as does the suddenness of the leap which lies within the compass of mimic art. Even were the word more terrible, even though it were a Shakespeare, a Byron, a Shelley, that breaks the silence, the word always conserves its saving power; for even all despair and all the horror of evil expressed in one word is not so horrible as silence. Mimic art is able to express the sudden, though this does not imply that this art as such is the sudden. In this respect Bournonville as Master of the Ballet deserves great credit for his representation of Mephistopheles. The horror which seizes one on seeing Mephistopheles leap in through the window and remain stationary in the attitude of the leap! This bound within the leap, recalling the plunge of the bird of prey and the bound of the wild beast, which are doubly terrifying because commonly they break forth from complete immobility, produces therefore an infinite impression. Hence Mephistopheles must walk as little as possible, for the walk itself is in a way a transition to the leap, suggests a presentiment of its possibility. This first appearance of Mephistopheles in the ballet of *Faust* is not a *coup de théâtre* but a very profound thought. Words and speech, short as they may be, have yet always, if we regard the thing abstractly, a certain continuity, because it is in time they are heard. But the sudden is completely detached from continuity, whether it be with the past or with the future. So it is with Mephistopheles. No one has yet seen him – when there he stands, wholly himself from head to feet, and speed cannot be expressed more strongly than by the fact that he stands there with one leap. If this passes into a walk, the effect is weakened. By the fact that Mephistopheles is represented in this fashion, his appearance upon the scene produces the effect of the demoniacal, which comes more suddenly than the thief in the night, for one commonly thinks of the thief as moving stealthily. By this then Mephistopheles reveals his nature, which, like the demoniacal nature, is the sudden. Thus in its forward movement the demoniacal is the sudden, thus it springs into existence in a man, and thus man himself is sudden in so far as he is demoniacal, whether it be that this power has possessed him wholly or that only a little part of it is present in him. Thus the demoniacal always is, and thus suddenly does unfreedom become dread, and such too is the movement of its dread. Hence the aptness of the demoniacal for the mimic art, not in the sense of the beautiful but of the sudden, the abrupt, something which life often gives us opportunity to observe.

17. The Scientist out on Søeborg Lake

A typical literary device of the period was to appear as 'Editor' of a bundle of papers found in some unlikely place. The section of Stages on Life's Way *called* 'Guilty?/Not Guilty?' – A Passion Narrative – A Psychological Experiment *purports to be edited by one Frater Taciturnus (The Silent Brother) and contains some of the most personal and provocative texts in the entire Kierke-gaardian oeuvre. The description of how the Frater comes across the Diary in the first place pushes the delight in serendipity to its limit.*

Every child knows that Søeborg Castle is a ruin which lies in the northern part of Seeland, about half a mile from the seashore, close to a little town of the same name. In spite of the fact that the castle was destroyed a long while ago, it still maintains itself in the memory of the nation and will continue to, for it has a rich historic and poetic background to live upon. Something of the sort might be said, in a way, of the Søeborg Lake which is contiguous to the castle. Originally it had a length of a couple of miles and a depth of several fathoms to live upon; for this reason it has not yet disappeared, and in spite of the fact that the mainland is encroaching upon it more and more and is constricting it more and more painfully, it will for a long time continue to vindicate its existence as a lake.

Last summer I fell in with an older friend of mine, a naturalist, who had followed the coast from Copenhagen north to this point for the sake of making observations upon marine plants. He had determined to visit the country about Søeborg, which he expected would yield rich results. He proposed that I should make the excursion with him, and I accepted the proposal.

It is not easy to get near the lake, for it is surrounded by a rather wide stretch of bog. Here it is that the border conflict is carried on day and night between the lake and the mainland. There is something sad about this conflict, which is not indicated, however, by any trace of destruction; for what the land gradually wins from the lake is transformed into smiling and exceedingly fruitful fields. But alas for the poor lake which is thus disappearing! No one has compassion upon it, no one feels for it; for neither the parson whose fields border upon it on one side, nor the peasants whose fields are on the opposite bank, are averse to winning one piece of land after the other. The poor lake is abandoned to its own resources on the one side and on the other!

What imparts to the lake a still more shut-in appearance is the fact that the bog is overgrown luxuriantly with rushes. There is nothing to match it in Denmark, so at least said my friend the naturalist. Only at one place is there a small open channel, and here is a flat-bottomed boat in which we two (he for the sake of science, and I for friendship and curiosity) punted our way out to the lake. With difficulty we got the boat started, for the channel has scarcely a foot of water. The thicket of rushes is as dense as a forest to the height of about four yards, and when hidden by it one is as though lost to the world forever, forgotten in the stillness which is broken only by our struggles with the boat, or when a bittern, that mysterious voice in the desert, thrice repeats its cry and then again thrice repeats it. Strange bird, why dost thou sigh thus and lament? Thine only desire after all is to remain in solitude!

Finally we got beyond the reeds, and before us lay the lake, clear as a mirror and sparkling in the radiance of the afternoon. Everything so still! Silence rested upon the lake. Whereas while we punted our way through the thicket of rushes I felt as though I were transported into the midst of the luxuriant fertility of India, now I felt as though I were out upon the Pacific Ocean. I was almost alarmed at being so infinitely far from men, at lying in a nutshell upon a vast ocean. Now there was a confused voice, a mingled cry of all kinds of fowls, and then stillness prevailed again, almost to the point of making me apprehensive when the sound suddenly ceased and the ear grasped in vain for a support in the infinite.

My friend the naturalist took out the apparatus with which he drew up submarine plants, cast it into the water and began his work. Meanwhile I sat at the other end of the boat dreamily absorbed in the beauties of nature. He already had drawn up a good deal of material and began to busy himself with his booty when I begged him to lend me the instrument. Resuming my former place I cast it out. With a muffled sound it sank to the depths. Perhaps it was because I did not know well how to use the apparatus, at all events when I wanted to pull it up I encountered so much resistance that I was almost afraid of proving the weaker of the two. I pulled again, then up rose a bubble from the depths, it lasted an instant, then burst – and then I succeeded. I had the strangest feeling, and yet I did not have the remotest notion what sort of a find it was I had made. Now when I reflect upon it I know all, I understand it, I understand that it was a sigh from below, a sigh *de profundis*, a sigh that I had wrested from the lake its treasure, a sigh from the shy and secluded lake from which I had wrested its secret. If two minutes earlier I had had a presentiment of this, I would not have ventured to pull.

The naturalist sat absorbed completely in his work, he merely inquired casually if I had got anything, an exclamation which did not seem to expect a reply, since with good reason he did not regard my fishing efforts as having any bearing upon science. In fact I had not found what he was after, but something altogether different. And so each of us sat at our respective ends of the boat, each preoccupied with his find, he for the sake of science, I for the sake of friendship and curiosity. Wrapped in oilskin and provided with many seals was a rosewood box. The box was locked, and when I opened it by force the key lay inside – thus it is that morbid reserve always is introverted. In the box was a manuscript written with a very careful and clear hand upon thin paper. There was orderliness and neatness in it all, and yet an air of solemn consecration as if it had been written before the face of God. To think that by my intervention I have brought disorder into the archives of heavenly justice! But now it is too late, now I crave forgiveness of heaven and of the unknown author. Undeniably the place of concealment was well chosen, and Søeborg Lake is more trustworthy than the most solemn declaration which promises 'complete silence,' for the lake makes no such declaration. Strangely enough, different as happiness and unhappiness are, they sometimes agree in wishing for . . . silence. The administration of the lottery when distributing the prizes of fortune is extolled for being silent about the names of the fortunate ones lest their good fortune might become an embarrassment to them; but the unfortunate who has gambled away all his fortune also desires to have his name passed over in silence.

In the box there were found also several pieces of jewelry, some being of considerable value: adornments and precious stones – ah, precious indeed, too dearly bought, would the owner say, in spite of the fact that he was allowed to keep them! It is a valuable find, and I feel that I am under obligation to advertise it. There was found a flat gold ring with a date engraved inside it, a necklace consisting of a diamond cross fastened to a light blue silk ribbon. The remainder was in part of no value at all: a fragment of a playbill, a scrap torn from the New Testament (each apart by itself in an envelope of vellum paper), a withered rose in a silver-gilt pyx, together with other things which only to the owner could have had a value equal to the diamonds of two carats each with which the pyx was adorned.

Herewith the owner of a box found in Søeborg Lake in the

summer of '44 is summoned to apply to me by the initials F.T. through Reitzel's Book Shop. In order to obviate betimes any delay I take the liberty of observing that the handwriting of this application must at once betray the owner, as well as that everyone who may do me the honor to write, when he receives no reply, can from this conclude securely that the handwriting is not the right one, for only this can properly claim a reply. On the other hand, for the comfort of the owner be it said, that even though I have taken the liberty of publishing his manuscript, its contents, unlike the handwriting, are of a sort that does not betray anybody, and be it said that I have not taken the liberty of showing to anyone, not to a single person, either the manuscript, or the diamond cross, or the other things.

*   *   *

Candidate Bonfils has published a table by the aid of which one can calculate the year when any day of the week and of the month is given. His merits in this respect redound also to my advantage; I have calculated and calculated and finally have discovered that the year corresponding to the dates engraved on the ring is 1751, the memorable year in which Gregory Rothfischer was converted to Lutheranism, a year which, for the man who with a profound eye contemplates Cyclopically the marvellous course of world history, was also remarkable for the fact that precisely five years later the Seven Years War broke out. So one is compelled to go back to a rather remote epoch in time, unless one is ready to assume that an error has crept into the data or into my calculation. If one refuses to do anything under compulsion, one might, for all I care, assume that a poor devil of a psychologist who can count upon but scanty sympathy for psychological experiments and unsubstantial constructions has made an attempt to give them both a little life by adding a touch of romanticism, the fiction that the thing belonged to a past age. For a sketch, however psychologically correct, which does not inquire whether such a person ever lived, is perhaps of less interest to our age, when even poetry has snatched at the expedient of trying to produce the effect of reality. A little psychology, a little observation of so-called real men, they still want to have, but when this science or art follows its own devices, when it looks away from the manifold expressions of psychic states which reality offers, when it slips away in order by itself alone to construct an individuality by means of its own knowledge, and to find in this individuality an object for its observations, then many people grow weary. As a matter of fact, in real life passions, psychic states, etc., are only carried to a certain point. This too delights the psychologist, but he has a different sort of delight in seeing passion carried to its utmost limits.

As for the reviewers, I could wish that my prayer might be understood in all simplicity and entirely in accordance with the tenor of the words as my honest meaning and that the result might correspond with the prayer's desire: namely, that the book may not be the object of any critical discussion, whether favorable or unfavorable. When one may acquire in so easy a way a claim upon a man's gratitude one surely might oblige him.

18. Keep on walking!

The importance of walking to Kierkegaard was both physical and metaphysical. It was his form of daily exercise. It kept him in touch with people (he was famous for his ability to stop and talk to anyone, picking up from the exact spot where they had stopped talking last time). It was a means of counterpointing his own texts. It was (with Kolderup- Rosenvinge) a means of keeping up to date with political talk, as well as being a literary form. But above all, it was for him a symbol of movement itself. For Kierkegaard as for Blake 'Energy is eternal delight'.

1847

DEAR JETTE,

Above all, do not lose your desire to walk: every day I walk myself into a state of well-being and walk away from every illness; I have walked myself into my best thoughts, and I know of no thought so burdensome that one cannot walk away from it. Even if one were to walk for one's health and it were constantly one station ahead – *I would still say: Walk!* Besides, it is also apparent that in walking one constantly gets as close to well-being as possible, even if one does not quite reach it – *but by sitting still, and the more one sits still, the closer one comes to feeling ill.* Health and salvation can be found only in motion. If anyone denies that motion exists, I do as Diogenes did, I walk. If anyone denies that health resides in motion, then I walk away from all morbid objections. *Thus, if one just keeps on walking, everything will be all right.* And out in the country you have all the advantages; you do not risk being stopped before you are safe and happy outside your gate, nor do you run the risk of being intercepted on your way home. I remember exactly what happened to me a while ago and what has happened frequently since then. I had been walking for an hour and a half and had done a great deal of thinking, and with the help of motion I had really become a very agreeable person to myself. What bliss, and, as you may imagine, what care did I not take to bring my bliss home as safely as possible. Thus I hurry along, with downcast eyes I steal through the streets, so to speak; confident that I am entitled to the sidewalk, I do not consider it necessary to look about at all (for thereby one is so easily intercepted, just as one is looking about – in order to avoid) and thus hasten along the sidewalk with my bliss (for the ordinance forbidding one to carry anything on the sidewalk does not extend to bliss, which makes a person lighter) – directly into a man who is always suffering from illness and who therefore with downcast eyes, defiant because of his illness, does not even think that he must look about when he is not entitled to the sidewalk. I was stopped. It was a quite exalted gentleman who now honored me with conversation. Thus all was lost. After the conversation ended, there was only one thing left for me to do: instead of going home, to go walking again.

As you see, there really is no more space in this letter, and therefore I break off this conversation – for a sense it has been a conversation, inasmuch as I have constantly thought of you as present. Do take care of yourself!

YOURS, S. KIERKEGAARD.

19. I can walk away from everything!

August 1848

DEAR CONFERENTSRAAD,
    'We did not get around to talking about politics,' you remark. No

wonder! You are so polite that you forget that I was so impolite as to hold forth by myself which, however, could not be otherwise during a – solitary walk in your company, and after all you are the person who is usually informed about politics while I remain all ears.

No, politics is not for me. To follow politics, even if only domestic politics, is nowadays an impossibility, for me, at any rate. Whenever anything happens very quickly – well, then one attempts to follow it; whenever anything goes very slowly – well, then one attempts to put up with the boredom of following it. But whenever something fluctuates back and forth, up and down and down and up, and then comes to a halt, and around and up and down and back again, then I am incapable of voluntarily following. If necessary I should prefer going to war as a 'coerced volunteer' to sitting at home – following it. I do not consider him who goes to war under such conditions as great a patriot as him who sits at home – following it. We have not been at war for a long time, but it has never impressed me as a real war. To me the whole thing seems more like a lecture (such as Ørsted's on physics) during which experiments are conducted, or during which the presentation is illustrated with experiments. To my way of thinking this war has really always been some sort of peace making or making of peace – the most peculiar sort of war I have ever known.

That is why I keep away from politics, however much I like to hear someone talk about it who after all is so well versed in these matters that he can keep up with them. It turns sour for me, probably because I know too little, so that I become like someone who wanted to go travelling around Sjælland with the help of an ordinary little map of Denmark. Politics is too much for me. I love to focus my attention on lesser things, in which one may sometimes encounter exactly the same.

Hence I leave the world's stage, the field of battle, and return to Copenhagen, but in a manner of speaking I even leave Copenhagen. I go for a walk, and yet I shall perhaps arrive at the same thing. I shall allow myself to escort you out to one of those neighborhoods *dicht an den neuen Buden* [close to the new cottages], where there is that quiet noise that emanates from the many little families there. – Act I – Two dogs have started fighting. This event causes an enormous sensation. An unbelievable number of heads appear at the windows to watch. While it lasts, all work stops. Everything is abandoned. – Act II – From the doors of the two houses closest to the battle emerge two housewives, each from her own. These two housewives appear to be the mistresses of the dogs. One maintains that the other's dog started the fight. The women become so angry over this that they start fighting. – I observed no more than this, but it could easily be continued. – So, Act III – Two men arrive, the husbands of the respective women. One of them maintains that the other's wife started it. The two husbands become so angry that they start fighting. Whereupon it may be assumed that other husbands and wives join in – and this is now a European war. The occasion is the question of who started it. In this you will perceive the formula for war in the second degree. War in the first degree is war; in the second degree it is a war occasioned by the question of who started the first war.

But now to something far more important. I see, to my horror, from what you write that you have stopped walking. Above all, this must not be so. For your own sake, dear *Conferentsraad*, and for mine so that I may have a clear conscience, I must emphatically request that you go on walking. Indeed, I have yet another reason for insisting so zealously on this. That little circle that is closest to you, whose sole desire is and will ever be for your well-being, may have occasionally almost thanked me silently for coming and persuading you to go out. Yes, that is how it is. I have the pleasure of walking with you and the gratitude of your family into the bargain. Accordingly I have an even greater responsibility – it may sound strange to say this – not to lead you *astray*, as I would if I were to make you *sit still* in order first to make you read – a letter from me – and then, and this would be even more irresponsible, to write to me. Oh no! You must walk. As those two lovers, Charles and Emeline, promise each other in parting to look at the moon whenever it is full, wherever they may find themselves in the world, so let us two walkers promise each other whenever we receive a letter – regardless of the weather and walking conditions – to go for a walk. Next time I write I shall purposely arrange it so that inside the outer envelope there will be another one on which it will say, 'from Magister Kierkegaard,' so that without opening the envelope you will be able to see whom it is from. Then, provided that you consider a letter from me a burden, please read it at once – and then off with you to overcome whatever damage you may have sustained from it. But on the other hand, provided you consider such a letter a relatively good thing when compared with the rest of the boredom and mediocrity of this best of all worlds, then please go for a walk first and then read. Whichever way you choose, what I request of you will take place – for that you walk is most important. I who do not understand politics, do, on the other hand, understand all about walking. My view of life is like that of the parson: 'Life is a path.' That is why I go walking. As long as I am able to go walking, I fear nothing, not even death. For as long as I am able to go walking I can walk away from everything. When I am unable to go walking, I fear everything, especially life, for when I am unable to go walking, nothing goes well for me.

I shall stop here, at your gate. I take my leave. Thank you for today, thank you for the walk, thank you for the kindness I know you bear me so readily, indeed with so much friendship. Now our ways are parting. The gate is closing. Once more I look back. Then I leave, but I remain

Your S. Kierkegaard

20. Fear of Germany

All this fear of Germany is a fancy, a game, a new attempt to flatter national vanity. A million people who honestly own up to being a small nation, and then if everyone is resolved before God to be what they are: is a tremendous strength; there is no danger there. No, the misfortune is quite another; the misfortune is that this little people is demoralized, divided against itself, disgustingly envious one of another, insubordinate towards everyone in power, petty towards everyone who is something, impertinent and unbridled, incited to a sort of tyranny of the plebs. That produces a bad conscience, and therefore people fear Germany. But no one dares to say where the misfortune lies – and so people flatter all these unhealthy passions and become self-important by fighting against the Germans.

Denmark is facing a loathsome period. Provincial-mindedness

and ill-natured pettiness fighting among themselves; in the end one will be suspected of being German unless one wears a particular kind of hat etc. etc. On the other side the Communist rising; everyone who owns a little will be marked out and persecuted through the press.

That is Denmark's misfortune – or the punishment which has come upon Denmark, a people without a true fear of God, a people whose national consciousness is small-town gossip, a people who idolize being nothing, where school-boys are the judges, a people where those who should govern are afraid and those who ought to obey are impertinent, a people among whom are to be found daily proofs that there is no public morality in the land – a people who can only be saved by a tyrant or a few martyrs.

21. Talks with the King of Denmark

All of Kierkegaard's arch humour and malicious wit is captured in these three Journal *entries about his conversations with the King of Denmark, Christian VIII. Enormously flattered to be so famous a citizen, Kierkegaard yet hardly lets the King maintain his dignity, but takes pleasure in showing up his limitations. With the Queen he is even more merciless. Their talk came to rest on Communism. Kierkegaard is, of course, a staunch royalist!*

I

It is a miserable existence, as I said at the time to Christian VIII, to be a genius in a provincial town. Naturally I said it in such a way as to compliment him, I said: Your majesty's only misfortune is that your wisdom and prudence are too great and the country too small; it is a misfortune to be a genius in a provincial town. To which he answered: One can do all the more for the individual. That was the first time I spoke to him. He said many flattering things to me and asked me to visit him, to which I answered: I visit no one, your majesty. Then he said: Yes, but I know that you will not object to my sending you word. To that I answered: 'I am a subject, it is for your majesty to command; but in return I shall make one stipulation.' 'Well, and what is it?' 'That I should be given permission to talk with you in private.' Thereupon he gave me his hand and we separated. In the course of conversation, at the beginning, he also said something to me about my having so many ideas and whether I could not surrender some to him, to which I answered that I considered that my whole endeavour was, among other things, to the advantage of every government, but that the point of it was that I should be a private individual, for otherwise people would at once insert a little interpretation. And I added furthermore: 'I have the honour to serve a higher power, for the sake of which I have staked my life.'

As I came in through the door and announced my name he said: it gives me particular pleasure to see you, I have heard so much good of you. To that I answered (I who had sat in fear and trembling in the antechamber not knowing whether I should get in on my head or on my feet. [Someone who was standing outside with me had just asked me whether I was going to bow three times on entering, to which I had answered that it was a ridiculous question to ask me, an old courtier might know that kind of thing beforehand but I did not know whether I should get in on my hands or on my feet] but then when I got into the room I went up so close to him that he took a step back, and I caught his eye, where I saw what he was looking for): 'and I your majesty, have always said to myself, in the end the man you will get on best with will be the King; for in order for that to happen I must find someone who has intelligence enough and who is placed so high that it could never occur to him to be petty towards me.'

Altogether my conversations with him were well worth noting down.

II

The second time I talked to Christian VIII was at Sorgenfrie many months later. Moreover his conversations were in a certain sense not very important to me, for he wished me to talk. But it was stimulating to talk with him and I have never seen an oldish man so animated, in a fever of excitement, almost like a woman. He was a sort of spiritual and intellectual voluptuary. I saw at once that here was danger, and I was therefore very careful to keep as far from him as possible. In the presence of a king I found it unsuitable to make my eccentricity into a pretext for not visiting him and so used different tactics, saying I was unwell.

Christian VIII was brilliantly gifted but ran to seed, lacking a moral background of corresponding proportions. If he had lived in a southern country, I can imagine that Christian VIII would have been the certain prey of a cunning priest. No woman would ever really have got power over him, not even the most gifted, partly because he was too intelligent and partly because he shared a little the manly superstition that man is more intelligent than woman.

But a Jesuit – he could have turned and twisted Christian VIII any way he liked, but the Jesuit would have had to have complete command of *the interesting*, for that was what he was really panting for. But without a doubt he was captivating, extraordinarily subtle, and had an unusual eye for whatever could please or satisfy the individual, just that particular individual.

And so I went in. He said: 'It is a long time since I have seen you here.' To that I answered, still at the door: 'Your majesty will perhaps first of all let me explain myself. I must ask your majesty to rest assured how much I appreciate the graces and favours which you show me; but I am poor in health and that is why I come so seldom, I cannot endure waiting in an antechamber, it exhausts me.' He answered that I need not wait, but that in any case I could write to him. I thanked him for that. Thereupon we began talking, walking about part of the time. He always preferred to talk about the government's affairs, or general remarks about some political theme or other. That day he led the conversation to communism of which he was plainly enough anxious and afraid. I explained to him that as I understood it the whole movement which was impending was a movement which did not come in contact with kings. It would be a fight between classes, but the fighting parties would always find it in their interest to be on good terms with the King. It was a return of the problems of antiquity and it was therefore easy to see that in a sense the king would stand outside them. It would be like the fights in a house between the cellar and the ground-floor, and between these and the first floor, but the landlord would not be attacked. I talked next of how to fight with 'the masses': simply remain quite quiet; that 'the masses' were like a woman with whom one never fought directly but indirectly, and helped them to put their foot in it, and since they were wanting in intelligence they would always lose in the end – but simply stand fast. Here he said:

'Yes, of all people a king should do that.' To that I answered nothing. And so I said that what the whole age needed was education, and that what became violence in a large country, in Denmark became rudeness. Then he said some complimentary things to me about my mind etc. I made use of the situation and said: Your majesty sees best of all from me that what I say is true, for where I am concerned everything really turns upon the fact that I am well brought up, and therefore really upon my father. And so we talked about Guizot, an attack which had just been made upon him. I explained how ambiguous the position was in modern states, where scandal has really been given an official position, and the right tactic was, consequently, to ignore it, but that they suddenly took it into their heads one day to take such an attack seriously. 'I imagine Guizot reading the attack, and then at the most, perhaps, looking in the glass to see that his smile and appearance were the same as usual – and then, then people hit upon the idea of taking it seriously; and if on the other hand he had taken such an attack seriously he would have been laughed out of court as a country bumpkin who was not used to life in a big city.'

Then he talked a little about Sorø, gave a sort of lecture on it, and questioned me: I answered that I had never thought about Sorø. He asked me whether I would not like to have a position there. Now I knew that he had been out fishing that very morning and so my answer contained an allusion to it. That in addition to the real line fishermen had a special little line on which they sometimes caught the best fish – and I was a little line of that kind.

Then he thanked me for the book I had lately brought him, he had read in it, 'it was very profound but above him'. I answered: 'Your majesty naturally has not got time to read books and what I write is not intended for you. On the other hand you have recently had the natural scientists with you, that is something for you, something which satisfies your sense of beauty at the same time.' At that he was obviously a little vexed and said: yes, yes, the other can also be good.

I had several times made as though to depart and said I would not keep him longer. Each time he answered: yes, yes, I have plenty of time. When it happened the third time I said: yes, your majesty will understand that I have enough time, I was afraid your majesty might not have time. Afterwards I learnt from a more experienced man, to whom I related it, that I had behaved like a bungler, that by trying to be polite in that way to a king one is being impolite, since one has only to wait till be bows.

In the end I got away. He said that it would be a great pleasure for him to see me. Thereupon he made a movement with his hand meaning, as I knew from the last time, that he wished to give me his hand; but as the same man told me it was the custom, when the king offered one his hand, to kiss his hand, and as I could not bring myself to do it, I behaved as though I did not understand and bowed.

In the meanwhile I resolved to visit him as rarely as possible.

III

The third time I visited him was at Sorgenfrie, I gave him a copy of *Works of Love*. Parson Ibsen had told me that he had once and for all got it into his head that he could not understand me, and I was unable to get that idea out again. That was what I had in mind. I came in, handed him the book, he looked at it a little, noticed the arrangement of the first part (Thou *shalt* love, thou shalt love thy *neighbour*, *thou* shalt love thy neighbour) and understood it immediately; he was really very gifted. Thereupon I took the book back from him and asked him whether I might read him a passage, choosing part one (p.150). It moved him, moreover he was always easily moved.

Then he walked over to the window and so I followed him. He began to talk about his government. I said that I could naturally tell him one or two things which perhaps he would not otherwise get to know, for I could tell him what he looked like from the street. 'But am I to speak, or am I not to speak; for if I am to speak I shall speak quite straight out.' He answered: 'Go on then.' And so I told him that he allowed himself to be seduced by his personal gifts and that a king should in this respect be like a woman, who ought to hide her personal talents and simply be the woman of the house – and he simply a king. 'I have often pondered over what a king should be. In the first place he can perfectly well be ugly; then he ought to be deaf and blind, or at least pretend to be so, for that gets over many difficulties, a tactless or stupid remark which being addressed to a king has a certain importance is best put off by a: "I beg your pardon" – i.e. that the king has not heard it. Finally the king ought not to say much but have some expression or other which he can use on every occasion, and which is consequently meaningless.' He laughed and said: a charming portrait of a king. So I said: 'Yes, it is true, one thing more: the king must take care to be ill every now and then, so as to arouse sympathy'. Then he broke in, with a peculiar expression which was almost one of joy and delight: 'Oh, that is why you go talking about being ill, you want to make yourself interesting.'

It was really like talking to a woman, he could get so animated. Then I showed him that he had done harm to himself by his audiences, that he was too familiar with Tom, Dick, and Harry, that by doing so he alienates the upper official class in particular, who are impatient at the fortuitous kind of influence of unauthorized people, that he would have to admit that it was impossible to rule by talking with all his subjects in that way. He did not perhaps realize that everyone he spoke to went away and gossiped. That the mistake must be apparent at this very moment as I stood here talking with him, though I was certainly an exception because I considered myself religiously bound not to divulge a single word. (That is moreover true, as long as he lived I never said a word about it to anyone, and afterwards only to one and then only partially.) He answered: that I must not think that it was only due to his possible gifts, but that when he came to the throne he was of the opinion that to be a king no longer meant prestige, but little by little he had changed his mind.

I had said that I had had occasion to make some of these observations the very first day he came to the throne. To which he said: yes, wasn't that the time when there was a general meeting of which you were president. – He certainly had a good memory. – At that moment a side door opened, but was immediately closed again. I stepped back a yard. He went to the door, but as he went he said it was sure to be the Queen: she very much wishes to see you, now I will fetch her. So he came leading the Queen by the hand – and I bowed. That was really not polite to the Queen, who did not get a chance of making a proper entry, she even looked rather insignificant – but what else can happen if a queen suddenly has to appear like that.

The King showed the Queen the copy of my new book, to which I answered: Your majesty makes me feel embarrassed at not having brought a copy for the Queen. He answered: Oh, we can share one.

The Queen said she already knew me, she had seen me once on the ramparts (where I ran away and left Tryde in the lurch), that she had read part of 'your *Either and Or*, but could not understand it'. To which I answered: Your majesty will easily understand that that is all the worse for me. But there was something even more notable about the situation. Christian VIII immediately heard the mistake 'Either *and* Or' and I certainly did; I was surprised to hear the Queen saying exactly what servant girls say. I caught the King's eye; I looked away. After we had spoken a few words the King said to the Queen: is Juliana alone in your room? She answered 'yes' – and went away.

I went on talking with the King. He asked me whether I was going away this year. I answered that if I did it would only be for a very short time, to Berlin. 'You are sure to know a lot of interesting people there.' 'No, your majesty, in Berlin I live completely isolated and work harder than ever.' 'But then you might just as well go to Smørum-Ovre' (and then he laughed at his own joke). 'No, your majesty, whether I go to Smørum-Ovre or to Smørum-Nedre I do not find an incognito, a hiding-place of 400,000 people.' Now that was a little pointed, he answered: yes, that is perfectly true.

Then he asked me about Schelling. I tried to give him a rough impression. He asked me about Schelling's personal attitude towards the court and his reputation at the university. I said that Schelling was like the Rhine at its mouth where it became stagnant water – Schelling was degenerating into a Prussian 'Excellency'. I talked a little more to him about Hegelian philosophy having been the government philosophy, and that now it was supposed to be Schelling.

This last visit was an example of Christian VIII's delicacy in showing exactly the right attentions to people, it was as flattering as could be to have made it into a sort of family visit.

I did not speak to him again. I had resolved to visit him as little as possible, preferably when I had a book to give him. But I did not regret having been to see him; it is a very pleasant memory. If he had lived longer it would have been awkward for me, for he could not bear anyone being a private individual, he thought it was part of the king's right to show everyone exactly what they had to do. And so it was when I first began to think of taking an official position that I went to see him.

The whole episode is a charming memory, he never had occasion

to receive anything but an impression of animation, and I only saw
him as charm and liveliness itself.

22. Oh, for an Eastern despotism!

That is the old story. A discovery is made – the human race
triumphs; full of enthusiasm everything is set in motion in order to
make the discovery more and more perfect. The human race is
jubilant and adores itself. At length there comes a pause – people
come to a halt: but is that discovery a good, particularly in its
extraordinary perfection! And so once again the most eminent
minds are obliged to think themselves almost silly in order to
discover safety-valves, dampers, drags etc., so as, if possible, to
stop again, so that that unparalleled and incomparably perfect
discovery, the pride of the human race, should not end by running
away and desolating the whole world. One has only to think of the
invention of book-printing, perfected down to the high-speed
press, which ensures our not missing any filth or sediment. Think of
the railways. Think of the liberal constitutions, those incomparably
perfect discoveries – the pride of the human race – and it arouses
longing for an Eastern Despotism as something more fortunate to
live under.

PART TWO

Women

I do not maintain, and have never maintained that I did not marry because it was supposed to be contrary to Christianity, as though my being unmarried were a form of Christian perfection. Oh, far from it. Had I been a man, the danger for me would certainly have been another, to have given myself all too much to women, and I might possibly have become a seducer.

1. The eight paths in the forest

To the north of Copenhagen, there is a wood called Gribskov. In the middle of that wood, there is a remarkable place where eight paths meet. That place is called the Nook of Eight Paths. Just nearby, legend has it, there was a very smart restaurant or banqueting hall, and once upon a time, a very special banquet took place there.

In Gribs-Forest there is a place called the Nook of Eight Paths; he alone finds it who worthily seeks it, for it is not indicated upon any map. The very name seems to involve a contradiction. For how can the junction of eight paths constitute a nook? how can that which implies travel in all directions accord with what is lonely and concealed? And what the solitary man shuns is named after the junction of only three paths: triviality – how trivial then must be the junction of eight paths! And yet it is so: there actually are eight paths, but very solitary paths. Though it is apparently remote, hidden and lonely, one is quite near the hedge of the enclosure, which is called Hedge of Ill Luck. So the contradiction in the name merely makes the place more solitary, as contradiction always does. The eight paths, the much traffic, are merely a possibility, a possibility for thought, since no one frequents these paths except a tiny insect which hurries across them *lente festinans*; no one frequents them except the cursory traveller who is continually looking about him on all sides, not in search of anyone but with the aim of avoiding everyone, that fugitive whom only the death-dealing bullet overtakes – which explains indeed why the stag now is still, but not why it was so restless; no one frequents them except the wind, of which no man knows whence it cometh and whither it goeth. Even the man who lets himself be deceived by the beguiling suggestion wherewith morbid reserve seeks to capture the wayfarer, even he who followed the narrow footpath which entices one into the recesses of the forest – even he is not so solitary as one is on the eight paths along which no one travels! It is in fact as if the world were extinct and the survivor confronted by the embarrassment of having no one to bury him; or as if the whole tribe had wandered away by the eight paths and left one of the members behind. – If it is true as the poet says, *bene vixit qui bene latuit*, then I have lived well, for my nook was well chosen. Certain it is too that the world and all that therein is never appears to better advantage than when it is seen from a nook and one must take a look at it by stealth; certain it is too that all one hears in the world or is able to hear sounds most enchanting and delicious when heard from a nook where one gives ear to it by stealth. So I often have resorted to my retired nook. I knew it before, long before, but now I have learned not to need the night in order to find quiet, for here it always is quiet, always beautiful, but most beautiful, as it seems to me, now when the harvest sun holds a vesper service, and the sky turns a languishing blue; when the creatures take breath after the heat, when coolness is released, and the leaves of the meadow shiver voluptuously, while the forest rustles; when the sun thinks of the evening when it will cool itself in the ocean, when the earth prepares itself for repose and thinks of thanksgiving, when before their parting the two come to an understanding with one another in the tender fusion which darkens the forest and makes brighter the green of the meadows.

2. Constantine's speech: Woman as a jest

Five brilliant, yet utterly diverse, speeches are made at that banquet. The second speaker, Constantine Constantius, we know already as the author of Repetition *(1843). He strikes a bold tone: woman for him is just a jest. (He is still suffering from the desperate and unexpected end of his love-affair, evidently).*

Constantine spoke as follows:

'There is a time to keep silence and a time to speak, and now, it seems to me, is a time to speak briefly, for our young friend has spoken very long and very strangely. His *vis comica* has brought us to the pass of fighting *ancipiti proelio*, for his speech was of as doubtful a character as he is himself, whom you now see sitting there, a puzzled man, not knowing whether he ought to laugh or weep, or whether to fall in love. Indeed, if I had had foreknowledge of his speech, such as he insists upon having about love, I would have forbidden him to speak, but now it is too late. So now I bid you, dear boon companions, "that ye merry and jovial here shall be", and if this is not a mood that comes by bidding, I bid you then to forget each speech as soon as it is delivered, washing it down with a single gulp.

'And now for woman, the subject on which I would speak. I too have pondered, and I have fathomed her category; I too have sought, but I have also found, making a peerless discovery which I impart to you herewith. She can only be rightly construed under the category of jest. It is man's part to be absolute, to act absolutely, to give expression to the absolute; woman has her being in relationships. Between two such different beings no genuine reciprocal action can take place. This incongruity is precisely what constitutes jest, and it is with woman jest first came into the world. It follows, however, as a matter of course that man must know how to keep himself under the category of the absolute, for otherwise nothing comes of it, that is to say, there comes of it something only too universal, that man and woman tally with one another, he as a half-man and she as a half-man.

'Jest is not an aesthetic but an imperfect ethical category. Its effect upon thought is like the effect upon one's frame of mind at hearing a man who begins a speech, and after reciting a phrase or two with the same eloquence, says, "H'm" – and then dead silence. So it is with woman. One aims at her with the ethical category, one shuts one's eyes, one thinks of the absolute in the way of requirements, one thinks the thought of man, one opens one's eyes, one fixes one's glance upon the demure little miss upon whom one is experimenting to see if she meets the specifications; one becomes uneasy and says to oneself, "Ah, this surely is jest." For the jest consists in applying the category, in subsuming her under it, because with her the serious never can become serious; but precisely this is jest, for if one might require seriousness of her, it would not be jest. To put her under a vacuum pump and pump all the air out of her would be cruel and would not be in the least amusing, but to pump air into her, to pump her up to supernatural size, to let her suppose she has attained all the ideality a little miss of sixteen years can imagine she wants to have – this is the beginning of the performance, and the beginning of a highly entertaining performance. No young man has half so much imaginary ideality as a young girl. But "there is a rebate on that," as said the tailor, for all her ideality is illusion.

'If one does not regard woman in this way, she may do irreparable harm; with my interpretation she becomes harmless and amusing. There is nothing more dreadful for a man than to catch himself in the act of twaddling. With this all genuine ideality is brought to naught; for to have been a knave is a thing one can repent of, not having meant one word of all one said one can regret, but to have meant all one said, and lo, it turned out to be twaddle – even repentance turns away from that in disgust. It is different with woman. She has a prescriptive right to be transformed in less than twenty-four hours into the most innocent and pardonable galimatias; far be it from her candid soul to want to deceive anyone, she meant all she said, now she says the contrary, but with the same lovable frankness, for she is ready to die for the contrary. In case a man in all seriousness surrenders himself to love, he can say that he has lots of assurance, if only he can get any assurance company to take the risk, for a material so inflammable as woman must always make the insurer suspicious. What has he done? He has identified himself with her: if on New Year's Eve she goes off like a rocket, he goes with her, or if that does not occur, he has nevertheless come into pretty close affinity with danger. And what does he stand to lose? He can lose everything; for there is only one absolute opposite to the absolute, and that is twaddle. He is not to seek asylum in a society for persons morally depraved, for he is not morally depraved, far from it, he is merely reduced *in absurdum* and rendered beatific by nonsense, he has made a fool of himself. Between man and man this situation can never occur. If in this fashion a man fizzles out in nonsense, I despise him; if he dupes me by his shrewdness, I have merely to apply to him the ethical category and the danger is very insignificant; if the thing is carried too far – well, then I put a bullet through his head. But to challenge a woman to a duel – what is that? Who does not know? It is jest – as when Xerxes gave orders to have the sea scourged. When Othello murders Desdemona, he gains nothing, even assuming that she really had been guilty; he had made a fool of himself in the first instance, and he remains a fool. For even in murdering her he only draws attention to the consequence of an act which originally makes him ridiculous, whereas, on the contrary, Elvira can always be pathetic when armed with a dagger to revenge herself. A man who becomes red in the neck might perhaps become tragic, but a man of whom one ventures to require *esprit* either doesn't become jealous, or be becomes comic when he does, and most of all when he comes running up with a dagger. What a pity that Shakespeare has not produced a play on such a theme, where the challenge implied in a woman's unfaithfulness was rejected by irony; for not everyone who can perceive the comic aspect of this situation or even can describe it is endowed with the talent for dramatizing it. But one has only to imagine Socrates accidentally discovering Xanthippe *in flagrante* – I say "accidentally" because it would be essentially unsocratic to imagine Socrates being profoundly concerned about Xanthippe's fidelity, or that he might even spy upon her. I believe that the subtle smile which changed the ugliest man in Athens into the handsomest must for the first time have been transformed into a roar of laughter. It is inconceivable that Aristophanes, who sometimes liked to hold Socrates up to ridicule, never thought of letting him run out upon the stage shouting, "Where is she? where is she? that I may murder her," viz. Xanthippe, the unfaithful Xanthippe. For whether Socrates was made cuckold or not is a question of no importance, for anything Xanthippe would do in that respect would be labor lost, like snapping one's fingers in one's pocket, and Socrates remains the same intellectual hero even with the horn upon his forehead. But that he might become jealous, that he might want to murder Xanthippe – alas, then would Xanthippe have power over him as the entire Greek state and the death-sentence did not have . . . to make him ridiculous. Hence a cuckold is comic in relation to his wife, but can be regarded as tragic in relation to other men. The most obvious illustration of this is the Spanish notion of honor. However, the tragic element here is essentially this, that the injured husband can get no real satisfaction, and that the smart of his suffering is meaningless – and that is dreadful enough. To shoot a woman, to challenge her to a duel, to show contempt for her, only makes the poor man more ridiculous, for woman is the weaker sex. This consideration is brought forward everywhere and brings everything to confusion. If she does something great she is more admired than a man would be, because people did not suppose they might venture to require it of her; if she is deceived, she has all the pathos in her favour, whereas when a man is deceived, people have a little sympathy and a little patience so long as he is present, only to laugh at him when he is gone.

'One had better be prompt, therefore, to regard woman as a jest. The entertainment is peerless. Let one regard her as a fixed quantity and make a relative quantity of oneself. One is not to contradict her, far from it, that would only be to play into her hands. Just because she is unable to set limits to herself, she shows off to the best advantage, seriously speaking, when one contradicts her a bit. One is never to doubt what she says, far from it, every word must be believed. With a rapturous look of blissful intoxication one must dance attendance upon her with the mincing step of an idolatrous worshipper – one falls upon one's knees, one pines, one raises one's eyes to her, one pines, one breathes again. One is to do everything she says, like an obedient slave. Now comes the spice of it. It requires no proof that a woman can talk, i.e. *verba facere*. Unfortunately, she does not possess sufficient power of reflection to insure her against self-contradiction for any considerable time, say a week at the maximum, if the male does not help her regulatively by contradicting her. So the consequence is that in a short while the confusion is in full swing. If one had not done what she told one to do, the confusion would have passed unnoticed, for she forgets again as promptly as she is prompt to talk. But since her adorer has done everything she wanted and been entirely at her service, the confusion is palpable. The more gifted a woman is, the more amusing. The more gifted, so much the more imagination has she. The more imaginative, so much the more potent is she at the instant, and so much the more does confusion reveal itself the next instant. This amusement is rarely witnessed in life because such blind obedience to a woman's whim is very rare. If it is to be found in the languishing shepherd, he hasn't wit enough to perceive the amusement.

'The amusement, as I have said, is priceless; indeed I know that, for sometimes I have not been able to sleep at night, merely for thinking what new confusions I might live to see, wrought by my lady and by my humble zeal to serve her; for no one who bets on the lottery can have experience of more extraordinary combinations than the man who has a passion for this game. For one thing is certain, that every woman possesses this possibility of flying up and being transfigured into nonsense, with an amiability, a noncha-

lance, an assurance, befitting the weaker sex. As a true lover one
discovers in one's lady every imaginable charm. Thereupon finding
that one has some talent for this, one does not let it lie fallow as a
mere possibility but develops it into virtuosity. I need say no more,
nothing more can be said in general terms, everybody understands
what I mean. Just as one man finds his amusement in balancing a
cane upon his nose, in swinging a glass of water in a circle without
its contents flying out, or in dancing among eggs, and other similar
exercises which are as entertaining as they are profitable – so and
not otherwise has the lover in commerce with his lady the most
incomparable amusement and the most interesting study. With
respect to erotic situations one is to believe her absolutely – not
only that she is faithful, for one soon tires of that game, but one is to
believe absolutely in all those outbursts of indefeasible romanticism from which presumably she would perish if one did not apply a
safety-valve through which the sigh and the smoke (which is the air
of romanticism) stream forth to the delectation of the adorer. One
has to raise her to the pinnacle of a Juliet – the only difference being
that no one has thought of touching a hair of Romeo's head. With
respect to intellect one has to credit her with everything, and if one
has been fortunate enough to find the right woman, in a trice he has
on his hands a brooding authoress, and one must admiringly shade
one's eyes with the hand to see what the little black hen is going to
lay next. It is inconceivable that Socrates did not choose this part
instead of scolding Xanthippe – well, after all, he wanted to keep in
practice, like the horse-trainer who, though he has the best trained
horse, knows how to tease it in such a way that there may be reason
sufficient for breaking it in again.

'I should like to speak a little more concretely in order to
illuminate a special and rather interesting case. Much is said about
woman's fidelity, but not often wisely. Regarded from a purely
aesthetic point of view, it belongs among the theatrical properties
of the poet, as a phantom which crosses the stage in search of the
loved one, or the phantom which sits by the spinning-wheel await-
ing the loved one – for when she has found him or he has come, then
aesthetics has lost interest in it. Her unfaithfulness, which can be
brought into the closest connection with her foregoing faithfulness,
is essentially regarded from an ethical point of view, and then
jealousy makes its appearance as a tragic passion. There are three
cases, and the situation is favourable to woman, inasmuch as two of

them are instances of faithfulness and only one of unfaithfulness. Inconceivably great is her faithfulness so long as she is not sure of the loved one, and just as inconceivably great when he declines her fidelity. The third case would be that of infidelity. Now if only one has enough *esprit* and detachment to think, one will find in what has already been said ample justification of the category "jest". Our young friend, the very beginning of whose speech misled me for a moment, made as if he wanted to start out with this theme but sprang back affrighted at the difficulty. Yet the explanation is not difficult if one really is serious in putting death and unhappy love in conjunction, if one has seriousness enough to hold this thought fast – and one ought to have at least as much seriousness as that . . . for the sake of the jest. All this sort of talk originates of course with a woman or with a womanish male. One recognizes it at once, for it is one of those absolute outbursts which, uttered with aplomb at the instant, is sure of great applause at the instant; although it is a matter of life and death, it is intended for instant enjoyment, like an omelet soufflé; although it concerns a whole lifetime, it lays no obligation whatever upon the dying person but only obliges the auditor to hasten that very instant to the aid of the dying. If a man were to deliver such a speech, it would not be in the least amusing, for he would be too despicable for anybody to laugh at him. Woman, on the other hand, is a genius, she is lovable for that quality, and is amusing from first to last. So then the lady dies of love. That is certain – for has she not said she would? Here lies her pathos; for woman is man – at least she is man enough to say what hardly any man is man enough to do. She is a real man! When I say this I have passed upon her an ethical judgment. Do ye likewise, dear boon companions, and thus understand Aristotle. He remarks justly that woman cannot well be used in tragedy. That indeed is obvious, she belongs in the pathetic and serious *divertissement*, in the half-hour farce, not in the five-act drama. Accordingly she dies. But for all that, might she not be able to love again? Why not? – in case anyone can bring her to life again. If she comes again to life she is in fact a new person, and a new person, another person, begins anew, loves for the first time, there is nothing remarkable in that. O death, great is thy power! Not the most violent emetic, not the strongest laxative could effect so clean a sweep.

'The confusion is marvellous, if only one is on the lookout and does not forget. A deceased person is one of the most amusing figures one can encounter in life. How strange that it is not more frequently employed on the stage, in real life one now and then sees such a thing. Even a man who has one time been taken for dead is essentially a comic object of interest, but a person actually deceased contributes to our amusement all that one can reasonably require. Be on the lookout. The fact is, my attention was first drawn to this one day when I was walking in the street with an acquaintance. A pair passed us by. Judging from the look of my acquaintance I inferred that he knew them and asked if it were so. "By Jove," he replied, "right well do I know them, especially the lady, for she was my deceased." "Your deceased what?" I enquired. "By Jove, my deceased first love. Yes, it's a strange story. She said, 'I am dying,' that very instant she departed – in death of course, I hadn't even time to take out insurance on her life, it was too late; dead she was and dead she remained; and now I rove about, as says the poet, seeking in vain the loved one's grave to offer her the sacrifice of a tear." So spake that dejected man who was left behind in the world all alone, though it comforted him nevertheless to find that his deceased love had got so far along, if not by the help of another, at least in the company of another. It is a good thing for the girls, thought I, that they don't have to be buried every time they die. In that case too the parents, who hitherto have regarded male children as the most expensive luxury, might easily find the girls still more expensive. A simple case of infidelity is not nearly so amusing – I mean, when a young woman falls in love with another man and says to her husband, "I cannot help it, save me from myself." But to die of sorrow because she cannot endure to have her lover separated from her by a journey to the West Indies, to have to put up with his departure, and then upon his return not only not to be dead but to be joined forever to another – that is really a strange fate for a lover. What wonder then that this dejected man sometimes comforted himself with the refrain of an old song: Hurrah for me and you, I say, that day is ne'er forgotten!

'Forgive me now, dear boon companions, if I have spoken too long, and now drain a glass to love and woman. Fair is she and lovely when regarded aesthetically – that no one can deny. But since it so often is said, I too will say: one should not remain standing, but "go further." So regard her ethically, and the thing becomes a jest. Even Plato and Aristotle take it that woman is an incomplete form, that is, an irrational quantity, which perhaps some time in a better existence might be brought back to the male form. In this life one must take her as she is. What this is will soon appear, for she too is not satisfied with the aesthetic sphere, she "goes further," she would be emancipated – that she is man enough to say. Let that come to pass, and the jest will be beyond all bounds.'

3. A couturier's contempt

The fourth speaker is the Ladies' Tailor or Fashion Designer. He is probably no admirer of women, and they have become the willing victims of his sadistic inclinations. Their servitude to fashion means that they are fair game for any manipulation. The ultimate trope of the lust for fashionableness, a ring through the nose, has today been given realization. In his discourse, suffered pain and imposed sadism are exactly balanced.

Hardly had Victor finished than the Ladies' Tailor sprang to his feet, upset a bottle of wine standing in front of him and began as follows:
'Well spoken, dear boon companions, well spoken, the more I hear you talk, the more I am convinced that you are co-conspirators; I hail you as such, I understand you as such, for conspirators understand one another from afar. And yet what do you know? What is your bit of theory worth to which you give the semblance of experience, your bit of experience which you revamp into a theory? And after all, you now and then believe in her for an instant and are captivated for an instant. No, I know woman on her weak side, that is to say, I know her. I shun no terror in the pursuit of my studies and shun no measures calculated to confirm what I have understood. For I am a madman, and one must be mad in order to understand her, and if one was not mad before, he must be so when he has understood her. As the robber has his haunt near the noisy highway, and the ant-lion his funnel in the loose sand, and the pirate his hiding-place near the roaring sea, so have I my *maison* of

fashion in the midst of the human swarm, seductive, irresistible to a woman, as the Venusberg is to man. Here in a *maison* of fashion one learns to know her practically and from the bottom up, without any theoretical fuss. Oh, if fashion meant nothing more than that a woman in the heat of desire were to throw off all her clothes, well, that would be something. But that is not all of it, fashion is not undisguised sensuality, not tolerated debauchery, but a contraband trade in indecency licensed as decorum. As in heathen Prussia a marriageable girl wore a bell which served as a signal to the men, so likewise is the existence of a woman of fashion a perpetual bell-ringing, not for debauchees but for lickerish voluptuaries. It is believed that fortune is a woman – oh, yes, it is changeable, to be sure, but it is changeable in something, for it is able to give much, and to that extent it is not a woman. No, it is fashion that is a woman, for fashion is changeable in nonsense, is logically consistent only in becoming more and more crazy. One hour in my *maison* is worth more than a year and a day outside of it, if one wants to learn to know woman. I say in my *maison*, for it is the only one in the capital of Denmark, no one thinks of competing. Who would dare to risk competition with one who has sacrificed himself completely and continues to sacrifice himself as high priest of this idolatrous worship? No, there is not a distinguished company where my name is not mentioned first and last, there is no middle-class company where my name when it is mentioned does not inspire holy awe like the name of the King, and there is no costume so crazy that, when it is from my *maison*, it is not accompanied by whispers as it walks through the salon; and there is not one lady of gentle birth who dares to pass by my *maison*, and not a single girl of the bourgeois class who passes it by without sighing and thinking, "If only I could afford it!" Well, she was not in the least deceived. I deceive no one; I furnish the finest, the most costly stuff at the lowest prices, indeed I sell below cost, so I am not eager to win a profit, no, I lay out large sums yearly. And yet I will win, I *will* to win, I am ready to spend my last farthing in bribing and underselling the organs of fashion so that my game may be won. To me it is a rapture beyond compare to bring out the most costly fabrics, to cut them up, to clip pieces out of genuine Brussels lace to make a fool's motley; I sell at the cheapest prices genuine material of the latest fashion. You think perhaps that it is only at particular instants she wishes to be in the fashion; far from it, that is what she wants all the time, and that is her one and only thought. For woman has spirit, but it is about as well employed as was the fortune of the Prodigal Son; and woman possesses reflection in an indescribably high degree, for there is nothing so sacred but in the same breath she finds it commensurable with finery in dress, and the proudest expression of finery is fashion. What wonder she finds it commensurable, for indeed fashion is the holy, and there is no detail so insignificant that she does not know how to relate it to finery in dress, and the most senseless expression of finery is fashion. And there is nothing, nothing whatever in all her attire, not the least ribbon, concerning which she has not a definite view of its relation to fashion and does not instantly detect whether the lady who passed her has noticed it. After all, for whom does she dress, unless it is for other ladies? Even in my *maison*, where she comes indeed to be shown what fashion is, even there she is in fashion. Just as there is a special bathing-costume and a special riding-habit, so also there is a particular kind of dress which it is *moderne* to wear in my *maison*. This costume is not so careless as the negligée in which a lady likes to be surprised early in the forenoon. The point then is her femininity and the coquetry involved in letting herself be surprised. The costume at the tailor's, on the other hand, is calculated to be careless and a bit frivolous without her seeming to be embarrassed by it, because the fashion tailor stands to her in a different relation than the cavalier. The coquetry now consists in displaying herself thus before a man who by reason of his position dare not claim the lady's feminine favor, but must be content with the chance perquisites, which accrue to him abundantly, but without her thinking of it, and without it ever occurring to her to want to be a lady in the eyes of a dressmaker. The point therefore is this, that femininity is in a way left out, and coquetry is nullified by the patronizing superiority of the distinguished lady, who would smile if anyone were to hint at the possibility of such a relationship. In her negligée on the occasion of a social visit she makes an attempt to conceal herself and betrays herself by the concealment; in my *maison* she exposes herself with the utmost nonchalance, for it is only a tailor – and she is a woman. Now her shawl drops a little and exposes her a little – in case I don't know what that means and what she wants, my renown is in jeopardy. Now she purses up her lips aprioristically, now she gesticulates aposteriorically, now she sways on her hips, now she looks at herself in the mirror and sees my admiring phiz behind her, now she lisps, now she minces, now she hovers, now she trails her foot lightly, now she sinks languidly into the armchair, while I in a humble posture offer her a flask of salts and by my adoration cool her heat, now she strikes at me roguishly with her hand, now she drops her handkerchief, without the slightest motion she lets her arm hang indolently, while I bow deeply and pick it up and tender it to her and receive a little patronizing nod. So it is a woman of fashion behaves when she is in my *maison*. Whether Diogenes made any impression upon the woman who in a rather indecent position was lying prostrate in prayer when he enquired whether she supposed the gods could not see her from behind, I do not know; but this I know, that if I were to say to her kneeling ladyship, "The folds of your gown do not fall in a fashionable way," she would be more afraid of this than of offending the gods. Woe to the scum, the Cinderella, who does not understand this. *Pro dii immortales*, what then is a woman when she is not in the fashion? *Per deos obsecro*, what is she when she is in the fashion?!

'You wonder whether it is true? Well, just put it to the test: at the moment his sweetheart sinks blissfully upon his breast and whispers incoherently, "Thine forever," as she hides her face against his bosom, let the lover say to her, "Dear Kitty, your curls are not in the fashion." Perhaps men don't think about this, but the man who knows it and has the reputation of knowing it is the most dangerous man in the kingdom. What blissful hours the lover passes with his sweetheart before the wedding, I do not know, but the blissful hours she passes in my *maison* he has no inkling of. Without my royal license and sanction a wedding is an invalid act, or at least it is a very plebeian affair. Suppose the moment has already arrived when they are about to meet in front of the altar, suppose she is marching up with the best conscience in the world, knowing that everything was bought in my place and was tried on in my presence, and I rush up and say, "But, my God! gracious lady, the myrtle wreath is all awry!" – perhaps then the ceremony would be postponed. But men know nothing about this sort of thing, one must be a *modiste* to know it. It requires such prodigious reflection to keep track of a woman's reflection that only a man who sacrifices himself to that task is sufficient for it, and then only in case he has a native gift. A man is fortunate therefore if he never takes up with any woman, in any case she doesn't belong to him, even if she doesn't belong to any other man, she belongs to that phantom which is formed by the unnatural intercourse of feminine reflection with feminine reflection, i.e. fashion. For this reason a woman ought always to swear by fashion, then her oath would have some force, for fashion after all is the one thing she is always thinking about, the one thing she is able to think together with and in everything else. From my *maison de mode* has gone out to the world of elegance the glad tidings for every lady of distinction that fashion commands the use of a special sort of headdress when one goes to church, and again that the headdress must be somewhat different for high mass and for evensong. When the bells are ringing the equipages begin to draw up at my door – for it has also been proclaimed that nobody can properly adjust the headdress but me, the arbiter of fashion. I rush out to meet her with a low bow and lead her into my salon. While she vegetates languidly I adjust everything as it should be. The work is finished, she has looked at herself in the glass. Swift as a messenger of the gods I hasten on before her, I have opened the door of the salon and bowed, I hasten to the door of the *maison*, I fold my arms upon my breast like an oriental slave, but encouraged by a gracious curtsy I venture even to throw her an adoring and admiring kiss – she takes her seat in the carriage, ah! she has forgotten her prayer-book, I make haste and hand it to her through the window, permitting myself to remind her once more to hold her head a little to the right and to rearrange things herself a little if in alighting her headdress should become a trifle disordered. She drives away and is edified.

'You think perhaps that only ladies in high society do homage to fashion. Far from it. Just look at my seamstresses, upon whose toilet I spare no pains in order that the dogmas of fashion may be emphatically proclaimed from my *maison*. They compose a chorus of nitwits, and I the high priest go before them as a shining example, prepared to squander everything if only by the help of fashion I may make every woman ridiculous. For when a seducer boasts that the virtue of every woman is vendible to the right bidder, I don't believe him, but I do believe that before long every woman will be satanized by the crazy and defiling self-reflection of fashion, which depraves her more thoroughly than if she were to be seduced. I have put it to the proof more than once. If I am not able to accomplish it by myself, I egg her on by the help of the female slaves of fashion who belong to her own class. For as one can train rats to bite rats, so is the bite of a satanized woman like that of a tarantula, and it is dangerous above all when a man takes part in it. Whether I am serving the devil or serving God, I do not know, but I am in the right, I will be in the right, I will it, I will it as long as I have a single farthing left, I will it until the blood spurts from my fingers. The physiologist draws the form of a woman to show the dreadful effect of corsets, and alongside of this he draws the normal form. That's all very well, but only the one drawing has the validity of truth – for they all wear corsets. Describe in this way the miserable stunted extravagance of the fashion-mad woman, describe the insidious self-reflection which consumes her, and describe the womanly modesty which knows about itself last of all; do this well, and with that thou hast passed judgment upon woman, and in reality hast passed a damning judgment. If ever I discover such a girl, contented and humble, who is not yet depraved by indecent intercourse with women, she shall fall nevertheless. I entangle her in my toils, now she stands at the place of sacrifice, i.e. in my *maison*. With the most disdainful look a haughty nonchalance can arm itself with I take her measures, she is ready to perish with fright, a peal of laughter from the adjoining room where my trained assistants sit annihilates her. Dressed up in the fashion she looks as crazy as a lunatic, as crazy even as one who could not be admitted into a lunatic asylum. Then she departs from me full of bliss, no man, nor even a god, could terrify her, for she is indeed in the fashion.

'You understand me now, you understand why I call you co-conspirators, though at a great distance from me. You understand now my interpretation of woman. Everything in life is a matter of fashion, the fear of God is a matter of fashion, and love, and hoop-skirts, and a ring in the nose. So with all my might I will abet the lofty genius who desires to laugh at the most ludicrous of all animals. Since woman has reduced everything to fashion, I by the aid of fashion will prostitute her as she deserves. I give myself no rest, I, the Ladies' Tailor; my soul chafes when I think of my task, she must yet come to the point of wearing a ring in her nose. Therefore seek no sweetheart, forego love as you would shun the most dangerous neighborhood, for also your sweetheart would have to come to the point of wearing a ring in her nose.'

4. Johannes the Seducer: Women are for use

The most erotic passage of writing in all Kierkegaard is this plunge into the mind of the professional seducer, the man for whom women are merely for pleasure and for use. Johannes the Seducer was perhaps partly modelled on the figure of P.L. Møller, a seducer whose ease in conquest Kierkegaard could not help but wrily admire. This speech of Johannes was to cost Kierkegaard dear.

Thereupon Johannes the Seducer spoke as follows:

'Esteemed boon companions, is Satan plaguing you? You talk like undertakers, your eyes are red with tears and not with wine. You move me almost to tears, for an unfortunate lover is very sadly situated in life. *Hinc illae lacrymae.* Now I am a fortunate lover, and my only desire is to remain such constantly. Perhaps this is a concession to woman, which Victor is so much afraid of? Why not? It is a concession. The fact that I undo the wire of this champagne bottle is also a concession, that I let its foam spurt into the goblet is also a concession, that I raise the goblet to my lips is also a concession – now I have drained it – *concedo.* Now, however, the goblet is empty, so I make no more concessions. Thus it is with the girls. If some unlucky lover has bought a kiss too dearly, that only proves to me that he knows neither how to help himself to a dish nor to abstain from it. I never buy it too dearly, I leave that to the girls. What is the meaning of this? To me it means the most beautiful, the most delicious, and pretty nearly the most persuasive *argumentum ad hominum*; but since every woman at least once in her life possesses this primitive power of argumentation, why should I not let myself be persuaded? Our young friend would like to *think* the thing. In fact he can buy what the confectioner calls a "kiss," just to look at it. I want to enjoy. No nonsense! Hence an old song says about a kiss, *Es ist kaum zu sehen, es ist nur für Lippen, die genau sich verstehen* – which understand one another so perfectly that reflection is impertinence and folly. The man who is twenty years old and does not comprehend that there is a categorical imperative: Enjoy thyself – that man is a fool. And he who does not seize the opportunity is a Wesleyan Methodist. But you are unfortunate lovers, hence you want to remodel woman. God forbid it. I like her as she is, exactly as she is. Even Constantine's notion that she is a jest implies a secret wish. I, on the other hand, am gallant – and why not? Gallantry costs nothing and brings in everything and is the condition of all erotic enjoyment. Gallantry is the Freemasonry of sensuousness and sensuality as between man and woman. It is a primitive language of nature, like love's language in general. It is not made up of sounds but of masked desires which are constantly changing their roles. I can understand very well that an unfortunate lover is ungallant enough to want to convert his deficit into a bill of exchange on eternity. Yet at the same time I do not understand it, for to me woman possesses abundant intrinsic value. That I will assert of every woman, and it is true, but it is certain also that I am the only one not deceived by this truth. As to whether a deflowered woman is worth less than man is an item not to be found in my price list. I do not pluck broken flowers, I leave that to married men for a decoration at Shrovetide. Whether Eduard, e.g., would think it over and fall in love again with Cordelia, or would recite his love affair by heart, I leave to him. Why should I get mixed up in other people's affairs? What I thought of her I explained to her at the right time, and she truly has convinced me, convinced me to my absolute satisfaction, that my gallantry was well placed. *Concedo. Concessi.* If a new Cordelia comes under my eye, I shall enact comedy "Ring No.2." But you are unfortunate lovers and conspirators and are more deceived than the girls, in spite of the fact that you have abundant talents. But resolution, the resolution of desire, is the gist of living. Our young friend always remains on the outside, Victor is an unpractical enthusiast, Constantine has purchased his common sense too dearly, the Ladies' Tailor is a madman. What's the good of all that? Though the four of you were after one girl, it would come to nothing but wind. Let one have enthusiasm enough to idealize, taste enough to take part in the festive enjoyment of clinking the glasses, sense enough to break off, to break off as absolutely as death, madness enough to want to enjoy again – then one is the darling of the gods and of the girls. But what's the use of talking here? I don't want to make proselytes, nor is this the place for it. I enjoy wine, to be sure, and I enjoy the abundance of the banquet, but let me have a girl for my company, and then I talk. So I thank

Constantine for the banquet and the wine and the excellent appointments, the speeches, however, were not much to boast of. But in order that it may not end thus I will speak in praise of women.

'As he who is to speak about the divine must be inspired by divinity in order to speak worthily, so that divinity itself teaches what one is to say, just so it is with women. For woman is further even than the deity from being the whim of a man's brain, a daydream, something one happens to think of all by oneself and can dispute about *pro et contra*. No, only from her does one learn how to talk about her. And the more women one has learned from, so much the better. The first time a man is simply a learner, the second time he has already been coached, just as in a learned disputation one can use the last opponent's complements against the next. Nevertheless there is no lost time. For the notion that a kiss is a smacking of the lips, that an embrace is an exertion, is no more absurd than that this lesson is exhausted like the proof of a proposition in geometry which remains the same though the letters are altered. Such notions only apply to mathematics and ghosts, not to love and to women, where every new experience is a new proof and demonstrates in another way the truth of the same proposition. It is my joy that the female sex, far from being more imperfect than man, is on the contrary the most perfect. However I will clothe my speech in a myth, and for woman's sake whom you have so unjustly offended I shall be glad if it may prove a judgment upon your souls for the fact that sensual pleasure is brought before your eyes but flees from you like the fruits from Tantalus, because you have fled from it and have offended woman. For only thus is she offended, though she is exalted high above offense and everyone is punished who ventures to offend her. I do not offend anyone. The idea that I do is the invention of married men and is a slander, whereas on the contrary I appreciate her much more than does the married man.

'Originally there was one sex, that of the man – so the Greeks report. Gloriously endowed was he, so that he reflected honor upon the gods who created him, so gloriously endowed that the gods were in the position in which a poet sometimes finds himself when he has expended all his forces upon a poetic creation: they became envious of man. Yea, what was worse, they feared him, lest he might bow unwillingly to their yoke. They feared, though it was without reason, that he might cause heaven itself to totter. So then they had conjured up a power they hardly thought themselves capable of curbing. Then there was concern and commotion in the council of the gods. Much had they lavished upon the creation of man, that was magnanimous; now everything must be risked, for everything was at stake, this was self-defense. So thought the gods. And it was impossible to revoke him, as a poet may revoke his thought. By force he could not be compelled, or else the gods themselves might have compelled him, but it was precisely about this they had misgivings. He must then be taken captive and compelled by a power which was weaker than his own and yet stronger, strong enough to compel. What a marvellous power that must be! Necessity, however, teaches the gods to surpass themselves in inventiveness. They sought and pondered and found. This power was woman, the miracle of creation, even in the eyes of the gods a greater miracle than man, a discovery for which the gods in their naïveté could not help patting themselves on the back. What more can be said in honor of her than that she should be able to do what even the gods did not think themselves capable of doing, what more can be said than that she was able? How marvellous she must be to be capable of it! This was a ruse of the gods. Cunningly the enchantress was fashioned; the very instant she had enchanted man she transformed herself and held him captive in all the prolixities of finiteness. This is what the gods wanted. But what can be more delicious, more pleasurable, more enchanting, than this which the gods as they were fighting for their own power devised as the only thing that could decoy man? And verily it is so, for woman is the unique and the most seductive power in heaven and on earth. In this comparison man is something exceedingly imperfect.

'And the ruse of the gods succeeded. However, it did not always succeed. In every generation there were some men, individuals, who became aware of the deception. They perceived her loveliness, it is true, more than did any of the others, but they had an inkling what it was all about. These are what I call erotics, and I reckon myself among them; men call them seducers, woman has no name for them, such a type is for her unmentionable. These erotics are the fortunate ones. They live more luxuriously than the gods, for they eat constantly only that which is more precious than ambrosia and drink what is more delicious than nectar; they dine upon the most seductive fancy which issued from the most artful thought of the gods, they dine constantly upon bait. Oh, luxury beyond compare! Oh, blissful mode of living! They dine constantly upon bait – and are never caught. The other men set to and eat bait as the vulgar eat caviar, and are caught. Only the erotic knows how to appreciate bait, to appreciate it infinitely. Woman divines this, and hence there is a secret understanding between him and her. But he knows also that it is bait, and this is a secret he keeps to himself.

'That nothing more marvellous, nothing more delicious, nothing more seductive can be devised than a woman, the gods vouch for, and the necessity which sharpened their invention; and in turn it vouches for them that they risked their all and in the forming of her nature set heaven and earth in commotion.

'I leave for a moment the myth. The concept of man corresponds exactly to the idea of man. One therefore can think of a single man existing and nothing more than that. On the other hand, the idea of woman is a generality which is not exhaustively exemplified in any single woman. She is not *ebenbürtig* with man but is later, is a part of man, and yet more complete than he. Whether it be that the gods took a part of him while he slept (fearful of awakening him if they took too much), or that they divided him in equal parts so that woman is a half – in any case it is man that was divided. So it is only as a subdivision she is related to man as his mate. She is a deception, but that she is only in her second phase and for him who is deceived. She is finiteness, but in her first phase she is finiteness raised to the highest power in the delusive infinity of all divine and human illusions. Not yet is the deception – but one more instant and a man is deceived. She is finiteness, and so she is a collective term, to say one woman means many women. This the erotic alone understands, and hence he is so prompt to love many, never being deceived, but sucking up all the voluptuous delights the cunning gods were capable of preparing. Therefore woman cannot be exhaustively expressed by any formula but is an infinity of finitudes. He who is bent upon thinking her idea is like one who gazes into a sea of nebulous shapes which are constantly forming, or like one who is bewildered by looking at the billows with their foaming crests which constantly elude him; for her idea is only a workshop of possibilities, and for the erotic these possibilities are the never-failing source of enthusiasm.

'Thus the gods fashioned her, delicate and ethereal as the mists of a summer's night and yet plump like a ripened fruit, light as a bird in spite of the fact that she carried a world of craving, light because the play of forces is unified at the invisible center of a negative relationship in which she is related to herself, slim of stature, designed with definite proportions and yet to the eye seeming to swell with the wave-lines of beauty, complete and yet as if only now she were finished, cooling, delicious, refreshing as new-fallen snow, blushing with serene transparency, happy as a jest which causes one to forget everything, tranquilizing as the goal whereunto desire tends, satisfying by being herself the incitement of desire. And this is what the gods had counted upon, that man upon catching sight of her should be amazed as one who gets a sight of himself in the glass, and yet again as if he were familiar with this sight, amazed as one who sees himself reflected in perfection, amazed as one who sees what he never had an inkling of and yet sees, as it appears to him, what must necessarily have occurred to him, what is a necessary part of existence, and yet sees this as the riddle of existence. Precisely this contradiction in his amazement is what elicits his desire, while amazement eggs him on nearer and nearer, so that he cannot desist from looking, cannot cease to seem familiar with this sight, without, however, quite daring to approach, although he cannot cease to desire.

'When the gods had thus forecast her form they were fearful lest even they might not be able to express it. But what they feared most was woman herself. They did not dare to let her know how beautiful she was, fearing that she might spoil their ruse if she were cognizant of it. Then was the crown placed upon the work. The gods made her perfect, but then they hid all this from her in the ignorance of innocence and hid it from her once more in the impenetrable mystery of modesty. She was perfect, and victory was assured. An enticing thing she was, at one moment she enticed by avoiding a man and betaking herself in flight, she was irresistible for the fact that she herself was resistance. The gods were jubilant. And indeed no allurement has been discovered in the world equal to woman, and there is no allurement so absolute as that of innocence, and no temptation so fascinating as that of modesty, and no deception so incomparable as woman. She knows nothing, and yet modesty contains an instinctive presentiment, she is separated from man, and the wall of modesty is a more decisive separation than the sword of Aladdin which separated him from Gulvare – and yet the erotic, who like Pyramis lays his ear against the separating wall of modesty, has a presentiment, remotely sensed, of all the lust of desire behind it.

'So it is that woman tempts. As food for the gods men present the most glorious things, they have nothing more glorious to offer. In the same manner woman is show-fruit, the gods know nothing to compare with it. She *is*, she is here, present, and yet she is infinitely remote, hidden in modesty, until she betrays her hiding-place, by what means she does not know, nature itself is the sly informer. She is roguish as a child at play who peeks from his place of concealment, and yet her roguishness is inexplicable, for she herself is not aware of it and is always inscrutable, inscrutable when she hides her eyes, inscrutable when she emits a glance as her messenger, which no thought, still less a word, is able to follow. And yet a glance is the interpreter of the soul – where then is the explanation when even the interpreter speaks unintelligibly? Placid is she as the stillness of the evening hour when no leaf is stirring, placid as a consciousness which is not yet aware of anything, the movements of her heart are as regular as if it did not exist, and yet the erotic who listens with stethoscopic precision discovers the dithyrambic beat of passion as an unconscious accompaniment. Careless as a puff of wind, content like the deep sea, and yet full of longing, as the inexplicable depths always are. Brothers, my mind is assuaged, indescribably assuaged; I conceive that my life too expresses an idea, even if you do not comprehend me. I too have found out the secret of existence. I too am in the service of something divine, and to a certainty I do not serve for naught. As woman is a deception on the part of the gods, this is the true expression of the fact that she wants to be seduced, and as woman is not an idea, therefore the truth is on the side of the erotic who wants to love as many as possible.

'What rapture it is to relish the deception without being deceived, only the erotic understands. How blissful it is to be seduced, only woman knows. I know it from women, though I have never given time to anyone to explain this to me, but have taken my revenge and served the idea by a breach as abrupt as death; for a bride and a breach correspond to one another as female and male. Woman only knows this, and knows it by means of her seducer. No married man comprehends such a thing; she never speaks to him about it. She puts up with her fate, she has a presentiment that thus it must be, that only once can she be seduced. Hence she is never really angry with her seducer. That is, if he actually did seduce her and expressed the idea. A broken marriage vow and things like that are of course galimatias and no seduction. So it is not so great a misfortune for a woman to be seduced, and she is lucky to be so. A girl who is admirably seduced may make an admirable wife. If I were not so good at seducing (though I feel deeply my inferiority in this respect), and if I wanted to be a married man, I would always choose a seduced woman, so that I might not have to begin by seducing my wife. Marriage also expresses an idea, but in relation to this idea that particular thing [i.e. innocence] is a matter of complete indifference which in relation to my idea is the absolute. A marriage therefore ought never to be planned to begin as if it were the beginning of a story of seduction. This much is certain, that for every woman there is a corresponding seducer. Her good fortune consists in encountering precisely him.

'By means of marriage, on the other hand, the gods conquer.' Then the aforetime seduced woman walks through life by the side of her husband, looks sometimes longingly backward, puts up with her fate until she has reached life's limit. She dies, but not in the same sense that men die; she is volatilized and resolved again into the inexplicable element from which the gods formed her, she vanishes like a dream, like a provisional form the time for which is past. For what is woman but a dream? – and yet she is the highest reality! So it is the erotic understands her and leads her and is led by her at the moment of seduction – outside of time, where she belongs as an illusion. With a husband she becomes temporal, and he through her.

'Oh, marvellous Nature, if I did not admire thee, she would teach me to do so, for she is the *venerabile* of existence. Gloriously hast thou fashioned her, but still more glorious for the fact that thou didst never make one woman like another. In the case of man the essential is the essential and therefore always the same; in the case of woman the accidental is the essential, hence the inexhaustible variety. Brief is her glory, but the pain I quickly forget as if I had not even sensed it, when the same glory is proffered to me again. Yes, I too perceive the uncomeliness which may make its appearance later, but she is not thus with her seducer.'

5. A delightful marriage

After the heady stuff spoken at the banquet, the pastoral mood is established. The revellers wander through Gribskov and come to a garden, where Judge Wilhelm (one of the characters of Either/Or*) is being served tea by his wife in the quiet stillness of the early morning. Such a profound ethical comment on the wild fantasies of the evening bring the revellers to a puzzled and respectful halt as they gaze over the hedge.*

They rose from the table. Only a hint from Constantine was needed; the participants understood among themselves with military punctuality when it was time for 'Right about! Face!' With the invisible wand of command, which in his hand was as elastic as a wishing-rod, Constantine touched them once again in order by a fleeting reminiscence to recall the banquet and the mood of sheer enjoyment which had been in a measure suppressed by the reasoning processes of the speakers, and in order that, as in the phenomenon of resonance, the tone of festivity which had vanished might return again to the guests for the brief instant of an echo, he gave the parting salute with a full glass, he emptied it, he flung it against the door in the wall behind him. The others followed his example and performed this symbolic act with the solemnity of initiates. The pleasure of breaking off was thus given its rights, this imperial pleasure which, though briefer than any other, is yet emancipating as no other is. With a libation every enjoyment of the table ought to begin, but this oblation wherewith one flings the glass away into annihilation and oblivion and tears oneself passionately away from every remembrance as if one were in mortal danger, this libation is made to the gods of the underworld. One *breaks* off, and it requires strength to do it, greater strength than to cut a knot with the sword, because the difficulty of the knot bestows passion, but the strength required for breaking off one must bestow upon oneself. In a certain outward sense the result is the same, but in an artistic respect there is a heaven-wide difference whether one leaves off (comes to an end) or breaks off by an act of freedom, whether it is an accident or a passionate decision, whether it is all over like the ballad of the schoolmaster when there is no more of it or is brought to an end by the imperial sword-stroke of pleasure, whether it is a triviality everybody has experienced or that mystery which escapes the majority.

It was a symbolic act of Constantine's when he threw away the goblet, and in another sense this throw was a decisive blow, for at the last blow the doors were thrown open and one saw, like him who has presumptuously knocked at the portal of death and sees when it is opened the puissance of annihilation, so one saw that crew of destruction prepared to lay everything waste – a memento which in a second changed the participants into fugitives from that place, and in the same second transformed as it were the whole environment into a ruin.

A carriage stood ready at the door. At Constantine's invitation they took their places and drove away in good spirits, for that tableau of destruction in the background had imparted a new elasticity to their souls.

A mile from the starting-place the carriage halted. Here Constantine took leave of them as host, informing them that there were five carriages at their service, so that each might follow his own inclination, drive whither he would, alone, or if he would in company, and with whomsoever he would. So it is that a rocket by the force of powder rises as a single shoot, stands for an instant still, collected as one entity, then disperses to all the winds.

While the horses were being hitched the nocturnal guests strolled a little way along the road. The fresh morning air purified their hot blood by its coolness, to the refreshment of which they abandoned themselves completely, whereas upon me their figures and the groups they formed made a fantastic impression. For that the morning sun shines upon field and meadow and upon every creature which at night found rest and strength to arise jubilant with the sun – with this we have a sympathetic and wholesome understanding; but a nocturnal party beheld by morning illumination, in the midst of a smiling rustic environment, makes an almost uncanny impression. One begins to think of ghosts which are surprised by the dawn of day, of elves which cannot find the crevice through which they are accustomed to vanish because it is visible only in the dark, of unfortunates for whom the difference between day and night has become obliterated by the monotony of their suffering.

A footpath led them through a bit of field to a hedged garden, behind which a modest country house betrayed itself in the distance. At the end of the garden next the field there was an arbor formed by trees. Noticing that there was someone in the arbor, they all became curious, and with the searching look of observers the beseigers closed in around this friendly hiding-place, looking as tense as the emissaries of the police when they are bent on outwitting somebody. Like emissaries of the police – well, I must confess that their outward appearance made possible the confusion that the emissaries of the police might be seeking them. Each had taken up his position to peek in, when Victor drew back a step and said to his neighbor, 'Why, my God! It's Judge William and his wife!'

They were surprised – I do not mean the two whom the foliage concealed, that happy pair, too much absorbed in domestic pleasures to be observers, too confident of their security to believe themselves the object of anyone's attention, except that of the morning sun which peeked in upon them with delight, while a gentle breeze rocked the boughs above them, and while the rural peace like everything else around them protected this little arbor. The happy married couple were not surprised and noticed nothing. That they were married people was clear enough, it was to be seen at a glance, alas, when one stands in a relation of consanguinity with an observer. Although nothing, nothing in the wide world, nothing evident, nothing hiddenly evident, nothing hidden, has any notion of wanting to disturb the happiness of the lovers, nevertheless when they are sitting alongside of one another they do not feel themselves thus secure; blissful they are, and yet it is as though there were some power that wished to separate them, so closely do they cling to one another, and yet it is as though there were an enemy at hand against whom they must protect themselves, and yet it is as though they never could be sufficiently assured. It is not thus with married people, and not thus with that married couple in the arbor. How long they had been married it was not possible, however, to determine precisely. The way the wife busied herself with the tea-table did seem to indicate the assurance acquired by long practice, and yet she showed an almost childish eagerness in this occupation, as if she were a recently wedded woman in that intermediate state where she does not yet know definitely whether marriage is play or earnest, whether being a housewife is a business or a game or a pastime. Perhaps she may have been married for a considerable time but did not as a rule preside at the tea-table, perhaps she did so only here in the country, or perhaps she did it only that morning, which may possibly have had a special significance for them. Who can decide? All reckoning is to a certain extent futile when it has to do with one who possesses originality of soul, for this prevents time from leaving its mark. When the sun shines in all its summer splendor, one thinks at once that it must be to celebrate some solemn occasion or another (it cannot surely shine thus for daily use), or that this is the first time it shines so brightly, or at least one of the first times (it surely could not be repeated during a long course of time). So thinks he who sees it only once, or sees it for the first time – and it was the first time I saw the Judge's wife. He who sees this sight every day may think differently – supposing he really sees the same thing. However, that is properly the Judge's business.

So then our amiable housewife was occupied: she poured boiling water into two tea cups (presumably to warm them thoroughly), she emptied that out, set the cup on a tray, poured in the tea, served the condiments, so all was ready – was this play or earnest? In case someone is not ordinarily a tea-lover, he ought to have sat in the Judge's place, for at that moment this drink seemed to me most inviting, and only the inviting look of the kind lady herself seemed more inviting.

Presumably she had not had time to talk until this moment, now she broke the silence, and as she passed the tea she said, 'Be quick now, dear, and drink while the tea is hot; after all, the morning air is rather cool, and so the least thing I can do is to be a little careful of you.' 'The least?' rejoined the Judge laconically. 'Well, or the most, or the only thing.' The Judge looked at her inquiringly, and while she was helping herself she continued, 'You interrupted me yesterday when I was about to say this, but I have thought it over again, many a time I have thought it over, and especially now – you know well enough what has suggested it to me – anyway it is certainly true that if you hadn't married you would have become a much greater person in the world.' With the cup still on the tray the Judge sipped the first mouthful with obvious delight and felt refreshed – or was it perhaps joy in the lovely woman. I believe it was that, but she seemed only to rejoice that it tasted so good to him. Then he put the cup on the table beside him, took out a cigar and said, 'May I light it at your samovar?' 'With all my heart,' she replied, taking a glowing coal with the teaspoon and handing it to him. He lit the cigar and put his arm about her waist while she leaned against his shoulder, he turned his head the other way to blow out the smoke, then his eyes rested upon her with all the devotion a look can express; he smiled, but this smile of joy had a little ingredient of sad irony; finally he said, 'Do you really believe that, my girl?' 'Believe what?' said she. He was silent again, the smile predominated, yet his voice was perfectly serious when he said, 'Then I forgive your former foolishness since you yourself have forgotten it so quickly, for you speak like one of the foolish women – what sort of a great person would I have become in the world?' His wife seemed for an instant embarrassed by this rejoinder, but she promptly collected herself and elaborated her point with feminine eloquence. The Judge looked straight ahead of him, he did not interrupt her, but as she went on he began to thrum on the table with the fingers of his right hand, he hummed a tune, the words of the ballad were momentarily audible; just as the woven pattern in a piece of damask in one aspect is visible and again disappears, so did the words fade again into the humming of the ballad's tune: 'Her husband went out to the forest and cut him the cudgels white.' After this melodramatic address, i.e. the wife's explanation of her cause accompanied by the humming of the Judge, the dialogue began again. 'You still are unaware,' he said, 'that the Danish law permits a man to beat his wife, the only trouble is that it doesn't specify on what occasions it is permissible.' His wife smiled at the threat and continued, 'But why can't I ever get you to be serious when I speak of this? You don't understand me. Believe me, I mean it honestly, it seems to me a very pretty thought. Of course, if you were not my husband, I shouldn't dare to think it, but here now I have thought it, for your sake and for my sake, so please be serious, for my sake, and answer me honestly.' 'No, you can't get me to be serious, and no serious answer do you get. I must either laugh at you and make you forget it as I have done before, or else thrash you, or you must stop talking about it, or I must find some other way of keeping you silent. You see it's a joke, and that is why there are so many expedients possible.' He arose, pressed a kiss upon her forehead, put her arm in his and disappeared in a heavily wooded path which led away from the arbor.

6. An indescribable joy

May 19. Half-past ten in the morning. There is an indescribable joy
which enkindles us as inexplicably as the apostle's outburst comes
gratuitously: 'Rejoice I say unto you, and again I say unto you
rejoice'. – Not a joy over this or that but the soul's mighty song
'with tongue and mouth, from the bottom of the heart': 'I rejoice
through my joy, in, at, with, over, by, and with my joy' – a heavenly
refrain, as it were, suddenly breaks off our other song; a joy which
cools and refreshes us like a breath of wind, a wave of air, from the
trade wind which blows from the plains of Mamre to the everlasting
habitations.

7. Oh, for the married life!

Yes, my good wise man, it is incredible what innate virtuosity a
woman possesses; she explains in the most interesting and beautiful
way the problem which has cost many a philosopher his reason, the
problem of time. A problem upon which in vain one seeks enligh-
tenment from many philosophers with all their prolixity, she
explains without ado at any time of the day. As she explains this
problem, so she explains many others in a way which arouses the
profoundest admiration. Although I am not a husband of many
years' standing I believe I could write a whole book about this. That
I will not do, but I will recount to you a story which to me has been
very suggestive. Somewhere in Holland there lived a learned man,
he was an orientalist and was married. One day he did not come to
the midday meal, although he was called. His wife waits longingly,
looking at the food, and the longer this lasts the less she can explain
his failure to appear. Finally she resolves to go over to his room and
exhort him to come. There he sits alone in his work-room, there is
nobody with him. He is absorbed in his oriental studies. I can
picture it to myself. She has bent over him, laid her arm about his
shoulders, peered down at the book, thereupon looked at him and
said, 'Dear friend, why do you not come over to eat?' The learned

man perhaps has hardly had time to take account of what was said, but looking at his wife he presumably replied, 'Well, my girl, there can be no question of dinner, here is a vocalization I have never seen before, I have often seen the passage quoted, but never like this, and yet my edition is an excellent Dutch edition. Look at this dot here! It is enough to drive one mad.' I can imagine that his wife looked at him, half-smiling, half-deprecating that such a little dot should disturb the domestic order, and the report recounts that she replied, 'Is that anything to take so much to heart? It is not worth wasting one's breath on it.' No sooner said than done. She blows, and behold the vocalization disappears, for this remarkable dot was a grain of snuff. Joyfully the scholar hastens to the dinner table, joyful at the fact that the vocalization had disappeared, still more joyful in his wife.

Do I need to draw out the moral from this story? If that scholar had not been married, he perhaps would have gone crazy, perhaps he would have taken several orientalists with him, for I doubt not that he would have raised a terrible alarm in the literary organs. You see why I say that one ought to live on good terms with the other sex, for (be it said between us) a young girl explains everything and doesn't give a fig for the whole consistory, and if a man is on good terms with her he delights in her information, but if not, she makes sport of him. But this story teaches also in what way one is to live on good terms with her. If that scholar had not been married, if he had been an aestheticist who had in his power all the requisites, perhaps then he would have become the lucky man to whom that marvelous maiden wished to belong. He would not have married, their sentiments were too superior for that. He would have built her a palace and would have spared no refinement to make her life rich in enjoyment, he would have visited her in her castle, for so she wished it to be; with erotic coquetry he would have made his way to her on foot while his valets followed him in a carriage, bringing rich and costly gifts. So, then, in the course of his oriental studies he stumbled upon that remarkable vocalization. He would have stared at it without being able to explain it. The moment, however, was come when he should make his visit to the ladylove. He would have cast this care aside, for how could he becomingly make a visit to a ladylove with thoughts of anything else but of her charms and of his own love? He would have assumed an air of the utmost amiability, he would have been more fascinating than ever, and would have pleased her beyond all measure because in his voice there was a distant resonance of many passions, because out of despondency he had to contend for cheerfulness. But when at dawn he left her, when he had thrown her the last kiss and then sat in his carriage, his brow was darkened. He arrived home, the shutters were closed in his study, the lamps lit, he would not be undressed but sat and stared at the dot he could not explain. He had indeed a girl whom he loved, yea, perhaps adored, but he visited her only when his soul was rich and strong, but he had no helpmeet who came in and called him at midday, no wife who could blow the dot away.

8. Crisis in the Life of an Actress

The Director of the Royal Theatre in Copenhagen, J.L. Heiberg, and his brilliant actress wife, Johanne Luise Heiberg, dominated Copenhagen cultural life. Kierke-gaard was fascinated by them, though since Heiberg was Denmark's leading Hegelian, he earned Kierkegaard's special contempt. Johanne Luise Heiberg had played Juliet in Shakespeare's Romeo and Juliet *when she was sixteen. In January 1847, she played the role again, this time aged thirty-four.*

The idea of a 'repetition' of this kind intrigued Kierke-gaard. The fact that a mature woman can act a fourteen-year-old's love affair better than a sixteen-year-old girl can, provided an illustration of his theme that he could not resist elaborating.

There is 'a potentiation, a more and more intensive return to the original condition'. At sixteen, perceived by the gallery as just a talented and pretty girl, she is now seen as portraying the essential idea of Juliet's passion. This 'metamorphosis', this potentiation through a return in ideality, is contrasted, in the last pages of the essay, with a different sort of 'metamorphosis', that of Asta Nielsen, Johanne Luise Heiberg's friendly lifetime rival

*on the Copenhagen stage. Her achievement is that of
'continuity'. At each age, she portrays 'the idea of femininity'. At sixty, we learn from a long footnote about her in*
Stages on Life's Way, *she will play the perfect grand-
mother. This backhanded compliment cannot help but
put Johanne Luise Heiberg into a class of her own: which
is doubtless where Kierkegaard intended her to be. A
woman who can enrich the idea of first love, while
negating the progress of time, keeps open the possibility
of 'repetition'. Once again the shadow of Regine Olsen
falls across the page.*

I

I suppose that when most people think of an actress of the first rank
they imagine her condition in life to be so enchanting and brilliant
that they generally quite forget its thorny side: the incredibly many
trivialities and all the unfairness or misunderstanding just at the
critical moment that an actress may have to contend with.

Let us conceive of the most favourable situation possible. Let us
imagine an actress who possesses everything she needs in order to
be absolutely of the first rank; let us suppose that she wins admiration and acclaim, and that she is fortunate enough (and this is
undoubtedly a great stroke of fortune) not to become the target for
one or another spiteful person's persecution. So she lives on year
after year, envied, successful, the perpetual object of open admiration. That seems just splendid; it looks as though that would
really be something. But when one looks closer and discovers the
sort of coin in which this open admiration is paid, discovers the
poor sum of shabby trivialities which in the world of the theatre
critics constitutes the fund *ad usus publicos* (and it is indeed from
this fund that the constant open admiration is regularly paid), then
it does seem just possible that even the most fortunate situation for
an actress is shoddy and poor enough. However true it may be, as
one hears, that the wardrobe of the Royal Theatre is very costly and
precious, one thing is certain: that the wardrobe of the newspaper
critics is appallingly shabby.

Further. The admired artist lives on, then, year after year. Just as
in a bourgeois household one knows beforehand exactly what the
dinner menu will be for each day, so she knows beforehand exactly
what the season has in store for her. Two or three times each week

she will be praised and admired, deafened with applause; already within the first three months she will more than once have undergone the newspaper critic's total repertoire of platitudes and – turns of phrase, as they can with special emphasis be called, since the same phrases keep turning up. Once or twice, or in good years three times, she will be celebrated in the song of one or another dissipated good-for-nothing or would-be poet. Her portrait will be painted for every art exhibit; she will be lithographed, and if her luck runs very high her portrait will even be printed on handkerchiefs and the crowns of hats. And she, who as a woman is sensitive regarding her name – as only a woman is sensitive – she knows that her name is on everybody's lips, even when they wipe their mouths with their handkerchiefs! She knows that she is the subject of everyone's admiring conversation, including those who are in the utmost distress for something to chatter about. She lives on in this way year after year. That seems just splendid; it looks as though that would really be something. But if in a higher sense she had to live on the rich nourishment of this admiration, take encouragement from it, receive strength and inspiration for renewed exertions – and since even the most highly talented person, and particularly a woman, can become despondent in a weak moment for want of some expression of genuine appreciation – at such a time she will really feel what she has doubtless realized often enough, just how fatuous all this is, and what a mistake it is to envy her this burdensome splendour.

Meanwhile, as the years go by, though not many in these prying and impatient times, the prattle already begins to stir to the effect that she is now beginning to get older. And so – oh yes, we live in a Christian land, but just as one often enough sees examples of aesthetic brutishness, so also the cannibalistic lust for human sacrifice has by no means gone out of fashion in Christendom. The same intense vulgarity which had never ceased beating the great drum of triviality in her praise and honouring her fondly on the cymbals, this same vulgarity has now become bored with the idolized artist. It wants to be rid of her, wants her out of its sight; she can thank God that it does not want her put to death. This same vulgarity has a new sixteen-year-old idol, and in her honour the former idol must feel vulgarity's full disfavour – for this is the great hardship which is involved in being an idol, that it is all but unthinkable that one should be allowed to resign this position in honour. Even if this does not happen, and nothing quite so crude is perpetrated, still something else sometimes happen, which seems much better but basically is just as bad. In this case the vulgar triviality is flowing along so briskly from the earlier admiration that the idol, even after she has grown older (as people express it), may still be carried along on its momentum for a while. No obvious change is observed in vulgarity's effusions concerning the idolized artist; yet one seems to detect a certain hesitancy, which betrays the fact that the worshipful Rosiflengius rather fancies that he has performed a service for the artist, that he is being *gallant* in continuing to say the same things. But to be gallant towards an artist is precisely the highest degree of insolence, a maudlin impertinence and a disgusting kind of intrusiveness. Anyone who is something, and is something essentially, poses *eo ipso* the claim to be recognized for exactly this special thing, and for nothing more nor less. If, as they say, the theatre is a sacred place, at least it is profaned often enough. How burdensome and painful in one's sixteenth year to have to endure hypocritical genuflections and declarations of love in the form of art criticism from bald and half-witted old reviewers; and how bitter later on to have to put up with the impudence of gallantry!

But now what is the reason for this inhumanity which directs so much injustice and even cruelty against women dedicated to the service of art? What reason except that aesthetic cultivation is so rare among people. Where the feminine is concerned, most people's appreciation of art is in its essential categories and its way of thinking like that of every butcher's apprentice, officer of the guard, or store-clerk, who talks enthusiastically about a damn pretty or a devil of a lively wench of eighteen. These eighteen years, this damnable prettiness and this devilish liveliness, that is the art-appreciation – and also its brutishness. On the other hand, when the aesthetic interest really begins, when inwardness comes into its own and is revealed with intensive significance in the metamorphosis: then the mass of people lose interest. If one does continue to admire, it means that one intends to be gallant or indulgent; for when she is only thirty years old she is essentially *passée*.

It is really to be wished, especially for people's own sakes, so that they would not be deprived or would not deprive themselves of the richest enjoyments, that this prejudice could be thoroughly eradicated. And it really is a prejudice, indeed a brutish prejudice, for a woman does not become an actress in her eighteenth year. She is more likely to become one in her thirtieth year or later, if she becomes one at all; for this play-acting in the eighteenth year is aesthetically of dubious merit. It is so far from gallantry to begin admiring an actress in the later period of her development, that the opposite is really the flattery: to admire a little girl of sixteen. I cannot believe that an essentially cultivated aesthetician could bring himself to make a sixteen-year-old actress the subject of a critique, especially if she were very pretty, etc. He would doubtless avoid such an ambiguous situation. True, it will often happen that one who has created a furore as a young girl never does come through. Maybe so, but then she has never essentially been an actress but has created a furore on the stage entirely in the same sense that a young girl creates a furore in social circles for one or two winters. On the other hand, it is also true that when the metamorphosis is successful there can be no talk of gallantry, for only then is admiration, aesthetically understood, really appropriate.

Of course, much is done for the actresses in the theatre to secure their future. I think it would also be very beneficial if this utterly unaesthetic superstition about the eighteen years could be done away with, and if it could be made quite clear that the most decisive juncture occurs much later – this, too, would provide a safeguard for the actresses' future. And the matter itself has not only an aesthetic, but also a great psychological interest. Indeed, I am surprised that it has not more often been made a subject for reflection. The interesting thing is to be able, in a purely aesthetic way but with the aid of psychology, to anticipate the metamorphosis or at least to explain it when it has set in.

However, a short article in a newspaper is not the suitable place for a detailed investigation into several cases. I shall merely attempt here, in a purely psychological and aesthetic manner, to describe one metamorphosis, certainly a difficult one but just for that reason one that is also beautiful and significant. For the more that has been devoted and the more that has therefore been committed to the first phase, the harder it is to develop a new phase. And the more an essentially unaesthetic public has given idolizing and noisy attention to the first, the easier it is for the attitude of that same public to be transformed into an anxious, distrustful, even sullen opposition to the metamorphosis. An actress who has never had the luck to be in unquestionable possession of that which so greatly captivates and enchants the unaesthetic spectators may as a compensation be lucky enough to enact her metamorphosis in all quietness. That, too, is beautiful, and precisely because it takes place so quietly. But it is also easier, simply because the quiet transformation leading up to the metamorphosis is neither ruined by inquisitiveness nor disturbed by misunderstanding, but is withdrawn from the whims of the public. For the public is peculiar. When in the course of ten years, for example, time has taken the liberty of making the acknowledged favourite ten years older: then the public gets angry – with the favourite.

II

So I am imagining an actress at the very beginning of her career, in the first triumph of her early youth, at the moment when she appears for the first time, and for the first time scores a brilliant success. It is aesthetically correct for me to speak of this situation, and to speak of it with pleasure, because my investigation is of an ideal sort and not concerned with any contemporary actress of sixteen. It is aesthetically proper for me to speak of such a youthful beginning for another reason as well: since the subject of this investigation is the metamorphosis itself, I am not concerned in this essay with her youthful phase as such. The portrayal of the first phase is for the sake of laying the groundwork, it is poetically and philosophically a recollection, but quite without sadness. We do not linger over the first phase, but rather hasten beyond it, since one always hastens on to that which is higher, and the author is aesthetically convinced that the metamorphosis is the highest.

She makes her début, then, in her seventeenth year. She is in possession of – well, what it is that she possesses is very difficult to define, just because it is something indeterminate, which nevertheless asserts itself overwhelmingly and demands an unconditional response. There is no use in even the dullest, most peevish person hardening himself against it, he must respond. Take a mathematician. He may rear up on his hind legs and demand to know what that proves, but it is no use, he must respond, at heart he is convinced: *ergo* she is in possession of – well, what it is that she possesses is very difficult to define, just because it is something indeterminate. It is astonishing. In other cases you can usually specify exactly what quality a person possesses, and when you have done that, then again you can see exactly how much that person is doing with – whatever he possesses. But on the contrary, a young actress who possesses this indefinable quality instantly makes all mere property-owners appear poor by comparison.

But to come a little closer to defining this indefinable possession, let us call it: *Luck*. She is in possession of luck. Luck does not signify here that she is fortunate enough to have good friends and influential connections, or fortunate enough to be engaged by the theatre on profitable terms, or so fortunate as to have the director and critics interested in her. No, luck signifies here what Caesar meant when he said to the ship captain: you are carrying Caesar – and his luck. Indeed, were it not for the fact that she would be tempting her luck, she might rashly dare each evening she plays to have printed on the playbill: Miss N.N. and her luck – to that degree is she in possession of luck. It is not merely that luck is on her side, though it is already a great deal that this almighty power is pleased to escort a young girl; but the luck is even at her beck and call. If she cannot be said to possess this luck, it is only because she is possessed by it. It attends her wherever she goes and wherever she stops, in everything she undertakes, in the least movement of her hand, in every wink of her eye or toss of her head, in every turn of her figure, in her motion, in her voice, in her facial expression. In short, luck dances attendance on her to such a degree that the sensitive critic is not permitted to detect, even for a second, what she would be like apart from her luck, even if he is already aesthetically aware of the extent to which the best aspects of her artistry do not in another sense belong to her at all.

To come still a little closer to defining her indefinable possession, let us further call it: *Youthfulness*. This is not to be taken in the statistical sense, that she completed her sixteenth year a week ago Monday. Nor does it mean that she is a young girl who is put on display of such things as her beauty, and to that extent cannot properly be called an actress at all. No, her youthfulness is again an indefinable treasure. First and foremost, it is the play of vital powers, what one could also call the vivacious, abundant restlessness of youth, of which one always speaks with spontaneous affection, as when it is said that a happily gifted child is the restless one in the family. Of course, you can soon have enough of restlessness, in the sense of finitude run riot. But restlessness in the pregnant sense, the restless of infinity, the joyous, vivacious originality which stirs the waters with rejuvenating, refreshing, healing powers, such restlessness signifies something further, something very great: it signifies the first flaring of an essential genius. And this restlessness is nothing fortuitous, it does not mean simply that she cannot stand still. On the contrary, it means that even when she does stand still one intuits this restlessness in her very repose. It does not mean that she comes running on to the stage, but means on the contrary that when she merely moves one can detect the swiftness of infinity. It does not mean that she speaks so rapidly that one cannot follow her, but means on the contrary that even when she speaks quite slowly one is able to sense the animation of her breath and spirit. This restlessness does not imply that she must quickly tire, but just the opposite: it reveals an elemental tireless-ness, like the wind or the sounds of nature. It reveals that her playfulness is inexhaustibly rich, that it only hints at how much more she possesses. It reveals that her coquetry (and such a personality utterly without coquetry is unthinkable) is nothing but an exuberant and innocent mind's happy, triumphant conscious-ness of its indescribable luck. It is therefore not really coquetry, but something that encourages the spectator still further; that is, it assures him of the reliability of the whole performance, makes him absolutely certain that her exuberance is secure.

It may be supposed that reliability on the one hand, and on the other playfulness, liveliness, luck, youthfulness, are utterly incon-gruous qualities that do not belong together at all. Yet that is by no means the case; they do absolutely belong together. If you cannot be perfectly sure of her playfulness and liveliness, if you cannot absolutely rely on her to have enough for herself and a dozen others besides, then her performance is *eo ipso* a failure and the pleasure is essentially lost. One can also recognize that these qualities are really inseparable from the fact that one naturally responds to playfulness by associating it with reliability: as when an older but still sprightly man says, with complete affection for a playful young girl, 'Goodness knows you can rely on that little lady!' He does not say that she is playful but that she is reliable, and yet that is also to say that she is playful. For this reliability is nothing he has invented, since she elicits this expression from him by her playfulness.

It may be supposed that exuberance on the one hand, and absolute assurance on the other, are again heterogeneous qualities which do not belong together at all, or which only blockheadedness

would think of putting together. And yet they are quite inseparable, and it is the dialectic which brings this combination about.
Anything which is an elemental fact of nature, and as such single
and simple, must be absolutely secure. Anything which is com-
pound can exist with something lacking; but something which is a
single unit, an immediacy, must be absolute, or, to say the same
thing, it is absolute whenever it is such. A little exuberance is to be
rejected as altogether unlovely. Real exuberance, therefore, precisely because of its absolute assurance, has above all a soothing
effect on the spectator; though this perhaps eludes the attention of
most people, who suppose that anything exuberant has a stimulating effect, which is true only of something artificially exuberant or a
little bit exuberant. Let us take an example from immediate
comedy, from whimsy. On a night when you see Rosenkilde come
on the stage, as if straight from the infinite and with its swiftness,
possessed by all the whimsical muses, when at the first sight of him
you find yourself saying, 'Well, this evening he's blowing up a
regular storm': then you feel *eo ipso* indescribably soothed. You
heave a sigh and settle down to relax; you assume a comfortable
posture, as if you intended to remain sitting for a long time in the
same position; you almost regret not having brought some food
along, because the situation induces such trust and assurance, and
therefore such tranquillity, that you forget that it is only a matter of
an hour in the theatre. While you laugh and laugh and quietly
rejoice in the whimsical exuberance, you feel constantly soothed,
indescribably convinced and lulled as it were by Rosenkilde's
absolute assurance, because his whimsy gives you the impression
that it can continue as long as you want. And if, on the contrary, a
comedian in the immediate mode is not first and foremost absolutely soothing, if the spectator is just a little bit anxious for fear his
whimsy may finally fall flat, then the enjoyment is essentially lost. It
is usually said that a comedian must be able to make the audience
laugh, but it might be better to say that he must first and foremost
be able absolutely to soothe, and then the laughter will follow of
itself. For real laughter, laughter that comes from the heart, does
not result from being stimulated, but precisely from being soothed.
So it is with exuberance also: it must above all soothe with its
absolute assurance; that is to say, if it is truly present in an actress it
functions primarily in an absolutely soothing way. It is in this
tranquillity, induced by her absolute assurance and trustworthi-

ness, that the spectator gives himself over to the exuberance. You see, here it is again: Exuberance and trustworthiness seems a strange combination, and it is odd to say of exuberance that it is trustworthy; and yet it is correct, and is only a new expression for playfulness, for this trustworthy exuberance is precisely playfulness.

To come still a little closer to defining her indefinable possession, let us further call it: *Soulfulness*. This means that in the temper of her immediate passion she is attuned to thought and idea; that her still unreflective inwardness is essentially in league with ideality; that every touch of a thought or idea strikes a note, giving a full-toned resonance; that she is an original, specific sensitivity. In this way she relates herself expressively to the playwright's words; but to herself she relates herself still further, in what might properly be called the tone modulated to each speech and the harmony modulated to the character as a whole. Not only does she take the author's words correctly off his lips, but she gives them back to him in such a way, in the accompanying sound of her playfulness and the self-awareness of her genius, that she seems to say in addition: Let me see you copy that.

Her indefinable possession signifies finally: *that she is in the right rapport with the tension of the stage*. Every tension, according to the dialectic's own dialectic, can have two different effects. It can reveal the strain it creates, but it can also do the opposite, can conceal the strain; and not only conceal it, but constantly transform it, change and transfigure it into lightness. Thus the lightness is invisibly grounded in the strain produced by the tension, but this strain is neither seen nor suspected; only the lightness is revealed. A heavy object can weigh something down. But conversely, it can also conceal the fact that it is heavy, and express its heaviness in the opposite way, by lifting something up in the air. People usually talk as though one became light by casting off one's burdens, and this view of the matter is the basis for all trivial outlooks on life. But in a higher, poetic or philosophical sense, the opposite is the case: One becomes light by means of – heaviness. One swings up high and free by means of – a pressure. Thus the celestial bodies soar through space by means of a great weight; birds fly with the help of tremendous pressure: the light soaring of faith is aided by a prodigious heaviness; the highest upswinging of hope is aided precisely by hardship and the pressure of adversity. However, it lays a prodigious burden on a person to have to support the illusion of the stage and the weight of everyone's eyes. In the absence of a happy rapport, therefore, even the highest degree of professional skill cannot quite conceal the heaviness of the burden; but where the happy rapport is present, the heaviness of the burden is continually transformed into lightness. That is the way it is with the young actress. She is in her element in the tension of the stage, just there does she become as light as a bird. It is precisely the weight that makes her light, and the pressure that swings her up so high. There is not a trace of anxiety. In the wings, she may be anxious, but on stage she is happy and light as a bird just set free; for only now, under the pressure, is she free and has received her freedom. That which manifests itself as anxiety when she is at home in her study or in the wings is not impotence, but quite the opposite. It is her elasticity which makes her anxious, just because there is no pressure on her. In the tension of the theatre this anxiety marvellously manifests itself as potency. The notion that an artist must not be anxious is in general very narrow-minded, and to be without anxiety is above all a false indication of artistic greatness. For the more powers he possesses, the greater is his anxiety so long as he is outside the tension which exactly corresponds to his powers. Suppose once that the force of nature which supports the heavenly bodies were personified, and imagine a situation in which it had been relieved of its task and were waiting to take it up again: it would be in the grip of the most deathly anxiety, and only at the moment it took up its burden would it become carefree and light. Hence, one of the greatest torments a human being can suffer is to have too great an elasticity in proportion to the tension of the little world in which he lives; such an unhappy person can never come to feel entirely free, just because he cannot get enough weight on him. The important thing is simply that there should be just enough anxiety, that so far as the actor is concerned it should be kept off-stage, and should never appear on-stage as it does with the person who is not anxious off-stage.

Her *definable possession* is of course easy to specify. She has not only natural grace, but also training. She possesses, as a subordinate aspect of her art, the larger part of a dancer's whole stock-in-trade. Her diction is correct, exact; her voice is not abused, but cultivated, moulding the words with fullness and clarity and without shrieking or breaking, not keeping them to herself or for herself, but projecting them from herself without inhibition. She articulates superbly, even when she whispers. She knows how to use the voice, and nothing testifies more to her qualifications than the way she is able to use it even in the insignificant lines, the casually dropped conversational digressions.

She makes her début in her seventeenth year. Her appearance is naturally a triumph; and in that instant her existence is transformed into a matter of national concern. Just as the daughter of the regiment is regarded as a daughter by the whole regiment, so she becomes the nation's daughter. The very first sight of her is enough to convince everyone that it would be difficult to find more than one woman in a generation who is so exceptionally and happily gifted. It therefore becomes a national duty to admire her and a common concern to preserve this rare flower. Furthermore, it must follow as a matter of course from human weakness that it becomes, if not quite a duty, at any rate a matter of inquisitive interest to see how long she will last. Yes, human rejoicing over the exception is strange; almost from the first and highest moment of rejoicing, inquisitiveness begins to plot the ambush. It is not envy, far from that, it is a kind of giddiness mingled in the admiration, which is beside itself for joy until it occurs to it already in the first year to develop this fatal tension, and out of pure admiration begins to admire in an almost suspicious way.

But let us recall what has already been suggested more than once: If there lived at the same time an essential aesthetician and he were called upon to attempt critically to evaluate this actress or one of her performances, he would certainly say: No, her time has not yet really come.

III

Fourteen years pass, and she is in her thirty-first year. Through all these years she has received constant recognition and admiration. Permit me to indicate this passing of time by using the interval to offer some observations. For let us not be deceived by a careless calculation of all her apparent privileges, and thereby be led unfairly to envy her this admiration. Let us rather consider how much blockheadedness is mixed into the constant mauling of this trivial recognition; and above all let us not forget what it signifies that during these fourteen years it has actually become a habit of her contemporaries to admire her; if we wish to consider the matter correctly, let us not be so unfair to her as to forget to subtract this factor from the supposed splendour of the admiration. Oh, how seldom is there found a person, let alone an age, that does not yield to the fraud of habit; so that even if the expression is not changed, this unchanged expression still becomes something different through force of habit; so that what is literally the same nevertheless sounds so weak, so mechanical, so toneless, even though the same thing is said. Oh, much is said in the world about seducers and seduction: but how many are there who do not deceive themselves through habit, so that they seem unchanged but actually are wasting away in the inner man; so that they still love the same people, love them, but so tamely, so shabbily; so that they still use the same tender expressions, but so feebly, so mechanically, so lifelessly. Suppose a king decided to visit a humble family -- yes, the family would feel honoured, proud, almost overwhelmed by its good fortune. But suppose His Majesty should decide to continue visiting the same family every day. How long would it be before the king must almost make an effort to give a little significance to the fact that he is visiting the family? While the family would remain unchanged, and from habit would continue to say: We thank you for the great honour. Of all sophists, time is the most dangerous, and of all dangerous sophists, habit is the most crafty. It is already difficult enough to notice that one is changed little by little over the years. But the fraud of habit is that one remains unchanged, that one says the same thing, while in fact he is utterly changed and says it in an utterly different way.

Just for that reason, all those who in truth serve the truth uselessly, that is, without putting it to selfish uses, for whom life is a sheer struggle with the sophisms of existence, whose concern is not how they can best profit for themselves, but how they can most truly serve the truth and in truth benefit mankind: such persons have been well-informed about the use of deceptions – in order to test mankind. For example, when an outstanding man lives in deep seclusion, when he only rarely shows himself, then people are not spoiled by too much exposure to him. On the contrary, there develops a splendid, and, if you will, an expedient deception: that this excellent man must really be something quite extraordinary. And why? Because people know how to value his splendid qualities? Oh, no – because they see him so rarely that this rare appearance produces a fantastic effect. Ample experience from the past shows that this can be done. The method, masterfully expressed by Shakespeare in Henry IV's address to Prince Henry, has been used successfully by a numerous host of kings and emperors and clerics and Jesuits and diplomats and shrewd pates, etc. Among them have probably been many superior persons, quite a number of whom have also wished to serve the truth, but all of them were nevertheless united in wishing to operate with the aid of a deception. Either they have simply sought to benefit themselves by arousing the awe of the masses, or they have perhaps piously but also shrewdly hoped to put the truth into general circulation with the aid of – a deception. The absolutely unselfish servants of the truth, on the other hand, have always followed the practice of moving about among people a great deal. They have never played hide and seek with the masses in order again to play the game of bedazzlement by exhibiting themselves on rare occasions as the objects of stunned amazement. They have on the contrary always shown themselves regularly, in everyday clothes, lived with the common man, chatted in the streets and byways, and renounced all prestige – for when the masses see a man every day, they think to themselves: Is that all? Oh well, '*mundus vult decipi*'. But the disinterested witnesses to the truth have never been willing to meet the masses half-way by adding the rest: '*decipiatur ergo*'. They have on the contrary deceived in the opposite way, that is, they have passed judgement on the world by seeming insignificant.

Suppose that an author who neither has a significant fund of ideas nor is very hard-working should once in a great while publish a decorative copybook, very dainty and elegantly put together, with many blank pages: then the masses would look upon this decorative phenomenon with wonder and admiration. They would think: since it has taken him so long to write it, and since there is so little written on the pages, it must be something really extraordinary. Suppose on the other hand a highly productive author, who has other things to think about than being decorative and profiting from a deception, should by exerting himself with greater and greater diligence find himself able to work with exceptional speed. The masses would soon get used to that, and would think: it must be a careless job. For of course the masses cannot judge whether something is really worked out or not, so they stick to – the deception. Suppose there were a pastor, who like the late Chaplain-to-the-Court in Berlin, the otherwise so highly-gifted Theremin, preached only every eighth Sunday or even just every twelfth, but who did so in the most regal and exalted presence of Their Majesties and the whole royal household: a deception would therefore immediately develop about such a Head-Chaplain-to-the-Court. He becomes – well, in truth he of course remains what he really is, a highly gifted man. But in the eyes of the masses he becomes not only the Head-Chaplain-to-the-Court but a Right Reverend Sir besides, or a Right Ruffled Head-Chaplain-to-the-Court, something Right Resplendent, like the king's golden coach, which one beholds with awe only a few times a year. The masses will be deeply impressed, and in their wisdom they will reflect as follows: such a preacher needs three months just to prepare one sermon and memorize it, so it must be extraordinary. And behold, the crowd of curiosity-seekers is so great on the long-awaited eighth or twelfth Sunday that the Head- Chaplain-to-the-Court is scarcely able to squeeze up into the pulpit – had he preached only once a year, the crowd would have been so huge that he would not have been able to squeeze down again at all, or policemen and armed sextons would have been needed to secure the Right Reverend Head-Chaplain's going out and coming in. And if the crowd were so great that someone were squeezed and trampled to death, then the next time the crowd would be still greater. For the dictum holds with regard not only to the truth, but also to curiosity: '*Sanguis martyrum est semen ecclesiae.*'

And now an actress, who for fourteen years has been a constant object of admiration. One has seen her many times, and has slept on one's admiration. One knows perfectly well that she is staying in the country. If only she were one of those personages who travel around Europe, then she could still hope for the assistance of the deception. But one knows that she must remain in the city, because in Denmark there is only one city and one theatre; indeed, one knows that she must play, because she is engaged to do so. Despite their admiration, many are perhaps even shameless enough to be quite aware that she *must* play, because that is the way she earns her living; one knows perfectly well that one can get to see her, generally twice a week. Granted that one continues constantly to admire; but how many are there in a generation who know how to preserve their fervour and discrimination with such vigilance that in their admiration's fourteenth year they can view her with the same originality, with the same freshness that she preserves! No, mankind is similar also in this respect to the children in the market place. When they realize that they possess something, that they are allowed to keep it, then they become ungrateful, or if not downright ungrateful then at least sluggish from the habit of admiration. Towards no one is mankind therefore so ungrateful as it is towards God, just because people have the sluggish notion that one can always have Him – why, He cannot even die some day, to let people feel what they have lost. O human admiration, you are nothing but vanity, and not the least so when you mean to remain constant!

There has been no change in the expression of admiration and recognition, except in its intonation. The *spiritus asper* of the first impression has slackened into the 'smooth breathing' of a vain, habitual admiration. The actress's stock stands unchanged at the quoted price, yet not quite so firm; a sneaking, anxious, basically well-meaning but in its inquisitiveness still treacherous reflection begins to mutter that she is getting older. No one wishes to admit it, and yet it is said, and yet no one wishes to admit having said it. The tension of the embarrassment is all the more painful, just because her existence has been a matter of national concern. People mean well so far as she is concerned (for we will not dwell here on the part that somebody's envy can play in the origin of such an opinion); they are really indignant against time for making her older, having once settled themselves comfortably in the habit of an admiration that would make her remain eighteen years old for ever. Nobody considers how ungrateful it is to make her metamorphosis more and more difficult, how ungratefully she is served when fond memory is transformed into opposition at the critical moment; and nobody considers that this whole thing is a galimatias, which has no place at all, especially in aesthetics, since only with the metamorphosis will her time really begin.

IV
(Last Article)

So now for the metamorphosis. This actress was constituted by feminine youthfulness, though not in the usual sense of the term. What is normally called youthfulness falls prey to the years; for the grip of time may be most loving and careful, but it seizes everything finite just the same. But in this actress there has been an essential genius which corresponds to the very idea: feminine youthfulness.

This is an idea, and an idea is something quite different from the phenomenon of being seventeen years old. A girl, after all, can be utterly devoid of any idea and still be seventeen years old. Without this correspondence of genius to an idea there could be no talk of a metamorphosis. But just because this is the case, and the idea is what it is without compromise, the metamorphosis is exceptional. Just as nature preserves its continuity by means of anticipation and recollection, foresight and hindsight, which naturalists have felicitously termed the Promethean and the Epimethean: so in the spiritual realm that which is to constitute the metamorphosis must be present from the beginning, but only after some time has passed can it be brought decisively into play or decisively manifest itself. Its manifestation is precisely the metamorphosis.

A woman who only possesses feminine youthfulness in the ordinary sense cannot receive the metamorphosis, since feminine youthfulness in this sense is not dialectical within itself. It has only a single life, which is simply consumed by the entrance of the dialectical rather than being set apart and singled out. Time is the dialectical which comes from without, which therefore consumes this undialectical youthfulness sooner or later. But suppose youthfulness is also alive in another dimension; then in destroying something of the natural youthfulness time simply makes the genius more manifest, and manifest in ideality's pure aesthetic relation to the idea. The actress will of course not become young again in the ridiculous sense, according to which butchers' apprentices and the public speak of a devilishly lively girl, but only in the sense of ideality will she become young or younger. She is now really a proper subject for an essential critique, now that she comes into relation to the same idea for the second time and raised to the second power; or more precisely expressed, precisely because it is the second time does she come to relate herself to the idea in a purely ideal way. The matter is quite simple. One might ask: which medium corresponds essentially to a genius whose idea is feminine youthfulness? Most people would presumably give the worst answer: it is feminine youthfulness itself, or being seventeen years old. But this is certainly a misunderstanding which conflicts with the dialectic's own movement of thought. The purely ideal and dialectical requirement is that the medium, or that in which the idea exists, is related to the idea at a distance from the idea. With respect to all natural characteristics it holds true that the first time is the highest, is the culmination. But it holds with respect to ideality that the second time is the highest; for what is ideality but precisely: the second time. From the standpoint of ideality, the fact of being quite young is not appropriate at all to the embodiment of the idea of youthfulness in a role. Unaesthetic spectators think otherwise because they suffer under a delusion; they confuse their enjoyment of Miss N.N.'s phenomenal youthfulness with an appreciation of the actress's essential ideality. Let us take another example. There is a form of lyricism which one may call the lyricism of youthfulness. Every young person who is *erectioris ingenii* has a little of it. But then there is a young person, who *qua* youth has this lyricism of youthfulness, and also possesses a genius the idea of which is the lyricism of youthfulness. Now let us ask, when will he produce his best lyrics, in his twentieth year do you suppose? By no means. His best lyrics will come just at some more mature age when time has taken away the happy accidents of his youthfulness, so that he will now relate himself to his idea in a purely ideal way, and thereby also in a deeper sense as its *servant*. Those who only have a taste for the happy accidents of his early youth are lacking in aesthetic cultivation, and therefore do not discover that these delights belong to the accidental, the transitory, while the genius and the relation to the idea are the eternal and the essential.

The most demanding role which can be assigned an actress who embodies the idea of feminine youthfulness in its most lyrical potentiation is certainly that of Juliet in *Romeo and Juliet*. I wonder whether it would really occur to an aesthetician that a seventeen-year-old actress could play Juliet? There is indeed much trumpeting about the complete play of powers, the fire, the ardour, and many other things of that sort, but these things are really spoken of in gallery-categories, which are hardly sufficient for judging an interpretation of Juliet. What the gallery wishes to see is of course not an ideal presentation, a portrayal of the ideal. The gallery wishes to see Miss Juliet, a devilishly pretty and damn lively girl of eighteen years, who plays at Juliet or passes herself off as Juliet, while the gallery is diverted by the thought that it is really Miss N.N. Therefore the gallery can naturally never get into its head that precisely in order to *portray* Juliet it is essential that an actress possess a distance in age from Juliet. And yet it is so, and that admired excess of powers in the eighteenth year is really, aesthetically, a misunderstanding. For in ideality it holds true that the prime power is consciousness and transparency, which knows how to be in control of the essential powers, in the service, be it well noted, of an idea. There certainly are roles in which the eighteen years are *quod desideratur* in an actress, but these roles are simply not the eminently demanding ones. There are roles in which this excess of powers which goes with the first youthfulness can be used as in a delightful game. Our actress may indeed undertake these roles, and the undertaking can be regarded as a lovely and also worthwhile way of passing the time until she becomes mature enough to acquire the necessary powers for sustaining the eminent assignments. To portray a little maiden of sixteen years in a French play would be a suitable role. But toying with this fleeting, teasing fragility is also to be considered as nothing compared with bearing the weight of Juliet's intensive fullness. It would of course be a misunderstanding to suppose that anyone who could once portray such an almost sketchy figure should therefore also be in a position eventually to undertake the eminent roles. No, far from it. But just for that reason it is the exception when a person who has trained herself in the light forms of fleeting fairy-tale creatures, absolutely happy and constantly fresh and rejuvenated, should in the fullness of time be transfigured into the eminent hypostasis.

The metamorphosis will be a return, in the eminent sense, to her first condition. This will now be elucidated more precisely by exhibiting the dialectical determinants in the metamorphosis. As we have said, time is the dialectical that comes from without, but she was originally dialectical within herself. Just for that reason she can stand in opposition to time, so that its dialectic only makes manifest the dialectical in her – in the metamorphosis.

Time has asserted its right; it has taken something away from her immediate, her first, direct, fortuitous youthfulness. But again, in so doing time simply makes her genius the more essentially manifest. She has lost in the eyes of the gallery, she has won in the ideal sense. The time of gallery-confusions is past; if she is to play Juliet, there can no longer be any talk of creating a furore as Miss Juliet. If she is to play Juliet, it must be an eminent presentation, or more correctly a presentation in the eminent sense. And this is just the metamorphosis. Might against might, it is said, and so also here: dialectic against dialectic, so that time has no power really to take away, but only a subservient power, which serves to make manifest.

Time has asserted its right; it has taken something away from the lucky accidents or accidental luck of that first youthfulness. But it has also developed her, cultivating and refining her, so that now, in full and conscious, well-earned and dedicated command over her essential powers, she can in truth be the handmaiden of her idea. This is the essential aesthetic relation, and it is essentially different from the seventeen-year-old's immediate relation to her own youthfulness. It is this subservient relation to the idea which really is the culmination, precisely this conscious self-abnegation under the idea is the expression for the eminent elevation of her presentation. The youthfulness of the seventeenth year is much too fastidious, much too arrogant, much too lucky to serve in the deepest or (which is the same) in the highest sense. But to be entirely subservient is real inwardness. The inwardness of the seventeenth year is essentially an aspiration directed outward, which for all its luck can never be secure against one or another accident; even if the accident can be avoided, still it is a constant possibility, so that one must say each time: that was a stroke of luck. Only in the absolutely subservient relation to the idea is the accident made absolutely impossible.

Time has asserted its right; there is something which has been consigned to the past. But then again an ideality of recollection will cast an illumination of the highest sort over the whole presentation, an incarnation that was not present in those days of the first youthfulness. Only in recollection is there absolute rest, and therefore the still fire of the eternal, its incorruptible glow. And she is soothed in the eternity of her essential genius. She will not childishly or sadly long for the blaze of times past, for precisely in the metamorphosis has she become both too warm and too rich for that. This pure, soothing and rejuvenating recollection, as an idealizing light, will permeate the whole presentation, which in this light will become completely transparent.

Such are the moments of this metamorphosis. In order once again to illuminate its characteristic quality from another side, let us now in conclusion juxtapose another kind of metamorphosis for purposes of comparison. We shall choose one which is qualitatively different; this will give the comparison an essential interest, meanwhile forestalling any inquisitive quantifying as to which is the rarest, etc. This other metamorphosis is one of continuity, which again more closely defined is a process, a succession, a steady transformation through the years, such that the actress, as she grows older, gradually shifts her field and assumes older roles, again with the same perfection with which in her earlier years she filled the younger. One could call this metamorphosis the direct perfectibility. It has an especially ethical interest, and it will therefore be in the highest degree pleasing and convincing to a certain ethicist, who in defence of his outlook on life proudly points to such a phenomenon as his triumph, and in quiet, intense gratitude regards such an actress as his almighty ally; for she proves his theory better than he, and at precisely one of its most perilous points. On the other hand, the metamorphosis of which we have spoken is one of potentiation, or a more and more intensive return to the original condition. This metamorphosis will be of absolute concern to an aesthetician, because the dialectic of potentiation is precisely the aesthetic-metaphysical dialectic. More joyfully than Archimedes will he utter the dithyrambic cry, 'Eureka!' as he points to this phenomenon. Drunk with admiration and yet sober in dialectical self-possession, he will only have eyes for this single one, and will understand it as his mission to create a situation in which this marvel can be seen and admired just as such.

The metamorphosis of continuity will in the course of the years extend itself uniformly over the essential range of roles included within the idea of femininity; that of potentiation will in the course of the years relate itself more and more intensively to the same idea, which, note well, is aesthetically understood the idea of femininity *sensu eminentissimo*. If one wishes to say of the actress who represents the metamorphosis of continuity that although she does not become older from the standpoint of temporality, she does become older from the standpoint of ideality, so one may say of the other that she becomes younger. But of both it may be said that time has no power over them. That is, there is one resistance against the power of the years, and that is perfectibility, which unfolds itself through the years, and there is another resistance to the power of the years, and that is potentiation, which precisely becomes manifest through the years. Both phenomena are essentially exceptions, and both have it in common that they become more exceptional with every year. Just because they are dialectically complex, their existence will also remain dialectical year after year. Each year will make the attempt to prove its thesis concerning the power of the years, but perfectibility and potentiation will triumphantly refute the years' thesis. This provides absolute tranquillity in the spectator, for the youthfulness of the seventeenth year is indeed fragile, but perfectibility and potentiation are absolutely dependable.

I hope this little article has succeeded in showing just how secure the essential actress's future really is, despite the years. If so it would be a fond satisfaction to me, so much the more because I am convinced that instead of the right conception of an actress's future there is manifold misunderstanding. For the same misunderstanding which misconstrues and unaesthetically overvalues the beginning also misconstrues and unaesthetically distorts what comes later, that is, the highest of all.

Summer 1847

Inter et Inter

PART THREE

The Midnight Hour

Do you not know that there comes a midnight hour
when everyone has to throw off his mask? Do you
believe that life will always let itself be mocked? Do you
think you can slip away a little before midnight in order
to avoid this? Or are you not terrified by it? I have seen
men in real life who so long deceived others that at last
their true nature could not reveal itself; I have seen men
who played hide and seek so long that at last madness
through them obtruded disgustingly upon others their
secret thoughts which hitherto they had proudly concealed. Or can you think of anything more frightful than
that it might end with your nature being resolved
into a multiplicity, that you really might become many,
become, like those unhappy demoniacs, a legion, and
you thus would have lost the inmost and holiest thing of
all in a man, the unifying power of personality? Truly,
you should not jest with that which is not only serious
but dreadful.

1. The black hole

1843

It is extraordinary how strictly, in a certain sense, I was brought up. Sometimes I was put into the black hole, there I would creep around in an agony of pain, seeing nothing, knowing no way out, then suddenly a thought would awaken in my soul, as alive as though I had never known it before, though it might not be unknown to me, but up till then I had, as it were, only been married to it with my left hand, and now with my right. When it had taken root in me I was caressed a little, was taken in its arms and I, who was all shrivelled up like a grasshopper grow as healthy, well-fed, happy, blood-warm, and limber as a new-born babe. Then I have to give my word that I will follow this thought to the very end, stake my life upon it, and then I am harnessed to it. I cannot stop, and my strength lasts. So I get to the end, and everything begins again from the beginning.

1847

The way of tribulation remains equally long and equally dark to the very end – it must be a different way which little by little gets lighter. Neither does one know when the change will come nor exactly whether nor how much nearer one has come to it (for that cannot be known in the dark). But one believes that the change will come, and then with the happiness of eternity. When the child in the dark room waits for the door to be opened and all the hoped-for glory to show itself, then even at the last second before the door is opened it is just as dark as before. And so long as there has been no agreement between the parents and the child as to how long he has to wait, he still does not know whether there may not be a long time to come. But it is quite certain that in the second the door is opened the glory will show itself. So it perhaps occurs to the child sadly that perhaps he has been forgotten. But then the child says to itself: how could I believe that my parents could behave like that. So the child endures in patience; for to make a noise for fear of being forgotten is, he knows quite well, to spoil everything. Oh, but it is so hard for a man to hold out thus and set everything upon the last moment, we should so much like it to show itself little by little, i.e. we should so much like to spoil it for ourselves by getting something in advance.

2. The little coffin

Why was I not born in Nyboder? Why did I not die in infancy? Then my father would have laid me in a little box, taken it under his arm, carried me out some Sunday afternoon to the grave, thrown the earth upon the casket himself, and softly uttered a few words, intelligible only to himself. It was only in the happy days when the world was young, that men could imagine infants weeping in Elysium, because they had died so early.

3. The idea for which I can live and die

> *Wandering alone, along the seashore in northern Sea-
> land, the young Kierkegaard, mentally tormented by
> people who do not understand him, decides to set himself
> a goal which will justify his whole existence: even if those
> people do not recognize what that goal is.*

Gilleleie, August 1, 1835

As I have tried to show in the foregoing pages, that is how things really appeared to me. But when I try to come to a clear under-standing of my own life, everything seems different. For just as it is a long time before the child learns to separate itself from other objects, to distinguish itself from its surroundings, and so stresses the passive side, saying for example, '*me hit.horse*', the same phenomenon repeats itself in a higher spiritual sphere.

I therefore believed that I might perhaps attain peace sooner by taking up another subject, or turning towards a definite aim. For a time I should undoubtedly have succeeded in driving away a certain unrest, but it would only have returned more violent than before, like fever after a drink of cold water.

What I really lack is to be clear in my mind *what I am to do*, not what I am to know, except in so far as a certain understanding must precede every action. The thing is to understand myself, to see what God really wishes *me* to do; the thing is to find a truth which is

true *for me*, to find *the idea for which I can live and die*. What would
be the use of discovering so-called objective truth, of working
through all the systems of philosophy and of being able, if required,
to review them all and show up the inconsistencies within each
system; – what good would it do me to be able to develop a theory
of the state and combine all the details into a single whole, and so
construct a world in which I did not live, but only held up to the
view of others; – what good would it do me to be able to explain the
meaning of Christianity if it had *no* deeper significance *for me and
for my life*; – what good would it do me if truth stood before me,
cold and naked, not caring whether I recognized her or not, and
producing in me a shudder of fear rather than a trusting devotion? I
certainly do not deny that I still recognize an *imperative of understanding* and that through it one can work upon men, *but it must be
taken up into my life*, and *that is* what I now recognize as the most
important thing. That is what my soul longs after, as the African
desert thirsts for water. That is what I lack, and that is why I am left
standing like a man who has rented a house and gathered all the
furniture and household things together, but has not yet found the
beloved with whom to share the joys and sorrows of his life. But in
order to find that idea, or better still, in order to find myself, it is no
use throwing myself still further into life. And that is just what I
have done hitherto. That is why I thought it would be a good thing
to throw myself into the study of the law so as to develop my
sharpness of mind in the complications of life. Here was a great
mass of detail in which I could lose myself; here perhaps I might be
able to work out a complete whole from given facts, an organum of
theft, following up its darker side (and here a certain spirit of
association is also extremely remarkable). I therefore wanted to be
a barrister so that by putting myself in another man's role I could, as
it were, find a substitute for my own life, and find distraction in
outward change. That was what I lacked in order to be able *to lead a
complete human life* and not merely one of the understanding, so
that I should not, in consequence, base the development of my
thought upon – well, upon something that is called objective –
something that is in any case not my own, but upon something
which grows together with the deepest roots of my life, through
which I am, so to speak, grafted upon the divine, hold fast to it,
even though the whole world fell apart. *That is what I lack and that
is what I am striving after*. It is with joy, and inwardly strengthened,

that I contemplate those great men who have thus found the precious stone, for the sake of which they sell all, even their lives, whether I see them intervene forcefully in life, and without faltering go forward on the path marked out for them, or discover them remote from the highway, absorbed in themselves and in working for their noble aim. And I look with reverence even upon the errors which lie so near by. It is this divine side of man, his inward action, which means everything, not a mass of information; for that will certainly follow and then all that knowledge will not be a chance assemblage, or a succession of details, without system and without a focusing point. I too have certainly looked for such a centre. I have looked in vain for an anchorage in the boundless sea of pleasure and in the depth of understanding; I have felt the almost irresistible power with which one pleasure reaches out its hand to the next; I have felt the kind of meretricious ecstasy that it is capable of producing, but also the *ennui* and the distracted state of mind that succeeds it. I have tasted the fruit of the tree of knowledge, and often delighted in its taste. But the pleasure did not outlast the moment of understanding and left no profound mark upon me. It seems as though I had not drunk from the cup of wisdom, but had fallen into it. I have searched with resignation for the principle of my life, by trying to believe that since all things proceeded according to unalterable laws things could not be otherwise, by dulling my ambition and the antennae of my vanity. And because I could not adapt everything to my own mind I withdrew, conscious of my own ability, rather like a worn-out parson resigning with a pension. What did I find? Not my Self, which was what I was looking for (thinking of my soul, if I may so express it, as shut in a box with a spring-lock which external circumstances, by pressing upon the lock, were to open). – And so the first thing to be decided, was the seeking and finding of the Kingdom of Heaven. But just as a heavenly body, if we imagine it in the process of constituting itself, would not first of all determine how great its surface was to be and about which other body it was to move, but would first of all allow the centripetal and centrifugal forces to harmonize its existence, and then let the rest take its course – similarly, it is useless for a man to determine first of all the outside and afterwards fundamentals. One must know oneself before knowing anything else ('Know thyself'). It is only after a man has thus understood himself inwardly, and has thus seen his way, that life acquires peace and significance; only then is he rid of that tiresome, ill-omened fellow-traveller, the irony of life, which shows itself in the sphere of understanding, bidding true understanding begin with ignorance (Socrates) like God creating the world out of nothing. But it really belongs in the waters of morality, with those who are still not in the trade winds of virtue. There man is hurled about in the most terrifying fashion; at one moment it makes him happy and contented to go forward with set purpose along the right path, at the next it hurls him into the abyss of despair. Often it lulls him to sleep with the thought 'things cannot, after all, be otherwise', only to wake him suddenly to the severest of tests. Often it draws a veil of forgetfulness over the past only to make every trifle stand out once more in a vivid light. While he fights his way along that road and rejoices at having overcome temptation, there follows, perhaps at the very same moment and hot upon the most complete victory, some seemingly insignificant outward circumstance that thrusts him straight down from the summit of the rock like Sisyphus. Often when a man has concentrated all his strength upon something he comes across some little outward circumstance that annihilates everything. (For example: a man who is tired of life and wants to throw himself into the Thames and is stopped at the decisive moment by the sting of a gnat). Like consumption it often suffers a man to feel at his very best when he is at his worst. In vain he turns against it; he has not the strength, and the fact that he has so often been through the same experience is no help to him; it is not the kind of experience he acquires in that way which matters. Just as no one, however much experience of swimming he may have, could keep afloat in a storm, but only a man who was absolutely convinced from experience that he was lighter than water, in the same way the man who has no inward hold on life cannot keep afloat in life's storm. Only when a man has understood himself in that way is he in a position to carve out an independent existence and thus escape abandoning his self. How often we see – (at a time when we praise the Greek historian to the skies who knew how to copy a foreign style with the most baffling likeness to the original, instead of censuring him because an author's most prized quality is always to have a personal style, i.e. a mode of expression and presentation shaped by his own individuality) – how often we see people who either from indolence of mind live on the crumbs that fall from the tables of others, or for more selfish reasons familiarize themselves with the lives of others, and finally, like the liar by the frequent repetition of his stories, believe them. Although I am still far from having reached so complete an understanding of myself, I have, with profound respect for its significance, tried to preserve my individuality – worshipped the unknown God. Warned by a premature apprehension I have tried to avoid coming in too close contact with those phenomena whose power of attraction would perhaps exercise too great an influence upon me. I have tried to master them, studied them individually and examined their importance in men's lives, but at the same time guarded against going, like the moth, too near the flame. I have had but little to win or lose from the ordinary run of men. Partly because everything which occupies them – so-called practical life – only interests me slightly; partly because the coldness and lack of interest with which they treat the more profound and spiritual emotions in man have estranged me still further. With few exceptions my associates have not exerted any particular influence upon me. A life which is not clear about itself inevitably displays an uneven surface; they have stopped short at particular facts and their apparent disharmony; they were not sufficiently interested in me to try to resolve them in a higher agreement or to perceive the inner necessity of it. Their opinion of me was therefore always one-sided,and I have, as a result, alternately laid too much, or too little weight upon their pronouncements. I have now withdrawn from their influence and their possibly misleading effect upon the compass of my life. And so I stand once again at the point where I must begin my life in a different way. I shall now try to fix a calm gaze upon myself and begin to act in earnest; for only thus shall I be able, like the child calling itself 'I' with its first conscious action, to call myself 'I' in any deeper sense.

But for that patience is necessary, and one cannot reap immediately where one has sown. I shall bear in mind the method of the philosopher who bade his disciples keep silence for three years after which time all would come right. One does not begin feasting at dawn but at sunset. And so too in the spiritual world it is first of all necessary to work for some time before the light bursts through and the sun shines forth in all its glory. For although it is said that God allows the sun to shine upon the good and the wicked, and sends down rain upon the just and the unjust, it is not so in the spiritual world. And so the die is cast – I cross the Rubicon! This road certainly leads me *to strife*; but I shall not give up. I will not grieve over the past – for why grieve? I will work on with energy and not waste time grieving, like the man caught in the quicksands who began by calculating how far down he had already sunk, forgetting that all the while he was sinking still deeper. I will hurry along the path I have discovered, greeting those whom I meet on my way, not looking back as did Lot's wife, but remembering that it is a hill up which we have to struggle.

4. Mount Moriah: four possible accounts

Mount Moriah, where Abraham prepared to sacrifice his son Isaac. Fear and Trembling *(1843), like the Mount Moriah of which it treats, is surrounded by a cloud of mystery. There is obviously some special coded message in this text which Kierkegaard has made sure cannot be finally elucidated.*

The story of Abraham and Isaac gave Kierkegaard an unparalleled opportunity to examine the relations between a sacrificing Father and a sacrificed Son. God and Christ; Abraham and Isaac; Michael Pedersen Kierkegaard and Søren Aabye Kierkegaard . . . and what if the Father has no right to sacrifice a son? Is it even in the power of Theology to abrogate Ethics?

The literary form of the work is little short of a cadenza. As an opening 'proem' or prelude, Johannes de Silentio offers four apparently simple descriptions of the same set of acts. But with repeated re-reading, it appears that each of the four accounts presents a different disaster as the result of the trip to Mount Moriah. The pendent paragraphs, variations on the theme of weaning, are themselves offers of disparate kinds of interpretation of cost.

Once upon a time there was a man who as a child had heard the beautiful story about how God tempted Abraham, and how he endured temptation, kept the faith, and a second time received again a son contrary to expectation. When the child became older he read the same story with even greater admiration, for life had separated what was united in the pious simplicity of the child. The older he became, the more frequently his mind reverted to that story, his enthusiasm became greater and greater, and yet he was less and less able to understand the story. At last in his interest for that he forgot everything else; his soul had only one wish, to see Abraham, one longing, to have been witness to that event. His desire was not to behold the beautiful countries of the Orient, or the earthly glory of the Promised Land, or that godfearing couple whose old age God had blessed, or the venerable figure of the aged patriarch, or the vigorous young manhood of Isaac whom God had bestowed upon Abraham – he saw no reason why the same thing might not have taken place on a barren heath in Denmark. His yearning was to accompany them on the three days' journey when Abraham rode with sorrow before him and with Isaac by his side. His only wish was to be present at the time when Abraham lifted up his eyes and saw Mount Moriah afar off, at the time when he left the asses behind and went alone with Isaac up unto the mountain; for what his mind was intent upon was not the ingenious web of imagination but the shudder of thought.

That man was not a thinker, he felt no need of getting beyond faith; he deemed it the most glorious thing to be remembered as the father of it, an enviable lot to possess it, even though no one else were to know it.

That man was not a learned exegete, he didn't know Hebrew; if he had known Hebrew, he perhaps would easily have understood the story and Abraham.

I

'And God tempted Abraham and said unto him, Take Isaac, thine only son, whom thou lovest, and get thee into the land of Moriah, and offer him there for a burnt offering upon the mountain which I will show thee.'

It was early in the morning, Abraham arose betimes, he had the asses saddled, left his tent, and Isaac with him, but Sarah looked out of the window after them until they had passed down the valley and she could see them no more. They rode in silence for three days. On the morning of the fourth day Abraham said never a word, but he lifted up his eyes and saw Mount Moriah afar off. He left the young men behind and went on alone with Isaac beside him up to the mountain. But Abraham said to himself, 'I will not conceal from Isaac whither this course leads him.' He stood still, he laid his hand upon the head of Isaac in benediction, and Isaac bowed to receive the blessing. And Abraham's face was fatherliness, his look was mild, his speech encouraging. But Isaac was unable to understand him, his soul could not be exalted; he embraced Abraham's knees, he fell at his feet imploringly, he begged for his young life, for the fair hope of his future, he called to mind the joy in Abraham's house, he called to mind the sorrow and loneliness. Then Abraham lifted up the boy, he walked with him by his side, and his talk was full of comfort and exhortation. But Isaac could not understand him. He climbed Mount Moriah, but Isaac understood him not. Then for an instant he turned away from him, and when Isaac again saw Abraham's face it was changed, his glance was wild, his form was horror. He seized Isaac by the throat, threw him to the ground, and said, 'Stupid boy, dost thou then suppose that I am thy father? I am an idolater. Dost thou suppose that this is God's bidding? No, it is my desire.' Then Isaac trembled and cried out in his terror, 'O God in heaven, have compassion upon me. God of Abraham, have compassion upon me. If I have no father upon earth, be Thou my father!' But Abraham in a low voice said to himself, 'O Lord in heaven, I thank Thee. After all it is better for him to believe that I am a monster, rather than that he should lose faith in Thee.'

When the child must be weaned, the mother blackens her breast; it would indeed be a shame that the breast should look delicious when the child must not have it. So the child believes that the breast has changed, but the mother is the same, her glance is as loving and tender as ever. Happy the person who had no need of more dreadful expedients for weaning the child!

II

It was early in the morning, Abraham arose betimes, he embraced Sarah, the bride of his old age, and Sarah kissed Isaac, who had taken away her reproach, who was her pride, her hope for all time. So they rode on in silence along the way, and Abraham's glance was fixed upon the ground until the fourth day when he lifted up his eyes and saw afar off Mount Moriah, but his glance turned again to the ground. Silently he laid the wood in order, he bound Isaac, in silence he drew the knife – then he saw the ram which God had prepared. Then he offered that and returned home . . . From that time on Abraham became old, he could not forget that God had required this of him. Isaac throve as before, but Abraham's eyes were darkened, and he knew joy no more.

When the child has grown big and must be weaned, the mother virginally hides her breast, so the child has no more a mother. Happy the child which did not in another way lose its mother.

III

It was early in the morning, Abraham arose betimes, he kissed Sarah, the young mother, and Sarah kissed Isaac, her delight, her joy at all times. And Abraham rode pensively along the way, he thought of Hagar and of the son whom he drove out into the wilderness, he climbed Mount Moriah, he drew the knife.

It was a quiet evening when Abraham rode out alone, and he rode to Mount Moriah; he threw himself upon his face, he prayed God to forgive him his sin, that he had been willing to offer Isaac, that the father had forgotten his duty toward the son. Often he rode his lonely way, but he found no rest. He could not comprehend that it was a sin to be willing to offer to God the best thing he possessed, that for which he would many times have given his life; and if it was a sin, if he had not loved Isaac as he did, then he could not understand that it might be forgiven. For what sin could be more dreadful?

When the child must be weaned, the mother too is not without sorrow at the thought that she and the child are separated more and more, that the child which first lay under her heart and later reposed upon her breast will be so near to her no more. So they mourn together for the brief period of mourning. Happy the person who has kept the child as near and needed not to sorrow any more!

IV

It was early in the morning, everything was prepared for the journey in Abraham's house. He bade Sarah farewell, and Eleazar, the faithful servant, followed him along the way, until he turned back. They rode together in harmony, Abraham and Isaac, until they came to Mount Moriah. But Abraham prepared everything for the sacrifice, calmly and quietly; but when he turned and drew the knife, Isaac saw that his left hand was clenched in despair, that a tremor passed through his body – but Abraham drew the knife.

Then they returned again home, and Sarah hastened to meet them, but Isaac had lost his faith. No word of this had ever been spoken in the world, and Isaac never talked to anyone about what he had seen, and Abraham did not suspect that anyone had seen it.

When the child must be weaned, the mother has stronger food in readiness, lest the child should perish. Happy the person who has stronger food in readiness!

Thus and in many like ways that man of whom we are speaking thought concerning this event. Every time he returned home after wandering to Mount Moriah, he sank down with weariness, he folded his hands and said, 'No one is so great as Abraham! Who is capable of understanding him?'

5. What if Abraham is wrong?

The central narrative in Fear and Trembling *is God's instruction to Abraham to sacrifice his son Isaac as a testimony of his faith (Genesis 22). But the problem Johannes de Silentio raises in a series of three* Problems, *is whether God had any right to demand such a proof of faith, and whether Abraham had any right to obey it. For God's demand does abrogate at a stroke the ethical, religious, civil, and family law. The moral law, which Johannes de Silentio called 'the universal', simply because it is the received, generally accepted moral law, surely does not admit of any exceptions at all? How then did God have the right to ask this particular act of Abraham? From this agonized conflict between moral law, and a presumed 'higher' law which sets the moral law aside, emerges the central Kierkegaardian category of 'the Individual': uniquely and terrifyingly responsible*

*uniquely and terrifyingly responsible for his actions –
responsible to God alone, and hence cut off from all
sympathy and understanding from his fellow men.
Behind its complex play of abstractions hover two questions so real for Kierkegaard that he made them central to
all his work: Did his father, the stern, guilt-ridden,
pietistic Michael Pedersen Kierkegaard, have the right to
'sacrifice' his son Søren as he did, to a joyless youth and
to a faith which was itself a crucifixion? And secondly,
was the 'sacrifice' of the young and beautiful Regine
Olsen by Kierkegaard himself really 'necessary'? Was
this really imperative, if the Kierkegaardian life-work
were to be carried out? And what if Abraham misheard?
What if Abraham got the instruction wrong?*

PROBLEM I
Is there such a thing as a teleological suspension of the ethical?

The ethical as such is the universal, and as the universal it applies to everyone, which may be expressed from another point of view by saying that it applies every instant. It reposes immanently in itself, it has nothing without itself which is its *telos*, but is itself *telos* for everything outside it, and when this has been incorporated by the ethical it can go no further. Conceived immediately as physical and psychical, the particular individual is the individual who has his *telos* in the universal, and his ethical task is to express himself constantly in it, to abolish his particularity in order to become the universal. As soon as the individual would assert himself in his particularity over against the universal he sins, and only by recog-nizing this can he again reconcile himself with the universal. Whenever the individual after he has entered the universal feels an impulse to assert himself as the particular, he is in temptation (*Anfechtung*), and he can labor himself out of this only by peni-tently abandoning himself as the particular in the universal. If this be the highest thing that can be said of man and of his existence, then the ethical has the same character as man's eternal blessed-ness, which to all eternity and at every instant is his *telos*, since it would be a contradiction to say that this might be abandoned (i.e. teleologically suspended), inasmuch as this is no sooner suspended than it is forfeited, whereas in other cases what is suspended is not forfeited but is preserved precisely in that higher thing which is its *telos*.

Faith is precisely this paradox, that the individual as the particular is higher than the universal, is justified over against it, is not subordinate but superior – yet in such a way, be it observed, that it is the particular individual who, after he has been subordinated as the particular to the universal, now through the universal becomes the individual who as the particular is superior to the universal, for the fact that the individual as the particular stands in an absolute relation to the absolute. This position cannot be mediated, for all mediation comes about precisely by virtue of the universal; it is and remains to all eternity a paradox, inaccessible to thought. And yet faith is this paradox – or else (these are the logical deductions which I would beg the reader to have *in mente* at every point, though it would be too prolix for me to reiterate them on every occasion) – or else there never has been faith . . . precisely because it always has been. In other words Abraham is lost.

That for the particular individual this paradox may easily be mistaken for a temptation (*Anfechtung*) is indeed true, but one ought not for this reason to conceal it. That the whole constitution of many persons may be such that this paradox repels them is indeed true, but one ought not for this reason to make faith something different in order to be able to possess it, but ought rather to admit that one does not possess it, whereas those who possess faith should take care to set up certain criteria so that one might distinguish the paradox from a temptation (*Anfechtung*).

Now the story of Abraham contains such a teleological suspension of the ethical. There have not been lacking clever pates and profound investigators who have found analogies to it. Their wisdom is derived from the pretty proposition that at bottom everything is the same. If one will look a little more closely, I have not much doubt that in the whole world one will not find a single analogy (except a later instance which proves nothing), if it stands fast that Abraham is the representative of faith, and that faith is normally expressed in him whose life is not merely the most paradoxical that can be thought but so paradoxical that it cannot be thought at all. He acts by virtue of the absurd, for it is precisely absurd that he as the particular is higher than the universal. This paradox cannot be mediated; for as soon as he begins to do this he has to admit that he was in temptation (*Anfechtung*), and if such was the case, he never gets to the point of sacrificing Isaac, or, if he has sacrificed Isaac, he must turn back repentantly to the universal. By virtue of the absurd he gets Isaac again. Abraham is therefore at no instant a tragic hero but something quite different, either a murderer or a believer. The middle term which saves the tragic hero, Abraham has not. Hence it is that I can understand the tragic hero but cannot understand Abraham, though in a certain crazy sense I admire him more than all other men.

Abraham's relation to Isaac, ethically speaking, is quite simply expressed by saying that a father shall love his son more dearly than himself. Yet within its own compass the ethical has various gradations. Let us see whether in this story there is to be found any higher expression for the ethical such as would ethically explain his conduct, ethically justify him in suspending the ethical obligation toward his son, without in this search going beyond the teleology of the ethical.

When Agamemnon, Jephtha, Brutus at the decisive moment heroically overcome their pain, have heroically lost the beloved and have merely to accomplish the outward sacrifice, then there never will be a noble soul in the world who will not shed tears of compassion for their pain and of admiration for their exploit. If, on the other hand, these three men at the decisive moment were to adjoin to their heroic conduct this little word, 'But for all that it will not come to pass,' who then would understand them? If as an explanation they added, 'This we believe by virtue of the absurd,' who would understand them better? For who would not easily understand that it was absurd, but who would understand that one could then believe it?

The difference between the tragic hero and Abraham is clearly evident. The tragic hero still remains within the ethical. He lets one expression of the ethical find its *telos* in a higher expression of the ethical; the ethical relation between father and son, or daughter and father, he reduces to a sentiment which has its dialectic in its relation to the idea of morality. Here there can be no question of a teleological suspension of the ethical itself.

With Abraham the situation was different. By his act he overstepped the ethical entirely and possessed a higher *telos* outside of it, in relation to which he suspended the former. For I should very much like to know how one would bring Abraham's act into relation with the universal, and whether it is possible to discover any connection whatever between what Abraham did and the universal . . . except the fact that he transgressed it. It was not for the sake of saving a people, not to maintain the idea of the state, that Abraham did this, and not in order to reconcile angry deities. If there could be a question of the deity being angry, he was angry only with Abraham, and Abraham's whole action stands in no relation to the universal, is a purely private undertaking. Therefore, whereas the tragic hero is great by reason of his moral virtue, Abraham is great by reason of a purely personal virtue. In Abraham's life there is no higher expression for the ethical than this, that the father shall love his son. Of the ethical in the sense of morality there can be no question in this instance. In so far as the universal was present, it was indeed cryptically present in Isaac, hidden as it were in Isaac's loins, and must therefore cry out with Isaac's mouth, 'Do it not! Thou art bringing everything to naught.'

Why then did Abraham do it? For God's sake, and (in complete identity with this) for his own sake. He did it for God's sake because God required this proof of his faith; for his own sake he did it in order that he might furnish the proof. The unity of these two points of view is perfectly expressed by the word which has always been used to characterize this situation: it is a trial, a temptation (*Fristelse*). A temptation – but what does that mean? What ordinarily tempts a man is that which would keep him from doing his duty, but in this case the temptation is itself the ethical . . . which would keep him from doing God's will. But what then is duty? Duty is precisely the expression for God's will.

Here is evident the necessity of a new category if one would understand Abraham. Such a relationship to the deity paganism did not know. The tragic hero does not enter into any private relationship with the deity, but for him the ethical is the divine, hence the paradox implied in his situation can be mediated in the universal.

Abraham cannot be mediated, and the same thing can be expressed also by saying that he cannot talk. So soon as I talk I express the universal, and if I do not do so, no one can understand me. Therefore if Abraham would express himself in terms of the universal, he must say that his situation is a temptation (*Anfechtung*), for he has no higher expression for that universal which stands above the universal which he transgresses.

Therefore, though Abraham arouses my admiration, he at the

same time appalls me. He who denies himself and sacrifices himself for duty gives up the finite in order to grasp the infinite, and that man is secure enough. The tragic hero gives up the certain for the still more certain, and the eye of the beholder rests upon him confidently. But he who gives up the universal in order to grasp something still higher which is not the universal – what is he doing? Is it possible that this can be anything else but a temptation (*Anfechtung*)? And if it be possible . . . but the individual was mistaken – what can save him? He suffers all the pain of the tragic hero, he brings to naught his joy in the world, he renounces everything . . . and perhaps at the same instant debars himself from the sublime joy which to him was so precious that he would purchase it at any price. Him the beholder cannot understand nor let his eye rest confidently upon him. Perhaps it is not possible to do what the believer proposes, since it is indeed unthinkable. Or if it could be done, but if the individual had misunderstood the deity – what can save him? The tragic hero has need of tears and claims them, and where is the envious eye which would be so barren that it could not weep with Agamemnon; but where is the man with a soul so bewildered that he would have the presumption to weep for Abraham? The tragic hero accomplishes his act at a definite instant in time, but in the course of time he does something not less significant, he visits the man whose soul is beset with sorrow, whose breast for stifled sobs cannot draw breath, whose thoughts pregnant with tears weigh heavily upon him, to him he makes his appearance, dissolves the sorcery of sorrow, loosens his corslet, coaxes forth his tears by the fact that in his sufferings the sufferer forgets his own. One cannot weep over Abraham. One approaches him with a *horror religiosus*, as Israel approached Mount Sinai. – If then the solitary man who ascends Mount Moriah, which with its peak rises heaven-high above the plain of Aulis, if he be not a somnambulist who walks securely above the abyss while he who is stationed at the foot of the mountain and is looking on trembles with fear and out of reverence and dread dare not even call to him – if this man is disordered in his mind, if he had made a mistake! Thanks and thanks again to him who proffers to the man whom the sorrows of life have assaulted and left naked – proffers to him the figleaf of the word with which he can cover his wretchedness. Thanks be to thee, great Shakespeare, who art able to express everything, absolutely everything, precisely as it is – and yet why didst thou never pronounce this pang? Didst thou perhaps reserve it to thyself – like the loved one whose name one cannot endure that the world should mention? For the poet purchases the power of words, the power of uttering all the dread secrets of others, at the price of a little secret he is unable to utter . . . and a poet is not an apostle, he casts out devils only by the power of the devil.

But now when the ethical is thus teleologically suspended, how does the individual exist in whom it is suspended? He exists as the particular in opposition to the universal. Does he then sin? For this is the form of sin, as seen in the idea. Just as the infant, though it does not sin, because it is not as such yet conscious of its existence, yet its existence is sin, as seen in the idea, and the ethical makes its demands upon it every instant. If one denies that this form can be repeated [in the adult] in such a way that it is not sin, then the sentence of condemnation is pronounced upon Abraham. How then did Abraham exist? He believed. This is the paradox which keeps him upon the sheer edge and which he cannot make clear to any other man, for the paradox is that he as the individual puts himself in an absolute relation to the absolute. Is he justified in doing this? His justification is once more the paradox; for if he is justified, it is not by virtue of anything universal, but by virtue of being the particular individual.

How then does the individual assure himself that he is justified? It is easy enough to level down the whole of existence to the idea of the state or the idea of society. If he does this, one can also mediate easily enough, for then one does not encounter at all the paradox that the individual as the individual is higher than the universal.

I return, however, to Abraham. Before the result, either Abraham was every minute a murderer, or we are confronted by a paradox which is higher than all mediation.

The story of Abraham contains therefore a teleological suspension of the ethical. As the individual he became higher than the universal. This is the paradox which does not permit of mediation. It is just as inexplicable how he got into it as it is inexplicable how he remained in it. If such is not the position of Abraham, then he is not even a tragic hero but a murderer. To want to continue to call him the father of faith, to talk of this to people who do not concern themselves with anything but words, is thoughtless. A man can become a tragic hero by his own powers – but not a knight of faith. When a man enters upon the way, in a certain sense the hard way of the tragic hero, many will be able to give him counsel; to him who follows the narrow way of faith no one can give counsel, him no one can understand. Faith is a miracle, and yet no man is excluded from it; for that in which all human life is unified is passion, and faith is a passion.

6. The necessity of silence

The third of the three Problems *developed in* Fear and Trembling *concerns the relation of speech and silence.* Problem III *runs:* 'Was Abraham ethically defensible in keeping silence about his purpose before Sarah, before Eleazar, before Isaac?' *Like 'Antigone' in* Either/Or *and 'Solomon' in* Stages on Life's Way, *Abraham has reasons why he cannot speak. He is bound to silence by the very nature of what it is he knows. The parallel with the silence that Kierkegaard forced himself to observe about his father, Michael Pedersen Kierkegaard, is directly at issue here.*

Genesis 22 records only one sentence spoken by Abraham: 'My son, God will provide Himself a lamb for a burnt offering' (verse 8). Otherwise he is silent. Johannes de Silentio chooses to regard this single utterance by the Biblical Abraham as an irony: 'for it always is irony when I say something and do not say anything'. But it is the silence of Abraham that fascinates Johannes de Silentio (John of Silence). For – what if Abraham was wrong?

But now as for Abraham – how did he act? For I have not forgotten, and the reader will perhaps be kind enough to remember, that it was with the aim of reaching this point I entered into the whole foregoing discussion – not as though Abraham would thereby become more intelligible, but in order that the unintelligibility might become more desultory. For, as I have said, Abraham I cannot understand, I can only admire him. It was also observed that the stages I have described do none of them contain an analogy to

Abraham. The examples were simply educed in order that while they were shown in their own proper sphere they might at the moment of variation [from Abraham's case] indicate as it were the boundary of the unknown land. If there might be any analogy, this must be found in the paradox of sin, but this again lies in another sphere and cannot explain Abraham and is itself far easier to explain than Abraham.

So then, Abraham did not speak, he did not speak to Sarah, nor to Eleazar, nor to Isaac, he passed over three ethical authorities; for the ethical had for Abraham no higher expression than the family life.

Aesthetics permitted, yea, required of the individual silence, when he knew that by keeping silent he could save another. This is already sufficient proof that Abraham does not lie within the circumference of aesthetics. His silence has by no means the intention of saving Isaac, and in general his whole task of sacrificing Isaac for his own sake and for God's sake is an offense to aesthetics, for aesthetics can well understand that I sacrifice myself, but not that I sacrifice another for my own sake. The aesthetic hero was silent. Ethics condemned him, however, because he was silent by virtue of his accidental particularity. His human foreknowledge was what determined him to keep silent. This ethics cannot forgive, every such human knowledge is only an illusion, ethics requires an infinite movement, it requires revelation. So the aesthetic hero can speak but will not.

The genuine tragic hero sacrifices himself and all that is his for the universal, his deed and every emotion with him belong to the universal, he is revealed, and in this self-revelation he is the beloved son of ethics. This does not fit the case of Abraham: he does nothing for the universal, and he is concealed.

Now we reach the paradox. Either the individual as the individual is able to stand in an absolute relation to the absolute (and then the ethical is not the highest) /or Abraham is lost – he is neither a tragic hero, nor an aesthetic hero.

Here again it may seem as if the paradox were the easiest and most convenient thing of all. However, I must repeat that he who counts himself convinced of this is not a knight of faith, for distress and anguish are the only legitimations that can be thought of, and they cannot be thought of in general terms, for with that the paradox is annulled.

Abraham keeps silent – but he *cannot* speak. Therein lies the distress and anguish. For if I when I speak am unable to make myself intelligible, then I am not speaking – even though I were to talk uninterruptedly day and night. Such is the case with Abraham. He is able to utter everything, but one thing he cannot say, i.e. say it in such a way that another understands it, and so he is not speaking. The relief of speech is that it translates me into the universal. Now Abraham is able to say the most beautiful things any language can express about how he loves Isaac. But it is not this he has at heart to say, it is the profounder thought that he would sacrifice him because it is a trial. This latter thought no one can understand, and hence everyone can only misunderstand the former. This distress the tragic hero does not know. He has first of all the comfort that every counter-argument has received due consideration, that he has been able to give to Clytemnestra, to Iphigenia, to Achilles, to the chorus, to every living being, to every voice from the heart of humanity, to every cunning, every alarming, every accusing, every compassionate thought, opportunity to stand up against him. He can be sure that everything that can be said against him has been said, unsparingly, mercilessly – and to strive against the whole world is a comfort, to strive with oneself is dreadful. He has no reason to fear that he has overlooked anything, so that afterwards he must cry out as did King Edward IV at the news of the death of Clarence:

> *Who su'd to me for him? who, in my wrath,*
> *Kneel'd at my feet and bade me be advised?*
> *Who spoke of brotherhood? who spoke of love?*

The tragic hero does not know the terrible responsibility of solitude. In the next place he has the comfort that he can weep and lament with Clytemnestra and Iphigenia – and tears and cries are assuaging, but unutterable sighs are torture. Agamemnon can quickly collect his soul into the certainty that he will act, and then he still has time to comfort and exhort. This Abraham is unable to do. When his heart is moved, when his words would contain a blessed comfort for the whole world, he does not dare to offer comfort, for would not Sarah, would not Eleazar, would not Isaac say, 'Why wilt thou do it? Thou canst refrain'? And if in his distress he would give vent to his feelings and would embrace all his dear ones before taking the final step, this might perhaps bring about the dreadful consequence that Sarah, that Eleazar, that Isaac would be offended in him and would believe he was a hypocrite. He is unable to speak, he speaks no human language. Though he himself understood all the tongues of the world, though his loved ones also understood them, he nevertheless cannot speak – he speaks a divine language . . he 'speaks with tongues.'

This distress I can well understand, I can admire Abraham, I am not afraid that anyone might be tempted by this narrative light-heartedly to want to be the individual, but I admit also that I have not the courage for it, and that I renounce gladly any prospect of getting further – if only it were possible that in any way, however late, I might get so far. Every instant Abraham is able to break off, he can repent the whole thing as a temptation (*Anfechtung*), then he can speak, then all could understand him – but then he is no longer Abraham.

Abraham *cannot* speak, for he cannot utter the word which explains all (that is, not so that it is intelligible), he cannot say that it is a test, and a test of such a sort, be it noted, that the ethical is the temptation (*Versuchung*). He who is so situated is an emigrant from the sphere of the universal. But the next word he is still less able to utter. For, as was sufficiently set forth earlier, Abraham makes two movements: he makes the infinite movement of resignation and gives up Isaac (this no one can understand because it is a private venture); but in the next place, he makes the movement of faith every instant. This is his comfort, for he says: 'But yet this will not come to pass, or, if it does come to pass, then the Lord will give me a new Isaac, by virtue viz. of the absurd.' The tragic hero does at last get to the end of the story. Iphigenia bows to her father's resolution, she herself makes the infinite movement of resignation, and now they are on good terms with one another. She can understand Agamemnon because his undertaking expresses the universal. If on the other hand Agamemnon were to say to her, 'In spite of the fact that the deity demands thee as a sacrifice, it might yet be possible that he did not demand it – by virtue viz. of the absurd,' he would that very instant become unintelligible to Iphigenia. If he could say this by virtue of human calculation, Iphigenia would surely understand him, but from that it would follow that Agamemnon had not made the infinite movement of resignation, and so he is not a hero, and so the utterance of the seer is a sea-captain's tale and the whole occurrence a vaudeville.

Abraham did not speak. Only one word of his has been preserved, the only reply to Isaac, which also is sufficient proof that he
had not spoken previously. Isaac asks Abraham where the lamb is
for the burnt offering. 'And Abraham said, God will provide
Himself the lamb for the burnt offering, my son.'

This last word of Abraham I shall consider a little more closely.
If there were not this word, the whole event would have lacked
something; if it were to another effect, everything perhaps would
be resolved into confusion.

I have often reflected upon the question whether a tragic hero, be
the culmination of his tragedy a suffering or an action, ought to
have a last rejoinder. In my opinion it depends upon the life-sphere
to which he belongs, whether his life has intellectual significance,
whether his suffering or his action stands in relation to spirit.

It goes without saying that the tragic hero, like every other man
who is not deprived of the power of speech, can at the instant of his
culmination utter a few words, perhaps a few appropriate words,
but the question is whether it is appropriate for him to utter them. If
the significance of his life consists in an outward act, then he has
nothing to say, since all he says is essentially chatter whereby he
only weakens the impression he makes, whereas the ceremonial of
tragedy requires that he perform his task in silence, whether this
consists in action or in suffering. Not to go too far afield, I will take
an example which lies nearest to our discussion. If Agamemnon
himself and not Calchas had had to draw the knife against
Iphigenia, then he would have only demeaned himself by wanting
at the last moment to say a few words, for the significance of his act
was notorious, the juridical procedure of piety, of compassion, of
emotion, of tears was completed, and moreover his life had no
relation to spirit, he was not a teacher or a witness to the spirit. On
the other hand, if the significance of a hero's life is in the direction
of spirit, then the lack of a rejoinder would weaken the impression
he makes. What he has to say is not a few appropriate words, a little
piece of declamation, but the significance of his rejoinder is that in
the decisive moment he carries himself through. Such an intellectual tragic hero ought to have what in other circumstances is too
often striven for in ludicrous ways, he ought to have and he ought to
keep the last word. One requires of him the same exalted bearing
which is seemly in every tragic hero, but in addition to this there is
required of him one word. So when such an intellectual tragic hero

has his culmination in suffering (in death), then by his last word he becomes immortal before he dies, whereas the ordinary tragic hero on the other hand does not become immortal till after his death.

One may take Socrates as an example. He was an intellectual tragic hero. His death sentence was announced to him. That instant he dies – for one who does not understand that the whole power of the spirit is required for dying, and that the hero always dies before he dies, that man will not get so very far with his conception of life. So as a hero it is required of Socrates that he repose tranquilly in himself, but as an intellectual tragic hero it is required of him that he at the last moment have spiritual strength sufficient to carry himself through. So he cannot like the ordinary tragic hero concentrate upon keeping himself face to face with death, but he must make this movement so quickly that at the same instant he is consciously well over and beyond this strife and asserts himself. If Socrates had been silent in the crisis of death, he would have weakened the effect of his life and aroused the suspicion that in him the elasticity of irony was not an elemental power but a game, the flexibility of which he had to employ at the decisive moment to sustain him emotionally.

What is briefly suggested here has to be sure no application to Abraham in case one might think it possible to find out by analogy an appropriate word for Abraham to end with, but it does apply to this extent, that one thereby perceives how necessary it is that Abraham at the last moment must carry himself through, must not silently draw the knife, but must have a word to say, since as the father of faith he has absolute significance in a spiritual sense. As to what he must say, I can form no conception beforehand; after he has said it I can maybe understand it, maybe in a certain sense can understand Abraham in what he says, though without getting any closer to him than I have been in the foregoing discussion. In case no last rejoinder of Socrates had existed, I should have been able to think myself into him and formulate such a word; if I were unable to do it, a poet could, but no poet can catch up with Abraham.

Before I go on to consider Abraham's last word more closely I would call attention to the difficulty Abraham had in saying anything at all. The distress and anguish in the paradox consisted (as was set forth above) in silence – Abraham cannot speak. So in view of this fact it is a contradiction to require him to speak, unless one would have him out of the paradox again, in such a sense that at the last moment he suspends it, whereby he ceases to be Abraham and annuls all that went before. So then if Abraham at the last moment were to say to Isaac, 'To thee it applies,' this would only have been a weakness. For if he could speak at all, he ought to have spoken long before, and the weakness in this case would consist in the fact that he did not possess the maturity of spirit and the concentration to think in advance the whole pain but had thrust something away from him, so that the actual pain contained a plus over and above the thought pain. Moreover, by such a speech he would fall out of the role of the paradox, and if he really wanted to speak to Isaac, he must transform his situation into a temptation (*Anfechtung*), for otherwise he could say nothing, and if he were to do that, then he is not even so much as a tragic hero.

However, a last word of Abraham has been preserved, and in so far as I can understand the paradox I can also apprehend the total presence of Abraham in this word. First and foremost, he does not say anything, and it is in this form he says what he has to say. His reply to Isaac has the form of irony, for it always is irony when I say something and do not say anything. Isaac interrogates Abraham on the supposition that Abraham knows. So then if Abraham were to have replied, 'I know nothing,' he would have uttered an untruth. He cannot say anything, for what he knows he cannot say. So he replies, 'God will provide Himself the lamb for the burnt offering, my son.' Here the double movement in Abraham's soul is evident, as it was described in the foregoing discussion. If Abraham had merely renounced his claim to Isaac and had done no more, he would in this last word be saying an untruth, for he knows that God demands Isaac as a sacrifice, and he knows that he himself at that instant precisely is ready to sacrifice him. We see then that after making this movement he made every instant the next movement, the movement of faith by virtue of the absurd. Because of this he utters no falsehood, for in virtue of the absurd it is of course possible that God could do something entirely different. Hence he is speaking no untruth, but neither is he saying anything, for he speaks a foreign language. This becomes still more evident when we consider that it was Abraham himself who must perform the sacrifice of Isaac. Had the task been a different one, had the Lord commanded Abraham to bring Isaac out to Mount Moriah and then would Himself have Isaac struck by lightning and in this way receive him as a sacrifice, then, taking his words in a plain sense,

Abraham might have been right in speaking enigmatically as he did, for he could not himself know what would occur. But in the way the task was prescribed to Abraham he himself had to act, and at the decisive moment he must know what he himself would do, he must know that Isaac will be sacrificed. In case he did not know this definitely, then he has not made the infinite movement of resignation, then, though his word is not indeed an untruth, he is very far from being Abraham, he has less significance than the tragic hero, yea, he is an irresolute man who is unable to resolve either on one thing or another, and for this reason will always be uttering riddles. But such a hesitator is a sheer parody of a knight of faith.

Here again it appears that one may have an understanding of Abraham, but can understand him only in the same way as one understands the paradox. For my part I can in a way understand Abraham, but at the same time I apprehend that I have not the courage to speak, and still less to act as he did – but by this I do not by any means intend to say that what he did was insignificant, for on the contrary, it is the one only marvel.

And what did the contemporary age think of the tragic hero? They thought that he was great, and they admired him. And that honorable assembly of nobles, the jury which every generation impanels to pass judgment upon the foregoing generation, passed the same judgment upon him. But as for Abraham there was no one who could understand him. And yet think what he attained! He remained true to his love. But he who loves God has no need of tears, no need of admiration, in his love he forgets his suffering, yea, so completely has he forgotten it that afterwards there would not even be the least inkling of his pain if God Himself did not recall it, for God sees in secret and knows the distress and counts the tears and forgets nothing.

So either there is a paradox, that the individual as the individual stands in an absolute relation to the absolute, or Abraham is lost.

7. The Knight of Faith

*The Knight of Faith, or the knight of 'infinite resigna-
tion', is a powerful and detailed description of the invisi-
bility of commitment. The knight who has carried out an
act of infinite resignation (such as giving up a fiancée)
does not hope to turn again, does not hope to re-receive
the beloved. His act, once carried out, is his own
responsibility.*

*The description is however particularly efficient
because it convinces the reader that there is nothing
unusual about a knight of faith, nothing to see, no little
'aura' or 'charisma' which would set him apart from the
rest of unregenerate mankind. He looks for all the world
like a tax-collector. Yet his entire life is based upon an
infinite, inward commitment which is invisible. The
theme of the contents of the writing-desk in* Either/Or
recurs here.

*Yet, mid-paragraph, disaster strikes. It turns out that
'the princess' (a transparent reference to Regine Olsen)
has got married. Now, the act of infinite resignation
would seem to have been deprived of its point. Is it indeed
so? No, because 'the individual' who is operating according to faith is, in a certain sense, infallible in his decisions:
at the very least, no merely social or human reckonings-
out can any longer affect his judgment.*

*But, built in even within this passage, is the possibility
of 'repetition' – for those with eyes to read. And this
book, like all the others, was written for Regine.*

I candidly admit that in my practice I have not found any reliable
example of the knight of faith, though I would not therefore deny
that every second man may be such an example. I have been trying,
however, for several years to get on the track of this, and all in vain.
People commonly travel around the world to see rivers and moun-
tains, new stars, birds of rare plumage, queerly deformed fishes,
ridiculous breeds of men – they abandon themselves to the bestial
stupor which gapes at existence, and they think they have seen

something. This does not interest me. But if I knew where there was such a knight of faith, I would make a pilgrimage to him on foot, for this prodigy interests me absolutely. I would not let go of him for an instant, every moment I would watch to see how he managed to make the movements, I would regard myself as secured for life, and would divide my time between looking at him and practising the exercises myself, and thus would spend all my time admiring him. As was said, I have not found any such person, but I can well think him. Here he is. Acquaintance made, I am introduced to him. The moment I set eyes on him I instantly push him from me, I myself leap backwards, I clasp my hands and say half aloud, 'Good Lord, is this the man? Is it really he? Why, he looks like a tax-collector!' However, it is the man after all. I draw closer to him, watching his least movements to see whether there might not be visible a little heterogeneous fractional telegraphic message from the infinite, a glance, a look, a gesture, a note of sadness, a smile, which betrayed the infinite in its heterogeneity with the finite. No! I examine his figure from tip to toe to see if there might not be a cranny through which the infinite was peeping. No! He is solid through and through. His tread? It is vigorous, belonging entirely to finiteness; no smartly dressed townsman who walks out to Fresberg on a Sunday afternoon treads the ground more firmly, he belongs entirely to the world, no Philistine more so. One can discover nothing of that aloof and superior nature whereby one recognizes the knight of the infinite. He takes delight in everything, and whenever one sees him taking part in a particular pleasure, he does it with the persistence which is the mark of the earthly man whose soul is absorbed in such things. He tends to his work. So when one looks at him one might suppose that he was a clerk who had lost his soul in an intricate system of book-keeping, so precise is he. He takes a holiday on Sunday. He goes to church. No heavenly glance or any other token of the incommensurable betrays him; if one did not know him, it would be impossible to distinguish him from the rest of the congregation, for his healthy and vigorous hymn-singing proves at the most that he has a good chest. In the afternoon he walks to the forest. He takes delight in everything he sees, in the human swarm, in the new omnibuses, in the water of the Sound; when one meets him on the Beach Road one might suppose he was a shopkeeper taking his fling, that's just the way he disports himself, for he is not a poet, and I have sought in vain to detect

in him the poetic incommensurability. Toward evening he walks
home, his gait is as indefatigable as that of the postman. On his
way he reflects that his wife has surely a special little warm dish
prepared for him, e.g. a calf's head roasted, garnished with veg-
etables. If he were to meet a man like-minded, he could continue
as far as East Gate to discourse with him about that dish, with a
passion befitting a hotel chef. As it happens, he hasn't four pence to
his name, and yet he fully and firmly believes that his wife has that
dainty dish for him. If she had it, it would then be an invidious sight
for superior people and an inspiring one for the plain man, to see
him eat; for his appetite is greater than Esau's. His wife hasn't it –
strangely enough, it is quite the same to him. On the way he comes
past a building site and runs across another man. They talk together
for a moment. In the twinkling of an eye he erects a new building,
he has at his disposition all the powers necessary for it. The stranger
leaves him with the thought that he certainly was a capitalist, while
my admired knight thinks, 'Yes, if the money were needed, I dare
say I could get it.' He lounges at an open window and looks out on
the square on which he lives; he is interested in everything that goes
on, in a rat which slips under the curb, in the children's play, and
this with the nonchalance of a girl of sixteen. And yet he is no
genius, for in vain I have sought in him the incommensurability of
genius. In the evening he smokes his pipe; to look at him one would
swear that it was the grocer over the way vegetating in the twilight.
He lives as carefree as a ne'er-do-well, and yet he buys up the
acceptable time at the dearest price, for he does not do the least
thing except by virtue of the absurd. And yet, and yet – actually I
could become furious over it, for envy if for no other reason – this
man has made and every instant is making the movements of
infinity. With infinite resignation he has drained the cup of life's
profound sadness, he knows the bliss of the infinite, he senses the
pain of renouncing everything, the dearest things he possesses in
the world, and yet finiteness tastes to him just as good as to one who
never knew anything higher, for his continuance in the finite did not
bear a trace of the cowed and fearful spirit produced by the process
of training; and yet he has this sense of security in enjoying it, as
though the finite life were the surest thing of all. And yet, and yet
the whole earthly form he exhibits is a new creation by virtue of
the absurd. He resigned everything infinitely, and then he grasped
everything again by virtue of the absurd. He constantly makes the

movements of infinity, but he does this with such correctness and assurance that he constantly gets the finite out of it, and there is not a second when one has a notion of anything else. It is supposed to be the most difficult task for a dancer to leap into a definite posture in such a way that there is not a second when he is grasping after the posture, but by the leap itself he stands fixed in that posture. Perhaps no dancer can do it – that is what this knight does. Most people live dejectedly in worldly sorrow and joy; they are the ones who sit along the wall and do not join in the dance. The knights of infinity are dancers and possess elevation. They make the movements upward, and fall down again; and this too is no mean pastime, nor ungraceful to behold. But whenever they fall down they are not able at once to assume the posture, they vacillate an instant, and this vacillation shows that after all they are strangers in the world. This is more or less strikingly evident in proportion to the art they possess, but even the most artistic knights cannot altogether conceal this vacillation. One need not look at them when they are up in the air, but only the instant they touch or have touched the ground – then one recognizes them. But to be able to fall down in such a way that the same second it looks as if one were standing and walking, to transform the leap of life into a walk, absolutely to express the sublime in the pedestrian – that only the knight of faith can do – and this is the one and only prodigy.

But since the prodigy is so likely to be delusive, I will describe the movements in a definite instance which will serve to illustrate their relation to reality, for upon this everything turns. A young swain falls in love with a princess, and the whole content of his life consists in this love, and yet the situation is such that it is impossible for it to be realized, impossible for it to be translated from ideality into reality. The slaves of paltriness, the frogs in life's swamp, will naturally cry out, 'Such a love is foolishness. The rich brewer's widow is a match fully as good and respectable.' Let them croak in the swamp undisturbed. It is not so with the knight of infinite resignation, he does not give up his love, not for all the glory of the world. He is no fool. First he makes sure that this really is the content of his life, and his soul is too healthy and too proud to squander the least thing upon an inebriation. He is not cowardly, he is not afraid of letting love creep into his most secret, his most hidden thoughts, to let it twine in innumerable coils about every ligament of his consciousness – if the love becomes an unhappy love, he will never be able to tear himself loose from it. He feels a blissful rapture in letting love tingle through every nerve, and yet his soul is as solemn as that of the man who has drained the poisoned goblet and feels how the juice permeates every drop of blood – for this instant is life and death. So when he has thus sucked into himself the whole of love and absorbed himself in it, he does not lack courage to make trial of everything and to venture everything. He surveys the situation of his life, he convokes the swift thoughts, which like tame doves obey his every bidding, he waves his wand over them, and they dart off in all directions. But when they all return, all as messengers of sorrow, and declare to him that it is an impossibility, then he becomes quiet, he dismisses them, he remains alone, and then he performs the movements. If what I am saying is to have any significance, it is requisite that the movement come about normally. So for the first thing, the knight will have power to concentrate the whole content of life and the whole significance of reality in one single wish. If a man lacks this concentration, this intensity, if his soul from the beginning is dispersed in the multifarious, he never comes to the point of making the movement, he will deal shrewdly in life like the capitalists who invest their money in all sorts of securities, so as to gain on the one what they lose on the other – in short, he is not a knight. In the next place the knight will have the power to concentrate the whole result of the operations of thought in one act of consciousness. If he lacks this intensity, if his soul from the beginning is dispersed in the multifarious, he will never get time to make the movements, he will be constantly running errands in life, never enter into eternity, for even at the instant when he is closest to it he will suddenly discover that he has forgotten something for which he must go back. He will think that to enter eternity is possible the next instant, and that also is perfectly true, but by such considerations one never reaches the point of making the movements, but by their aid one sinks deeper and deeper into the mire.

So the knight makes the movement – but what movement? Will he forget the whole thing? (For in this too there is indeed a kind of concentration.) No! For the knight does not contradict himself, and it is a contradiction to forget the whole content of one's life and yet remain the same man. To become another man he feels no inclination, nor does he by any means regard this as greatness. Only the lower natures forget themselves and become something new.

Thus the butterfly has entirely forgotten that it was a caterpillar, perhaps it may in turn so entirely forget it was a butterfly that it becomes a fish. The deeper natures never forget themselves and never become anything else than what they were. So the knight remembers everything, but precisely this remembrance is pain, and yet by the infinite resignation he is reconciled with existence. Love for that princess became for him the expression for an eternal love, assumed a religious character, was transfigured into a love for the Eternal Being, which did to be sure deny him the fulfilment of his love, yet reconciled him again by the eternal consciousness of its validity in the form of eternity, which no reality can take from him. Fools and young men prate about everything being possible for a man. That, however, is a great error. Spiritually speaking, everything is possible, but in the world of the finite there is much which is not possible. This impossible, however, the knight makes possible by expressing it spiritually, but he expresses it spiritually by waiving his claim to it. The wish which would carry him out into reality, but was wrecked upon the impossibility, is now bent inward, but it is not therefore lost, neither is it forgotten. At one moment it is the obscure emotion of the wish within him which awakens recollections, at another moment he awakens them himself; for he is too proud to be willing that what was the whole content of his life should be the thing of a fleeting moment. He keeps this love young, and along with him it increases in years and in beauty. On the other hand, he has no need of the intervention of the finite for the further growth of his love. From the instant he made the movement the princess is lost to him. He has no need of those erotic tinglings in the nerves at the sight of the beloved etc., nor does he need to be constantly taking leave of her in a finite sense, because he recollects her in an eternal sense, and he knows very well that the lovers who are so bent upon seeing 'her' yet once again, to say farewell for the last time, are right in being bent upon it, are right in thinking that it is the last time, for they forget one another the soonest. He has comprehended the deep secret that also in loving another person one must be sufficient unto oneself. He no longer takes a finite interest in what the princess is doing, and precisely this is proof that he has made the movement infinitely. Here one may have an opportunity to see whether the movement on the part of a particular person is true or fictitious. There was one who also believed that he had made the movement; but lo, time passed, the princess did something else, she married – a prince, let us say – then his soul lost the elasticity of resignation. Thereby he knew that he had not made the movement rightly; for he who has made the act of resignation infinitely is sufficient unto himself. The knight does not annul his resignation, he preserves his love just as young as it was in its first moment, he never lets it go from him, precisely because he makes the movements infinitely. What the princess does, cannot disturb him, it is only the lower natures which find in other people the law for their actions, which find the premises for their actions outside themselves. If on the other hand the princess is like-minded, the beautiful consequence will be apparent. She will introduce herself into that order of knighthood into which one is not received by balloting, but of which everyone is a member who has courage to introduce himself, that order of knighthood which proves its immortality by the fact that it makes no distinction between man and woman. The two will preserve their love young and sound, she also will have triumphed over her pains, even though she does not, as it is said in the ballad, 'lie every night beside her lord.' These two will to all eternity remain in agreement with one another, with a well-timed *harmonia praestabilita*, so that if ever the moment were to come, the moment which does not, however, concern them finitely (for then they would be growing older), if ever the moment were to come which offered to give love its expression in time, then they will be capable of beginning precisely at the point where they would have begun if originally they had been united. He who understands this, be he man or woman, can never be deceived, for it is only the lower natures which imagine they were deceived. No girl who is not so proud really knows how to love; but if she is so proud, then the cunning and shrewdness of all the world cannot deceive her.

8. Socrates' favourable appearance

Like the Writing Cabinet in Either/Or, *whose internal content was so dramatically different from what the external appearance might lead one to believe, Socrates' rough and gnarled exterior belies the richness of the subjectivity within.*

But back to Socrates. He did not have quite so favorable an appearance as that described; he was very ugly, had clumsy feet, and, above all, a number of growths on the forehead and elsewhere, which would suffice to persuade anyone that he was a demoralized subject. This was what Socrates understood by his favorable appearance in which he was so thoroughly happy that he would have considered it a chicane of the divinity to prevent him from becoming a teacher of morals, had he been given an attractive appearance like an effeminate cithara player, a melting glance like a shepherd lad, small feet like a dancing master in the Friendly Society, and *in toto* as favorable an appearance as could have been desired by any applicant for a job through the newspapers, or any theologue who has pinned his hope on a private call. Why was this old teacher so happy over his favorable appearance, unless it was because he understood that it must help to keep the learner at a distance, so that the latter might not stick fast in a direct relationship to the teacher, perhaps admire him, perhaps have his clothes cut in the same manner. Through the repellent effect exerted by the contrast, which on a higher plane was also the role played by his irony, the learner would be compelled to understand that he had essentially to do with himself, and that the inwardness of the truth is not the comradely inwardness with which two bosom friends walk arm in arm, but the separation with which each for himself exists in the truth.

That subjectivity, inwardness, is the truth was my thesis, and that the pseudonymous authors sustain a relationship to it is readily perceived, if from nothing else than from their sensitiveness to the comical. The comical is always the mark of maturity; but it is important that the new shoot should be ready to appear under this maturity, and that the *vis comica* should not stifle the pathetic, but rather serve an indication that a new pathos is beginning. The power to wield the weapon of the comic I regard as an indispensable legitimation for everyone who in our age is to have any authority in the world of the spirit. When an age is so thoroughly reflective as our age is, or is said to be, the comical must in so far as this is true have been discovered by everyone, and primitively discovered by everyone who proposes to have anything to say. But the *Docents* are so wanting in comic sense that it is terrifying; even Hegel, according to the assertion of a zealous Hegelian, is totally wanting in a sense of the comical. A ludicrous stiff solemnity and air of paragraph-importance that gives a *Docent* a striking resemblance to a bookkeeper out of Holberg, is what the *Docents* call seriousness. Everyone who does not have this terrible solemnity is frivolous. Perhaps. But what does it mean when a man says that he has actually reflected himself out of the sphere of the immediate, without attaining mastery in the realm of the comic: what does that mean? Why, it means that the man lies. What does it mean for a man to affirm that he has reflected his way out of the immediate, and then communicates this as information in direct form? Why, it means that the man is talking through his hat. In the world of the spirit the various stages are not like towns on a route of travel, which it is quite in order for the traveller to tell about directly: as for example, 'we left Pekin and came to Canton, on the 14th of the month, we were in Canton.' Such a traveller changes places but not himself, and hence it is in order that he tells about it in the direct unaltered form, and thus *relates* the change. But in the world of the spirit a change of place means a change in oneself, for which reason all direct assurances about having reached this or that stage are attempts à la Munchhausen. That a man has arrived at this or that distant place in the world of the spirit is proved by the mode of presentation itself; if this testifies to the contrary, all direct assurances become merely a contribution to the comical. The power to wield the weapon of the comic is the policeman's shield, the badge of authority, which every agent who in our time really is an agent must carry. But this comic spirit is not wild or vehement, its laughter is not shrill; on the contrary, it is careful of the immediacy that it sets aside. The scythe of the harvest hand is equipped with a cradle, some wooden rods that run parallel with the sharp blade; and while the scythe cuts the standing grain it sinks almost voluptuously down upon the supporting cradle, to be laid neatly and beautifully on the stubble. Such is also the legitimate comic spirit in relation to the immediacy that is ripe for the cutting. The task of cutting is a festive deed, the cutter is not a surly harvest hand, and though it is the sharp blade of the comical and its biting edge that compels the immediate to yield, its yielding is not unbeautiful, and even in falling it is supported by the cutter. This comic spirit is essentially humor. When the comic is cold and comfortless it is a sign that there is no new immediacy in the shoot, and then the comical does not function as a harvest, but as the contentless passion of an unfruitful wind raging over the naked ground.

It is always good to be distinguished by something; I ask nothing better than to be pointed out as the only one in our serious age who is not serious. Far from hoping for any modification of this judgment, it is rather my wish that the honorable *Docents*, both those who gesticulate *ex cathedra* and those whose voices ring loud about the tea tables, would stand by their judgment and not suddenly have forgotten the frequent private declamations of earnest phrases directed against the pseudonymous authors, but on the contrary clearly remember that it was these authors who proposed to make the comical a determination in earnestness, and to find in the jest a release from the sorriest of all tyrannies: the tyranny of moroseness, stupidity, and inflexibility of spirit. The pseudonymous authors including myself are all subjective; I ask nothing better than to be distinguished as the only one in our objective age who is incapable of being objective.

9. The limits of endurance

The engagement to Regine Olsen was broken off. Constantine Constantius is, however, hoping against hope that there can be a 'Repetition'. Nevertheless, a repetition is what he most fears. Only the figure of Job can console him, for his agony too was incapable of explanation, and Job too was misunderstood by all around him.

I

October 11

MY SILENT CONFIDANT:

My life has been brought to an *impasse*, I loathe existence, it is without savor, lacking salt and sense. If I were hungrier than Pierrot, I should not be inclined to eat the explanation people offer. One sticks one's finger into the soil to tell by the smell in what land one is: I stick my finger into existence – it smells of nothing. Where am I? What is this thing called the world? What does this word mean? Who is it that has lured me into the thing, and now leaves me there? Who am I? How did I come into the world? Why was I not consulted, why not made acquainted with its manners and customs but was thrust into the ranks as though I had been bought of a 'soul-seller'? How did I obtain an interest in this big enterprise they call reality? Why should I have an interest in it? Is it not a voluntary concern? And if I am to be compelled to take part in it, where is the director? I should like to make a remark to him. Is there no director? Whither shall I turn with my complaint? Existence is surely a debate – may I beg that my view be taken into consideration? If one is to take the world as it is, would it not be better never to learn what it is? What is a deceiver? Does not Cicero say that a deceiver can be found out by asking the question *cui bono*? I allow everyone to ask, and I ask everyone, whether I have had any profit by making myself and a girl unhappy. Guilt – what does that mean? Is it witchcraft? Is it not definitely known how a person becomes guilty? Will anybody respond? Is it not then of the utmost importance to the gentlemen involved in the thing?

My mind is at a standstill, or rather I am going out of it. One moment I am tired and weary, yes, dead for sheer indifference; at another moment I am frantic and travel bewildered from one end of the world to the other, to find one person upon whom I could expend my wrath. The whole content of my being shrieks in contradiction against itself. How did it come about that I became guilty? Or am I not guilty? Why am I then so called in all human tongues? What a wretched invention human language is: it says one thing and means another!

Is it not something that has simply happened to me, is not the whole thing an accident? Could I know beforehand that my whole nature would undergo a change, that I should become another man? Did that perhaps break out which lay obscurely hidden in my soul? But if it lay there obscurely, how could I foresee it? But if I could not foresee it, then I am not guilty. If I had had an attack of apoplexy, would I then too have been guilty? What is the human speech they call language, what is it but a miserable jargon understood only by a clique? Are not the dumb beasts wiser for the fact that they never talk about such things? – Am I unfaithful? In case she were to continue to love me and would never love anyone else, she would be faithful to me. If I continue to wish to love her only, am I unfaithful? We both do in fact the same thing; how then do I become a deceiver if I show my faithfulness by deceiving? Why must she be in the right, and I in the wrong? If we both are true, why then is this expressed in human language by saying that she is faithful, and I a deceiver?

Though the whole world were to rise up against me, though all the scholastics were to dispute with me, though my life were at stake, I nevertheless maintain that I am in the right. No one shall wrest this conviction from me, though there is no language in which I can give utterance to it. I have acted correctly. My love cannot express itself in a marriage. If I were to marry her, she would be crushed. Perhaps the possibility of marriage appeared alluring to her. I cannot help that – so it was to me. The very instant reality comes into question, all is lost, it is then too late. The reality in which she is to find her significance is for me only a shadow which runs alongside of my proper spiritual reality, a shadow which at one moment would make me laugh, at another would intrude disturbingly in my existence. It would end in my wanting to touch her, fumblingly, as if I were grasping a shadow, or stretching out my hand after a shadow. Would not her life be ruined? Indeed she is as if dead to me, yea, she might awaken in my soul the temptation to wish her dead. In case I were to crush her, she would be volatilized precisely at the instant I would make her a reality – whereas in the other case I retain her as a genuine reality, though in a sense it is a reality full of dread. What then? Why, then language says that I am guilty, for I ought to have foreseen this. – What sort of power is this which would take from me my honor and my pride, and would do it in such a senseless way? Am I then a victim of fate? Must I then be guilty and be a deceiver, whatever I do, even if I do nothing? – Or am I crazy? Then the best thing would be to shut me up; for human cowardice is especially afraid of the pronouncements of crazy people and of the dying. Crazy – what does it mean? What am I to do in order to enjoy public esteem and to be regarded as wise? Why no answer? I offer a reasonable *douceur* to anybody who invents a new word. I have stated the alternatives. Is anybody so wise that he knows more than two? But if he knows more, then it is nonsense that I am crazy, unfaithful, and a deceiver, whereas the girl is faithful, sane, and esteemed by everybody. Or is it to be laid to my charge that I made the first period of our relationship so beautiful? Thanks for the compliment! When I saw her joy in being loved, I put myself and everything she pointed to under the magic power of love's enchantment. Is it a fault that I could do this or that I did it? Who is at fault that I could do this or that I did it? Who is at fault in this, unless it be the girl herself and the third party whom no one knows, from whence it came that I was touched with the stroke of a wand and transformed? What I have done they praise in others. – Or is it my compensation that I became a poet? I decline any compensation, I demand my rights, i.e. my honor. I have not prayed to become a poet, and I would not buy the gift at that price. – Or, if I am guilty, then surely I must be able to repent of my guilt and make amends. Tell me how. Should I perhaps repent furthermore of the fact that the world takes the liberty of playing with me like a child with a June bug? – Or is it best to forget the whole thing? Forget! I have ceased to be if I forget this. Or what a life it would be if along with the loved one I have lost honor and pride – and lost them in such a way that no one knows how this thing came about for which I can make no reparation! Shall I let myself then be pushed out? But why was I then pushed in? I didn't demand it.

He who is put on bread and water is better off than I. My reflections are, humanly speaking, the scantiest diet imaginable; and yet, in spite of my microcosmic proportions, I experience a satisfaction in comporting myself as macrocosmically as possible.

I do not talk to anybody; and yet, not to break off all communication with men, or to give them fudge for their money, I have made a considerable collection of poems, pithy sayings, proverbs, and brief extracts from the immortal Greek and Latin writers who in all ages have been admired. To this anthology I have added several capital quotations from Balle's Lesson Book, published under the auspices of the Orphan Asylum. So if anybody puts a question to me, I have the answer ready. I can quote the Classics just as well as Peer Deacon could, and in addition to that I can quote Balle's Lesson Book. 'Even though we have attained all the honor one could desire, we ought not to let ourselves be carried away into pride and arrogance.' I do not deceive anyone. How many people are there after all who speak a truth or make a good remark? 'Under the word "world" is comprehensively included heaven and earth and all that in them is.'

What good would it do if I were to say something? There is no one who would understand me. My pain and my suffering are nameless, as I myself am – I who, though I have no name, nevertheless remain perhaps something to you, and in any case remain

DEVOTEDLY YOURS

II

September 19

MY SILENT CONFIDANT:

Job! Job! Job! Job! Didst thou indeed utter nothing but these beautiful words, 'The Lord gave, the Lord hath taken away, blessed be the name of the Lord'? Didst thou say nothing more? In all thy distress didst thou merely continue to repeat these words? Why wast thou silent for seven days and nights? What went on in thy soul? When the whole world fell to pieces above thy head and lay in potsherds around thee, didst thou at once possess this superhuman composure, didst thou at once have love's interpretation and the frankheartedness of confidence and faith? Is thy door then closed against the afflicted man, can he expect from thee no other relief than that pitiable consolation which worldly wisdom offers by reciting a paragraph about the perfection of life? Hast thou nothing more to say? Dost thou not dare to say more than what the false comforters laconically mete out to the individual, what the false comforters, rigid as a master of ceremony, prescribe to the individual, that in the hour of distress it is seemly to say, 'The Lord gave, the Lord hath taken away, blessed be the name of the Lord' – neither more nor less, just as one says 'Prosit' when a person sneezes! No, thou who in the ripeness of thy days wast a sword for the oppressed, a cudgel to protect the old, a staff for the decrepit, thou didst not fail men when all was riven asunder – then thou wast a mouth for the afflicted, and a cry for the contrite, and a shriek for the anguished, and an assuagement for all who were rendered dumb by torments, a faithful witness to the distress and grief a heart can harbor, a trustworthy advocate who dared to complain 'in anguish of spirit' and to contend with God. Why do people conceal this? Woe to him who devours the widow and the fatherless and defrauds them of their inheritance, but woe also to him who would slyly defraud the afflicted of the momentary consolation of relieving the oppression of his heart and 'contending with God.' Or in our time is godly fear so great that the afflicted man does not need what was customary in those old days? Does one perhaps not dare to complain before God? Is it now godly fear that has become greater, or fear and cowardice? Nowadays people are of the opinion that the natural expression of sorrow, the desperate language of passion, must be left to poets, who as attorneys in a lower court plead the sufferer's cause before the tribunal of human compassion. Further than this no one ventures to go. Speak therefore, O Job of imperishable memory! Rehearse everything thou didst say, thou mighty advocate who dost confront the highest tribunal, no more daunted than a roaring lion! There is pith in thy speech, in thy heart there is godly fear, even when thou dost complain, when thou wouldst justify thy despair against thy friends who rise up like robbers to assault thee with their speeches, and even when incited by thy friends thou dost tread their wisdom under foot and despise their defense of the Lord, accounting it the finite shrewdness of a veteran courtier or a worldly-wise minister of state. Thee I have need of, a man who knows how to complain aloud, so that his complaint echoes in heaven where God confers with Satan in devising schemes against a man.

Complain! The Lord is not afraid, he is well able to defend himself, but how might he be able to speak in his defense if no one ventures to complain as it is seemly for a man to do? Speak, lift up thy voice, speak aloud, God surely can speak louder, he possesses the thunder – but that too is an answer, an explanation, reliable, trustworthy, genuine, an answer from God himself, an answer which even if it crush a man is more glorious than gossip and rumor about the righteousness of providence which are invented by human wisdom and circulated by effeminate creatures and eunuchs.

My benefactor of imperishable memory, tormented Job, dare I join myself to thy company, may I listen to thee? Do not repel me, I am not standing here as an impostor beside thy ash heap, my tears are not false, although all I am able to do is to weep with thee. The joyful man seeks the company of gladness, although what gladdens him most intimately is the joy which dwells within him; and so the afflicted man seeks the company of sorrow. I have not been in possession of the world, have not had seven sons and three daughters, but he too may have lost all who possessed but little, he too may as it were have lost sons and daughters who lost his loved one, and he too was so to speak 'smitten with sore boils' who has lost honor and pride, and along with that the will to live and the meaning of life.

YOUR NAMELESS FRIEND

PART FOUR

1848:1984

THE NOOK OF THE EIGHT PATHS REVISITED
What I do lack is physical strength. My mind is calm. I
have always thought of myself as having to be sacrificed;
now I have received my orders and I will abide by the
command I have been given. Ordinarily I can take it.
But when, for example, seeking recreation, I take a
drive of 15–20 miles and sit in the carriage in the happy
ferment of thought, my body gradually becomes somewhat weak, partly from the riding, partly from the
purely mental exertion, and then when I get out and it so
happens I am received by a smirking, grinning crowd,
and some of those present are even nice enough to call
me names, then my physical state is powerfully affected.
Or when I have taken a long walk out on some solitary
path, lost in my own thoughts, and then suddenly meet
three or four louts way out there where I am all alone
and they start to call me names, my physical state is
powerfully affected. I do not have the physical strength
for a fight—and I know nothing that makes me more
depressed than such a scene. I have the ability to make
any man listen to reason, except the raw boor—to say
nothing of three of them who have orders from the
press—there can be no discussion with him.

1. Conversation with a Hegelian walking-stick

Perhaps I may here venture to offer a little remark, one which would seem to be not wholly superfluous in an objective age. The absence of inwardness is also madness. The objective truth as such, is by no means adequate to determine that whoever utters it is sane; on the contrary, it may even betray the fact that he is mad, although what he says may be entirely true, and especially objectively true. I shall here permit myself to tell a story, which without any sort of adaptation on my part comes direct from an asylum. A patient in such an institution seeks to escape, and actually succeeds in effecting his purpose by leaping out of a window, and prepares to start on the road to freedom, when the thought strikes him (shall I say sanely enough or madly enough?): 'When you come to town you will be recognized, and you will at once be brought back here again; hence you need to prepare yourself fully to convince everyone by the objective truth of what you say, that all is in order as far as your sanity is concerned.' As he walks along and thinks about this, he sees a ball lying on the ground, picks it up, and puts it into the tail pocket of his coat. Every step he takes the ball strikes him, politely speaking, on his hinder parts, and every time it thus strikes him he says: 'Bang, the earth is round.' He comes to the city, and at once calls on one of his friends; he wants to convince him that he is not crazy, and therefore walks back and forth, saying continually: 'Bang, the earth is round!' But is not the earth round? Does the asylum still crave yet another sacrifice for this opinion, as in the time when all men believed it to be flat as a pancake? Or is a man who hopes to prove that he is sane, by uttering a generally accepted and generally respected objective truth, insane? And yet it was clear to the physician that the patient was not yet cured; though it is not to be thought that the cure would consist in getting him to accept the opinion that the earth is flat. But all men are not physicians, and what the age demands seems to have a considerable influence upon the question of what madness is. Aye, one could almost be tempted sometimes to believe that the modern age, which has modernized Christianity, has also modernized the question of Pontius Pilate, and that its urge to find something in which it can rest proclaims itself in the question: What is madness? When a *Privatdocent*, every time his scholastic gown reminds him that he ought to say something, says *de omnibus dubitandum est*, and at the same time writes away at a system which offers abundant internal evidence in every other sentence that the man has never doubted anything at all: he is not regarded as mad.

Don Quixote is the prototype for a subjective madness, in which the passion of inwardness embraces a particular finite fixed idea. But the absence of inwardness gives us on the other hand the prating madness, which is quite as comical; and it might be a very desirable thing if an experimental psychologist would delineate it by taking a handful of such philosophers and bringing them together. In the type of madness which manifests itself as an aberrant inwardness, the tragic and the comic is that the something which is of such infinite concern to the unfortunate individual is a particular fixation which does not really concern anybody. In the type of madness which consists in the absence of inwardness, the comic is that though the something which the happy individual knows really is the truth, the truth which concerns all men, it does not in the slightest degree concern the much respected prater. This type of madness is more inhuman than the other. One shrinks from looking into the eyes of a madman of the former type lest one be compelled to plumb there the depths of his delirium; but one dares not look at a madman of the latter type at all, from fear of discovering that he has eyes of glass and hair made from carpet-rags; that he is, in short, an artificial product. If you meet someone who suffers from such a derangement of feeling, the derangement consisting in his not having any, you listen to what he says in a cold and awful dread, scarcely knowing whether it is a human being who speaks, or a cunningly contrived walking stick in which a talking machine has been concealed. It is always unpleasant for a proud man to find himself unwittingly drinking a toast of brotherhood with the public hangman; but to find oneself engaged in rational and philosophical conversation with a walking stick is almost enough to make a man lose his mind.

2. All corruption will come from Science

Almost everything that flourishes nowadays under the name of science (particularly natural science) is not science at all but curiosity. – *In the end all corruption will come from the natural sciences.* – Many of its admirers believe that if an examination is conducted microscopically then it is serious science (*un sot trouve toujours un autre sot qui l'admire*). A foolish, superstitious belief in the microscope; microscopic observation only makes curiosity more absurd than ever.

That a man should simply and profoundly say that he cannot understand how consciousness comes into existence – is perfectly natural. But that a man should glue his eye to a microscope and stare and stare and stare – and still not be able to see how it happens – is ridiculous, and it is particularly ridiculous when it is supposed to be serious. Looked upon as an amusement, as a way of killing time, the discovery of the microscope is reasonable enough, but to take it seriously is utterly stupid. Even the art of printing is an almost satirical discovery, for since when, oh God, have there been so many people with something to say. The result of that tremendous discovery has simply been to disseminate all the twaddle which would otherwise have died at birth.

If God were to go about with a stick in his hand things would go particularly hard with all those solemn people who make discoveries with the help of the microscope. God would beat all the hypocrisy out of them and the natural scientists. For the hypocrisy of it is that natural science is said to lead to God. Of course it leads to God – in a *superior way*, and that is impertinence. It is easy to see that the scientists are hypocritical, for if one were to say to them that Luther's little catechism and his conscience are sufficient for everyone, they would turn up their noses. They want to make God into a superior person, into the devil of a fellow whom not everyone can understand – but the divine and simple truth is that no one, no one at all can understand him, and the wise cling humbly to *the same* as the simple man.

This is where the profundity of Socratic ignorance can be seen: to give up all inquisitive knowledge with *passion* in order to be simply ignorant before God; to give up this appearance which is after all something between man and man: observing things through a microscope – Goethe, on the other hand, who was not religious, clung cravenly to that differentiating knowledge.

All such scientific methods become particularly dangerous and pernicious when they encroach upon the spiritual field. Plants, animals, and stars may be handled in that way, but to handle the spirit of man in such a fashion is blasphemy which only weakens moral and religious passion. Even eating is far more reasonable than speculating on the digestion with the help of the microscope. And to pray to God is not, like eating, something lower than observation, but the highest of all things.

Thus we learn from physiologists that the unconscious comes before the conscious, but how is it that the relationship is reversed and the conscious exercises a partial formative influence on the unconscious? Then physiology becomes aesthetic and sentimental and speaks of the nobility of a cultivated personality, behaviour, etc. What, in the name of heaven, does it all mean? A little misery and at the most a little paganism (the inside is the outside). St Paul does not talk of becoming beautiful through prayer and preaching. Let the outward man perish, the inward man is renewed.

Materialistic physiology is comic (that anyone should believe that the way to find the spirit which gives life is to put to death); the more modern, spiritual physiology though cleverer is mere sophistry. It admits that it cannot explain the miracle, and yet it wants to go on; it becomes more and more voluminous and the volumes deal with this that and the other thing, all of which is most curious and interesting – but nevertheless does not explain the miracle.

Thus sophistical physiology says that it is a miracle that the conscious should exist, a miracle that the idea should become soul, and soul spirit (in short the qualitative changes). But if that is to be taken absolutely seriously then the whole science is at an end – and so the science is nothing but a lot of jokes. Its real problem is the miracle, which it cannot explain; what, then, is the use of all it does explain? And so in order to have an opportunity of being sophistical, or rather in order to become a voluminous science, this is what physiology does: Certainly it says, the transition is a miracle (from unconsciousness to consciousness, etc.) but it happens so gradually, little by little. Dialectically it is easy to see where the sophistry lies. The question is not whether it happened in a long or a short time but whether, when it happened, it was a miracle. That is the sophistry; the whole of science is a parenthesis. It is not more or less of a miracle because it lasted a long time or a short time before it occurred. One can therefore see why it was quite consistent with that science for a doctor to write the history of trepanning in two parts, the first part dealing with the time when it was not known. The whole of physiology really deals with that which is qualitatively beside the point. But to call that a science is sophistry.

That 'gradually' may mean different things in relation to different spheres; it may mean the plant kingdom or the animal kingdom, or the world's 6,000 years; it may mean the statistics of procreation and God knows what; but qualitatively it means nothing at all if it is true that the miracle cannot be explained. The whole thing is an approximation: almost, as good as, it is almost as though as good as . . . and that is what is dealt with in all those volumes where the microscope is put to use.

We learn from this sophistical physiology that 'the key to the knowledge of the conscious life of the soul lies in the unconscious' (Carus). But what precisely does the key mean if the transition from unconsciousness to consciousness is not explained? The transition is a leap (which answers to marvelling) which no key can open.

Again we learn that *das Gesetz des Geheimnisses* is to help to explain. But that law can hardly do anything but posit the miracle – what does it explain then? Dogmatically one can understand that the miracle is explained as a miracle, and that it cannot be understood; but an exact science cannot behave like that. Consequently it likes to juggle with the appearance that it can almost, and as good as, and practically – explain the miracle.

And so physiology spreads out over the kingdom of plants and animals showing more and more analogies which are not really analogies, since man is qualitatively different from plants and animals.

Oh horrible sophistry, spreading microscopically and telescopically abroad in folio upon folio and which qualitatively speaking produces absolutely nothing, but certainly fools men into giving up a simple and profoundly passionate admiration and wonder of things which is the motive power of ethics.

Ethics and religion are the only certainties. They say: Thou shalt believe. And should anyone ask me whether with the help of that belief life was a bed of roses, I should answer: no, and yet the certainty that all is well and God is love is indescribably blessed; either it is my fault that things go badly – and so God is love; or else things will come right and evil will be seen to have its meaning – but then too God is love.

Let us simply ridicule that hypocritical sentimentality, saying: does the whole question not turn on the fact that you have not had an evacuation? Let us never forget to laugh at that meaningless microscopic solemnity.

But when it really comes to the point, in the medium of reality, and of becoming, what do physiology and the doctor really know? It is easy enough to observe and explain (in the medium of the imagination, where everything is at rest) that body and soul are not contradictions but a developing idea, and the relation between them therefore one within the other. But in the real situation what is to be done? Is the sufferer to begin by taking drops, or is he to believe first? Oh thou oft repeated and masterly satire on a doctor who does not know which way to turn. But the moralist says, 'Thou shalt believe'. Only the moralist can speak with enthusiasm, the doctor believes neither in his medicaments nor – in faith. The moralist can say with enthusiasm that in a certain sense the whole of medicine is a joke. The fun of saving a man's life for a few years is only a joke: the serious thing is to die blessed.

3. In Australia, in the moon

There is no use at all in going in for natural science. One stands there defenceless and without any control. The scientist begins at once to distract one with all his details, at one moment one is in Australia, at another in the moon, in the bowels of the earth, and the devil knows where – chasing a tape worm; at one moment one has to use a telescope and at the next a microscope, and who the devil can stand that kind of thing.

But joking apart; the confusion lies in the fact that it is never dialectically clear what is what, how philosophy is to make use of natural science. Is the whole thing a brilliant metaphor (so that one might just as well be ignorant of it)? is it an example and analogy? or is it of such importance that theory should be formed accordingly?

There is no more terrible torture for a thinker than to have to continue living under the strain of having details constantly uncovered, so that it always looks as though the thought is about to appear, the conclusion. If the natural scientist does not feel that torture he cannot be a thinker. Intellectually that is the most terrible tantalization! A thinker is, as it were, in hell until he has found spiritual certainty: *his Rhodus, hic salta*, the sphere of faith where, even if the world broke to pieces and the elements melted, thou shalt nevertheless believe. There one cannot wait for the latest news, or till one's ship comes home. That spiritual certainty, the most humbling of all, the most painful to a vain spirit (for it is so superior to look through a microscope), is the only certainty.

The main objection, the whole objection to natural science may simply and formally be expressed thus, absolutely: it is incredible that a man who has thought infinitely about himself as a spirit could think of choosing natural science (with empirical material) as his life's work and aim. An observant scientist must *either* be a man of talent and instinct, for the characteristic of talent and instinct is not to be fundamentally dialectical, but only to dig up things and be brilliant – not to understand himself (and to be able to live on happily in that way, without feeling that anything is wrong because the deceptive variety of observations and discoveries continuously conceals the confusion of everything); *or* he must be a man who, from his earliest youth, half unconsciously, has become a scientist and continues out of habit to live in that way – the most frightful way of living: to fascinate and astonish the world by one's discoveries and brilliance, and not to understand oneself. It is self-evident that such a scientist is conscious, he is conscious within the limits of his talents, perhaps an astonishingly penetrating mind, the gift of combining things and an almost magical power of associating ideas, etc. But at the very most the relationship will be this: an eminent mind, unique in its gifts, explains the whole of nature – but does not understand itself. Spiritually he does not become transparent to himself in the moral appropriation of his gifts. But that relationship is scepticism, as may easily be seen (for scepticism means that an unknown, an X, explains everything. When everything is explained by an X which is not explained, then in the end nothing is explained at all). If that is not scepticism then it is superstition.

4. 1848 – walking and politics – three letters

It is often asserted that Kierkegaard was a-political. Nothing could be further from the truth. He followed the events of 1848 with passionate interest and great acumen. It so happened that, at this period of his life, he was in the habit of taking long literary and political walks with his friend J.L.A. Kolderup-Rosenvinge. Indeed, the 'walk' became itself a literary form, with its setting out, its development, and its conclusion – which usually coincided with some geographical point in Copenhagen which formed an equally convenient point for them both, to say farewell. Kolderup-Rosenvinge entered fully into the fun of this new literary form, and, for once in his life, and for a very short time (for Kolderup-Rosenvinge died in 1850) Kierkegaard could enjoy ordinary human banter and wit with an intelligent companion. The letters testify, however, to the deep-seated loneliness of Kierkegaard, for whom such a friendship was only a brief interruption in a lifetime of solitary walking, through the streets and squares, and along the lonely ramparts, of old Copenhagen.

I

To J.L.A. Kolderup-Rosenvinge

1848

DEAR *Conferentsraad*,

As I was walking down the street the other day, it occurred to me – not as it occurs to Sibbern that people may be saying, 'I wonder what Sibbern is saying?' – no, it occurred to me to wonder what Holberg's Jeronymus, if he were living now, would say of these times, he who already in his own time believed the world could not last until Easter. This notion was conceived as follows: In a newspaper I had read that on railroad trains something called 'a gadfly' is employed in order – yes, is this not crazy? – *to stop*. Indeed, the crazier the better. Can you imagine anything more insane? Is it not accordingly impossible for the world to last until Easter – that is, if one can employ a gadfly in order to stop? It is true enough that the carpenter was only partially successful – presumably you have read the same account yourself – in stopping the train by means of the gadfly, for he was on the contrary run over by means of the very gadfly he wanted to use. *Berlingske Tidende* concludes its account by saying that further information has not yet been forthcoming. Oh, unknown to *Berlingske Tidende*, it has told more than enough to furnish a thinker with material for a long time to come. For inasmuch as the carpenter did not know how to use the gadfly properly, the case remains the same: the world has advanced so far in madness that it employs a gadfly in order to stop, and, that being so, to return to Jeronymus, it cannot possibly last until Easter. Because of this one actually feels less sorry for the poor carpenter, for since the whole world will have perished by Easter anyway, or, and this seems particularly appropriate, will have been run over, then the carpenter is not to be lamented that much. Indeed the world will perish before Easter, unless one can say that it already has perished and that the misfortune is and certainly will be the wish to stop by means of a gadfly – either because this is impossible or because one does not know how to use the gadfly properly.

I intend, you see, to use the following sentence: 'How could a gadfly possibly be used to stop?' as the basis for my reflections. And although it may not seem so at first, it will on closer inspection become apparent that this consideration is related to and coheres with what we spoke about during our last hour of meditation.

For you are quite correct, *Conferentsraad*, in saying that I 'belong to the movement party,' although not secretly, no, quite openly, as I always undertake my motions out in the open. Yet, however inviting it might seem to a walker, this talk of party followers, one thing is a certainty: no one belongs less to any party than I do, precisely because I keep on walking. Just as different as I am *qua* walker from the kind of people who cannot go walking or get outside unless it is to go to some particular place, just so indifferent am I to everything that has to do with a party! – Every party follower, everything that has to do with a party, goes to a particular place, goes in order to be seated. And scarcely has the party follower been given a seat – in the ministry – before he settles himself as though he wanted and intended to stay seated for the rest of his life, so that one must believe that he has (*ad modum*: to lose one's nose, to lose one's mind, etc.) lost his legs, or that, like certain insects that have wings only for a certain period, he had legs only for a certain period. He stays seated, he does not leave the spot – indeed, to make him move, one must (here it comes again!), one must, as they say, give him legs and feet to walk on.

But now back to the gadfly and to wanting to stop by means of a gadfly, and you will see that this is related to what we spoke of last time. For is this not the law of confusion that governs recent European events? They wish to stop by means of a revolution and to stop a revolution by means of a counterrevolution. But what is a counterrevolution if it is not also a revolution? And to what can we compare a revolution if not to a gadfly? Thus they want to stop by means of a gadfly? I am sure you will agree that I am right in considering the whole development in Europe as an enormous skepticism or as a vortex. What does a vortex seek? – A fixed point where it can stop. (Therefore, you see, I seek – said *in parenthesi* – 'that single individual.') We all seem to agree that a stop is necessary. But that person who, while wishing to stop, fails to find a fixed point – that person who in other words wants to stop by means of the moved or the moving only enlarges the vortex. For a long time now there has been so much discussion of the need for movement relative to what is established that the need of the established relative to movement has been completely forgotten. Yet throughout Europe nothing is really established at this moment – everything is movement. One gets tired, becomes dizzy, yearns for a foothold, a stop. One grabs at thin air and uses 'a gadfly' rather like the woman who, panicking because her house was on fire, saved her fire-tongs. That is what happened in France. Lamartine wanted to stop corruption etc. by means of – a gadfly, alas, and so, just like the carpenter, he was run over. Citizens had been shot at – still, the Republic was also bought at that price, so probably the defense could be made that they caused the shooting. Therefore, they wanted to stop by means of a law, the first one decreed by the Republic, which abolishes capital punishment for political crimes.

But alas, the Republic itself was not an established order, it was a gadfly – and so they wanted to stop by means of a gadfly. That became quite obvious, for now a stop was effectuated by shooting down citizens by the thousands. Still, once again it was a stop by means of a gadfly –

And I too shall stop, for by now both of us are probably tired of pursuing this thought any further. This, you see, was a reliable stop. But no, wait! Although I suppose France tired of revolutions long ago, they have not yet stopped for that reason. Alas, it will not be so easy. There is a nemesis over Europe. And thus there may also be a nemesis over you, *Conferentsraad*, because you became acquainted with me, and now, although long tired of listening to me, you cannot make me stop.

So I proceed. All this about stopping and the mistaken belief that one can stop by means of a gadfly is related to *walking*. Only he who fundamentally understands walking (and you know I do, I who do not understand politics), understands also how it is bound up with stopping. If I have systematized walking as you remarked last time, then please permit me to essay a little theory of 'motion,' to which category stopping in turn belongs. Most people believe that so long as one has a fixed point *to which* one wants to get, then motion is no vortex. But this is a misunderstanding. It all depends on having a fixed point *from which to set out*. Stopping is not possible at a point *ahead*, but at a point *behind*. That is, stopping is in the motion, consolidating the motion. And this is the difference between a political and a religious movement. Any purely political movement, which accordingly lacks the religious element or is forsaken by God, is a vortex, cannot be stopped, and is a prey to the illusion of wanting a fixed point ahead, which is wanting to stop by means of a gadfly; for the fixed point, the only fixed point, lies behind. And therefore my opinion about the whole European confusion is that it cannot be stopped except by religion, and I am convinced that – as so strangely happened once with the Reformation, which appeared to be a religious movement but turned out to be a political one – in the same way, the movement of our time, which appears to be purely political, will turn out suddenly to be religious or the need for religion.

And still, still, that which must agree perfectly with Jeronymus's opinion that the world cannot last until Easter, that which is the secret within the confusion of wanting to stop by means of a gadfly, is indeed, if understood at a deeper level, after all a paradox containing the truth, inasmuch as the truth is always a paradox. We know that Socrates called himself a 'gadfly.' Admittedly he explains this in the sense of awakening (and he too was a revolutionary). But yet in another sense it is clear that he was also a person who stopped, for he stopped a Sophist vortex. He ambushed the Sophists; with his gadfly's sting he drove them forward in such a way that they really moved backward, or in such a way that Sophistry perished and the single individual came to his senses at the fixed point behind. Sophistry also sought to fix a point ahead *to which* the movement would go and reasoned that it would thereby be safe from becoming a vortex. But the Socratic dialectic was inexhaustible in making it apparent that nothing remained fixed in this way. On the contrary, Socrates had the fixed point *behind*. His point of departure lay in himself and in the god. That is to say, he knew himself, he possessed himself. By this means he stopped Sophistry, which, like politics, always asks whither one should go instead of asking whence one should depart. Oh, that there might be such a gadfly in the confused struggle of our times who with Socratic *ataraxie* [peace of mind] would directly oppose the 'whither' of modern haste, who would turn time back to this, that inasmuch as the question concerns whence one should depart, that inasmuch as all knowledge, Socratically speaking, was a recollecting, so all genuine motion is a return to or a departure from the fixed point behind. It is true that Socrates was also run over, as everyone must be who is to be used in this way. But the difference, which also determines whether this desire to stop by means of a gadfly is an insane impossibility or the profundity of truth, the difference lies in this: whether he who is going to be used for stopping accepts the fact that he must be sacrificed or deceives himself into believing that he will conquer. For both will be run over, but when he who deceived himself into thinking that he would conquer is run over, everything is lost, whereas he who accepted in advance the fact that he must be sacrificed has one more thought, his best thought, and as he is being run over, he conquers. The martyr's superiority consists in laying down his life. He conquers as the dead man who returns. The dead Socrates stopped the vortex, something the living Socrates was unable to do. But the living Socrates understood intellectually that only a dead man could conquer, as a sacrifice – and he understood ethically how to direct his whole life to becoming just that.

Dear *Conferentsraad*, I hope I have not walked you weary for now you must set out. For the agreement was that if you considered my letter a burden you would read first and then walk. – Therefore, Goodbye! I hope the walk agrees with you, and that when you have returned and assumed your favorite position, that of lying on the sofa, letting the imagination go for a walk, hastening through the giant realms of possibilities, or, if you so choose, letting it run errands in town, I hope that then you will not regret the exertions caused by the letter and the walk. And above all I hope that you do not impatiently damn me to hell – alas! alas! then it would become even more insane inasmuch as I cannot do otherwise than remain

YOUR S. KIREKEGAARD

II

To J.L.A. Kolderup-Rosenvinge

August 1848

DEAR *Conferentsraad*,

First, a little story by way of introduction. It is said that great comic actors often occupied themselves, for their own private amusement, with seeing to what extent one could make the other laugh during a performance. Thus it is also told of Frydendahl that he made a bet with another older actor, whose name I cannot determine, as to which of them could make the other laugh first during a particular performance. I cannot remember what play it was, and besides it does not matter. Frydendahl acted the part of Zoroaster or someone like him, some sort of oriental high priest with a long beard, a turban on his head, and dressed in some kind of robe. Even though I did not see it, Frydendahl stands vividly before me, a figure who must irresistibly make every spectator laugh, even though he did not succeed in making the other comedian laugh. Two acts had already been performed and still Frydendahl had not succeeded. But in the third act he had the following line, which he had to address to the other comedian who accordingly must also have been some sort of Zoroaster: 'You fancy yourself a saint, but you worship false gods!' Having said this, Frydendahl was supposed to walk off stage, expressing the greatest contempt for the other. And so he did. But just as he reached the wings, he turned around once more and, summoning all his *vis comica* [comic strength], he said, 'Phooey!' This was not in the script, and combined with the high pathos of his line ('You worship false gods') and with Frydendahl's mastery, it brought about the desired effect: the other burst out laughing.

Oh, dear *Conferentsraad*, I would do the same if I were to meet you in person in the bad mood you complained about last time. I would try everything to chase away this bad mood. If I did not succeed, I would finally say 'Phooey!' Somehow I have gotten the *idée fixe* that you are becoming and must continue to become younger – but when you thus (pardon me for speaking this way, but it is connected with my *idée fixe*) yield in any way to that bad mood, then you do not become younger. But it is over now, is it not? It was a little cat's paw – and now you are once more in the process of getting younger, and I look forward with longing to the moment when I shall assure myself of it in person, when I walk by your side as an 'audience.'

But now on to something else. You who heed the events of the day and who still keep up, surely it cannot have escaped your attention how appropriate it is that the newest public assemblies here in town take place in a hippodrome. To him who knows how to interpret the signs of the times (if not as profoundly as Cand. Christensen, who, said *in parenthesi*, for me has the distinction of having first been my secretary who copied *Either/Or* and later of attacking me bluntly in *Kirketidenden*, strangely enough 'in order to show me that he dared write against me'), to him it must be remarkable that more recent times are gradually doing away with the designation 'man' in order to substitute the designation 'horse.' Thus nowadays one does not speak of manpower as in former times, of the strength of Holger the Dane, or the like; no, one always speaks of horsepower, of so and so much horsepower. But a group of people who will function only as a crowd, as *numerus*, also really function only as a machine. Accordingly I propose that a new linguistic usage be introduced. Assuming that fifty men = one horsepower, then, if this is so, rather than saying, 'Last night in the hippodrome there was a meeting of one thousand men,' one would say instead, 'Last night in the hippodrome there was a meeting of twenty horsepower – Balthasar Christensen presiding.' And further, it would be very much in keeping with the times if someone could work out a table, or a kind of *regula Petri*, which one would consult in order to see how much horsepower would be necessary relative to the various purposes. Here is just one example of a *regula Petri* sum in this manner: If ten to fifteen thousand people in the streets – that is, between 200 and 300 horsepower – are sufficient for a change of ministry, how much horsepower is required to bring about a change of councilor of chancery [*Cancelliraad*], i.e., to have one *Cancelliraad* dismissed and another installed? Yes, indeed! Horsepower, this horsepower, is a splendid invention and the pride of modern times. The question is not so much one of the power of spirit and brain at these big meetings, for it is really just as Lichtenberg so excellently puts it, 'Ohne Hände (that is, for the purpose of balloting) ist nichts anzufangen, aber der Kopf ist nur eine Art von Hut, den man zwar zuweilen trägt, der aber bei den eigentlichen Galla-Begebenheiten unsers Lebens abgelegt werden muss.'

But before we proceed, or maybe more correctly, as we proceed, for we are of course on a walk: it is true that when we spoke together last time there was something you asked me to clarify the next time: 'What is the difference between a foundry worker and a tinker?' – You will remember Rahbeck's reply to Lars Mathiesen when he had to answer the question about the difference between him (L.M.) and an ass. L.M. answered, 'I don't know,' and then R. said, 'Neither do I!' – The difference does not consist in education, for they have both studied, and basically they have both been educated by means of that political stockfish, that strange pamphlet that keeps being published as 'printed in this year.' Nor does the difference consist in the fact that one casts iron stoves and the other tankards, for that is only an accidental difference, whereas the similarity is the essential factor, inasmuch as they both mold states, and again the similarity is the essential factor, that in doing so they may both forget how to mold iron stoves or tankards, thus completely cancelling out the erstwhile difference. Still, there is a small difference after all. Insofar as one can judge, the tinker is an autodidact who has studied the political stockfish on his own, while the foundry worker on the other hand certainly has a tutor who goes over the assignment with him and then rehearses until he has memorized the stockfish and can spew it out again. To that extent the foundry worker almost seems to resemble the tinker's future son-in-law, whom the tinker wants to rehearse every night. Accordingly the foundry worker is the tinker's son-in-law. Furthermore, there is this difference, that with a certain grandeur the tinker utterly forgets the tinker and everything that brings the tinker and tinkers to mind, whereas the foundry worker can by no means forget about the foundry worker and wants to mold the state to favor foundry workers.

But apropos of foundry workers, it is in other words your opinion that if not a foundry worker, then surely an iron fist or a tyrant with an iron fist, a military despot with an iron fist, is needed to bring order into European affairs. However, you yourself are dubious about Cavaignac, and indeed with good reason. As we know, he has only one arm, but that might suffice, provided he had an iron fist on that one arm. For one needs only one arm in order to have an iron fist; what is the point of having so many arms? That might easily become a contradiction, just as it once seemed a contradiction to me that everyone was so busy knitting stockings for the army, while *Berlingske Tidende* every day assured us, and *Fædrelandet* as well, that we were all determined to die united as one man – so that accordingly only one pair of stockings would be required. But to return to Cavaignac's one arm. You have indeed discovered the trouble: he has married, and so he does not even have the freedom of that one arm – while at the same time he has been relieved of the other arm. The man who has to rule with an iron fist should never be married, but if it does come to that, then he should never contract more than a marriage to his left hand. But he has no left hand, and accordingly, by marrying he has given away his right hand – unless he let his beloved marry his stump. If that is the case, then this is such an 'offhand marriage vow' and such a stumpy relationship that there might still be hope for Cavaignac, for whom I, by the way, have no hope at all, because I only think of him as Thiers' new tool.

But all jesting aside. For where could I have learned that you are expecting a tyrant while I am expecting a martyr? I have learned this from a little poem, the significance of which and the significance to me I genuinely appreciate in more than one way. You say that you do not know if I am a friend of political poetry, but I do not know how you can think of calling this little poem political poetry. For it is so clearly marked with the essence of a serene spirit that although it perceives the political in an idea, it is still as far removed from all political uproar and noise – as far removed from them as your country house is, indeed even farther removed – as far removed as that remoteness in which *you* reside is from the bustle of politics. Rather, one designates as political poems those that do not seek the remoteness of the idea, but want to roar into the midst of the uproar. As to your poem: it is a mood born in secret and communicated in secret. And therefore I again see in this one more proof of the kindness you bear me, for you send me your poem in all confidence.

Thank you, then! Thank you for every so very welcome communication from you. Thank you for letting it signify to me that I may remain

YOUR S. KIREKEGAARD

III

To J.L.A. Kolderup-Rosenvinge

July 28, '49

DEAR *Conferentsraad,*

It was indeed a remarkable year, that year of 1848. In this I agree completely with Professor Lamartine, who is already, I notice, busily engaged in cutting it up and preparing it for history. Marvelous! Ultimately, I suppose, the same thing will happen to history as to New Year's gift books and the like, which usually make their appearance the preceding year – so in the end we shall see the history of '51 appearing in the guise of a New Year's gift for '50. Who knows, perhaps Lamartine will take this next step and do so. And perhaps it is not impossible either, for since '48 everything has in a certain sad sense become possible. And it is not surprising that Professor Lamartine should become so excited. Just imagine a history professor who in the year of '48 almost becomes historical subject matter himself for a couple of months. He probably thinks, 'Let other historians choose their own subject matter – I shall choose my own, something I know quite *extra ordinem* and which, well prepared, I must therefore hand over to history at once.'

As I say, it was a remarkable year, that year of '48. It has, as we have often noted, in all respects turned everything upside down or 'topsy-turvied' everything. Also in a way that has just occurred to me. Suppose a writer were to recreate *The Catastrophe* of '48 in dramatic form and had to make his drama conform in some way to actuality, he would then have to create a wholly new kind of drama, a monstrosity, a drama that makes a mockery of all the rules, a drama in five and a half acts. This half act is just what is most characteristic about it, this half act, which is not to say that there is half an act left and then it is over, not at all, but that there is always half an act left. The catastrophe cannot be said to have lacked a head or a tail, for although it had no head – in a manner of speaking – it definitely had a tail. What is most characteristic about it is – that there is always some tail left. One imagines that it is over – but behold, there is the tail! – and so it continues all the time. In a way there is both something inhuman and something exhausting about it. It seems to me rather like eating some dish (*Gemüse* [vegetables], for example) in which there are long, long stringy bits. One takes a forkful, but look out! Just as one is about to put it in one's mouth, a whole lot remains dangling outside so that one must resort to the fork again to gather up the loose ends; but that is not enough, one also has to resort to the knife, one has to use both hands; but that is not enough, and in the end a waiter has to hold a plate or bowl underneath – *Ich möchte rasend werden* [It is enough to drive one mad]. Do you call this eating! And so it is with the events of our time. Lucky the man who like me declined at once the invitation to keep up with the times. Do you think the war is over yet?

But enough of this. What is going to become of our walks? Ye friendly powers, ye benevolent spirits who protect those who walk and who help them to get together! Can you not take pity on me and help me arrange a walk with the *Conferentsraad*? But to tell the truth, unless something extraordinary occurs, I can see no possibility of it, all the worse for me. One would think that it would certainly be easy enough for two walkers – to get together. One might say that surely it is a different matter altogether for someone who is in prison or for someone who is prevented by some external force, but for two walkers nothing should be easier for them than to get together first (the coinciding) in order then to go walking in each other's company. However, this does not apply to me *qua* walker. It is a very simple matter. That which wise and learned men have enjoined and recommended to all, nature has benevolently placed very close to me: that is, not to exceed my limit. It has placed it very close – alas, in setting my limit so close it has practically left me no *spatium* at all – for going astray and the like. So one day while I am sitting at home, the desire awakens and beckons. I say to myself: 'Today I would really enjoy going for a walk with the *Conferentsraad*. But how? Well, I might walk out to his place,' I think to myself, and so the walk begins. Still, that limit, that limit I cannot exceed! It cannot be done, for after having gone all the way out there, I will not feel fresh enough to begin going for a walk. Whereupon I sit pondering this and become quite exhausted from pondering. 'Well,' I think, 'you might drive out there – marvelous, that can be managed. But then what? That limit, that limit, *respice finem* [consider the goal]! Either I shall have to drive home again or I shall have to walk home. If I drive home after having walked, I am afraid of catching cold. If I walk home, I will arrive home so tired that I forfeit the pleasure of the walk.' Then I sit pondering this until I become quite tired from pondering.

At last I reach a decision. On the assumption that you live several miles from town – I give up hope of a real walk; I pick up the pen and now it *currente calamo* [proceeds on the run] – and so long as you do not tire, I will surely not tire either.

5. The Present Age

In 1846, Kierkegaard considered that his activity as an author was over. Nevertheless, he could not get rid of the urge to write. So he invented a way of writing without writing: the review. Thomasine Gyllembourg's novel Two Ages *(1845) gave him the ideal opportunity. Against the brilliance and passion of the Age of Revolution could be set a description of his own Age. But that description seems, in an act of prophetic power, to generate a kind of meta-description, the description of a third Age – which we recognize as the Twentieth Century.*

Our age is essentially one of understanding and reflection, without passion, momentarily bursting into enthusiasm, and shrewdly relapsing into repose.

If we had statistical tables of the consumption of intelligence from generation to generation as we have for spirits, we should be astounded at the enormous amount of scruple and deliberation consumed by small, well-to-do families living quietly, and at the amount which the young, and even children, use. For just as the children's crusade may be said to typify the Middle Ages, precocious children are typical of the present age. In fact one is tempted to ask whether there is a single man left ready, for once, to commit an outrageous folly.

Nowadays not even a suicide kills himself in desperation. Before taking the step he deliberates so long and so carefully that he literally chokes with thought. It is even questionable whether he ought to be called a suicide, since it is really thought which takes his life. He does not die *with* deliberation but *from* deliberation.

It would therefore be very difficult to prosecute the present generation in view of its legal quibbles: in fact, its ability, virtuosity and good sense consists in trying to reach a judgement and a decision without ever going as far as action. If one may say of the revolutionary period that it runs wild, one would have to say of the present that it runs badly. Between them, the individual and his generation always bring each other to a standstill, with the result that the prosecuting attorney would find it next to impossible to get any fact admitted – because nothing really happens. To judge from innumerable indications, one would conclude that something quite exceptional had either just happened or was just about to happen. Yet any such conclusion would be quite wrong. Indications are, indeed, the only achievements of the age; and its skill and inventiveness in constructing fascinating illusions, its bursts of enthusiasm, using as a deceitful escape some projected change of form, must be rated as high in the scale of cleverness and of the negative use of strength as the passionate, creative energy of the revolution in the corresponding scale of energy. But the present generation, wearied by its chimerical efforts, relapses into complete indolence. Its condition is that of a man who has only fallen asleep towards morning: first of all come great dreams, then a feeling of laziness, and finally a witty or clever excuse for remaining in bed.

However well-meaning and strong the individual man may be (if he could only use his strength), he still has not the passion to be able to tear himself from the coils and seductive uncertainty of reflection. Nor do his surroundings supply the events or produce the general enthusiasm necessary in order to free him. Instead of coming to his help, his *milieu* forms around him a negative intellectual opposition, which juggles for a moment with a deceptive prospect, only to deceive him in the end by pointing to a brilliant way out of the difficulty – by showing him that the shrewdest thing of all is to do nothing. For at the bottom of the tergiversation of the present age is *vis inertiae*, and every one without passion congratulates himself upon being the first to discover it, and so becomes cleverer still. During the revolution arms were distributed freely, just as during the Crusades the insignia of the exploit were bestowed upon men, but nowadays people are supplied with rules of careful conduct and ready-reckoners to facilitate judgement. If a generation were given the diplomatic task of postponing any action in such a way as to make it seem as if something were just about to happen, then we should have to admit that our age had performed as remarkable a feat as the revolutionary age. Let anyone try forgetting all he knows of the age and its actual relativity which is so enhanced by familiarity, and then arrive, as it were, from another world: if he were then to read a book or an article in the papers, or merely to speak to some passer-by, his impression would be: 'Good heavens, something is going to happen to-night – or perhaps something happened the night before last.'

An age of Advertisement

A revolutionary age is an age of action; ours is the age of advertisement and publicity. Nothing ever happens but there is immediate publicity everywhere. In the present age a rebellion is, of all things, the most unthinkable. Such an expression of strength would seem ridiculous to the calculating intelligence of our times. On the other hand a political virtuoso might bring off a feat almost as remarkable. He might write a manifesto suggesting a general assembly at which people should decide upon a rebellion, and it would be so carefully worded that even the censor would let it pass. At the meeting itself he would be able to create the impression that his audience had rebelled, after which they would all go quietly home – having spent a very pleasant evening. Among the young men of today a profound and prodigious learning is almost unthinkable; they would find it ridiculous. On the other hand a scientific virtuoso might draw up a subscription form outlining an all-embracing system which he purposed to write and, what is more, in such a way that the reader would feel he had already read the system; for the age of encyclopaedists, when men wrote gigantic folios with unremitting pains, is gone. Now is the turn of those light-weight encyclopaedists who, *en passant*, deal with all the sciences and the whole of existence. Equally unthinkable among the young men of today is a truly religious renunciation of the world, adhered to with daily self-denial. On the other hand almost any theological student is capable of something far more wonderful. He could found a society with the sole object of saving all those who are lost. The age of great and good actions is past, the present is the age of anticipation when even recognition is received in advance. No one is satisfied with doing something definite, everyone wants to feel flattered by reflection with the illusion of having discovered at the very least a new continent. Like a young man who decides to work for his examination in all earnest from September 1st, and in order to strengthen his resolution decides to take a holiday during August, so the present generation seems – though this is decidedly more difficult to understand – to have made a solemn resolution that the next generation should set to work seriously, and in order to avoid disturbing or delaying the next generation, the present attends to – the banquets. Only there is a difference: the young man understands himself in the light-heartedness of youth, whereas our generation is serious – even at banquets.

'Something must be done!'

There is no more action or decision in our day than there is perilous delight in swimming in shallow waters. But just as a grown-up, struggling delightedly in the waves, calls to those younger than himself: 'Come on, jump in quickly' – the decision in existence, so to speak (of course it is in the individual), calls out to the young who are not as yet worn out by over-reflective thought or overburdened by the illusions of reflective thought: Come on, leap cheerfully, even if it means a light-hearted leap, so long as it is decisive. If you are capable of being a man, then danger and the harsh judgement of existence on your thoughtlessness will help you to become one.

If the jewel which everyone desired to possess lay far out on a frozen lake where the ice was very thin, watched over by the danger of death, while, closer in, the ice was perfectly safe, then in a passionate age the crowds would applaud the courage of the man who ventured out, they would tremble for him and with him in the danger of his decisive action, they would grieve over him if he were drowned, they would make a god of him if he secured the prize. But in an age without passion, in a reflective age, it would be otherwise. People would think each other clever in agreeing that it was unreasonable and not even worth while to venture so far out. And in this way they would transform *daring and enthusiasm* into a *feat of skill*, so as to do something, for after all 'something must be done.' The crowds would go out to watch from a safe place, and with the eyes of connoisseurs appraise the accomplished skater who could skate almost to the very edge (i.e. as far as the ice was still safe and the danger had not yet begun) and then turn back. The most accomplished skater would manage to go out to the furthermost point and then perform a still more dangerous-looking run, so as to make the spectators hold their breath and say: 'Ye Gods! How mad; he is risking his life.' But look, and you will see that his skill was so astonishing that he managed to turn back just in time, while the ice was perfectly safe and there was still no danger. As at the theatre, the crowd would applaud and acclaim him, surge homeward with the heroic artist in their midst, to honour him with a magnificent banquet. For intelligence has got the upper hand to such an extent that it transforms the real task into an unreal trick and reality into a play. During the banquet admiration would reach its height. Now the proper relation between the admirer and the object of admiration is one in which the admirer is edified by the thought that he is a man like the hero, humbled by the thought that he is incapable of such great actions, yet morally encouraged to emulate him according to his powers; but where intelligence has got the upper hand the character of admiration is completely altered. Even at the height of the banquet, when the applause was loudest, the admiring guests would all have a shrewd notion that the action of the man who received all the honour was not really so extraordinary, and that only by chance was the gathering for him, since after all, with a little practice, everyone could have done as much. Briefly, instead of being strengthened in their discernment and encouraged to do good, the guests would more probably go home with an even stronger predisposition to the most dangerous, if also the most respectable, of all diseases: to admire in public what is considered unimportant in private – since everything is made into a joke. And so, stimulated by a gush of admiration, they are all comfortably agreed that they might just as well admire themselves.

Formerly it was agreed that a man stood or fell by his actions; nowadays, on the contrary, everyone idles about and comes off brilliantly with the help of a little reflection, knowing perfectly well what ought to be done. But what two people talking together, or the speakers at a meeting, understand perfectly presented to them as a thought or as an observation, they cannot understand at all in the form of action. If someone were to overhear what people said ought to be done, and then in a spirit of irony, and for no other reason, proceeded to act accordingly, everyone would be amazed. They would find it rash, yet as soon as they had talked it over they would find that it was just what should be done.

The Comic

The present age with its sudden enthusiasms followed by apathy and indolence is very near the comic; but those who understand the comic see quite clearly that the comic is not where the present age imagines. Now satire, if it is to do a little good and not cause immeasurable harm, must be firmly based upon a consistent ethical view of life, a natural distinction which renounces the success of the moment; otherwise the cure will be infinitely worse than the disease. The really comic thing is that an age such as this should try to be witty and humorous; for that is most certainly the last and most acrobatic way out of the impasse. What, indeed, is there for an age of reflection and thought to defy with humour? For, being without passion, it has lost all feeling for the values of eros, for enthusiasm and sincerity in politics and religion, or for piety, admiration and domesticity in everyday life. But even if the vulgar laugh, life only mocks at the wit which knows no values. To be witty without possessing the riches of inwardness is like squandering money upon luxuries and dispensing with necessities, or, as the proverb says, like selling one's breeches to buy a wig. But an age without passion has no values, and everything is transformed into representational ideas. Thus there are certain remarks and expressions current which, though true and reasonable up to a point, are lifeless. On the other hand no hero, no lover, no thinker, no knight of the faith, no proud man, no man in despair would claim to have experienced them completely and personally. And just as one longs for the clink of real money after the crackle of bank-notes, one longs nowadays for a little originality. Yet what is more spontaneous than wit? It is more spontaneous, at least more surprising, even than the first bud of spring and the first tender shoots of grain. Why, even if spring came according to agreement it would still be spring, but wit upon agreement would be disgusting.

But, now, supposing that as a relief from feverish and sudden enthusiasms things went so far that wit, that divine accident – an additional favour which comes as a sign from the gods, from the mysterious source of the inexplicable, so that not even the wittiest of men dares to say: tomorrow, but adoringly says: when it pleases the gods – but supposing that wit were to be transformed into its shabbiest contrary, a trivial necessity, so that it became a profitable branch of trade to manufacture and make up and remake, and buy up old and new witticisms – what an epigram on a witty age!

In the end, therefore, money will be the one thing people will desire, which is moreover only representative, an abstraction. Nowadays a young man hardly envies anyone his gifts, his art, the love of a beautiful girl, or his fame; he only envies him his money. Give me money, he will say, and I am saved. But the young man will not run riot, he will not deserve what repentance repays. He would die with nothing to reproach himself with, and under the impression that if only he had had the money he might really have lived and might even have achieved something great.

Reflection

After these general observations, and having compared the present age with the revolutionary age, it will be in order to go back to the dialectical and categorical definitions of the present age, regardless whether they are present at a given moment or not. We are concerned here with the 'how' of the age, and this 'how' must be defined from a universal standpoint, the final consequences of which can be reached by deduction, *a posse ad esse*, and verified by observation and experience *ab esse ad posse*.

As far as its significance is concerned it is, of course, possible that the work of reflection, which is the task before the present age, may ultimately be explained in a higher form of existence. As for its quality, there is no doubt that the individual resting in his reflection can be just as well-intentioned as a passionate man who has made his decision; and conversely there may be just as much excuse for the man whose passions run away with him as for a man whose fault is never apparent, though he is cleverly aware that he lets himself be deceived by his reflection. The results of reflection are both dangerous and unforeseeable because one can never tell whether the decision which saves a man from evil is reached after thorough consideration, or whether it is simply the exhaustion resulting from reflection which prevents him from doing wrong. One thing, however, is certain, an increased power of reflection like an increased knowledge only adds to man's affliction, and above all it is certain that for the individual as for the generation no task is more difficult than to escape from the temptations of reflection, simply because they are so dialectical and the result of one clever discovery may give the whole question a new turn, because at any moment reflection is capable of explaining everything quite differently and allowing one some way of escape; because at the last moment of a reflective decision reflection is capable of changing everything – after one has made far greater exertions than are necessary to get a man of character into the midst of things.

But these are only the excuses of reflection and the real position in reflection remains unchanged, for it is only altered *within* reflection. Even if a certain injustice is done to the present age when it is compared to a complete and closed period (the present age is still struggling with all the difficulties of 'becoming'), such a qualification is only a reflective qualification; and then, in return, its uncertainty is filled with *hope*.

A passionate tumultous age will *overthrow everything, pull everything down*; but a revolutionary age, that is at the same time reflective and passionless, transforms that expression of strength into *a feat of dialectics: it leaves everything standing but cunningly empties it of significance. Instead of culminating in a rebellion it reduces the inward reality of all relationships to a reflective tension which leaves everything standing but makes the whole of life ambiguous: so that everything continues to exist factually whilst by a dialectical deceit*, privatissime, *it supplies a secret interpretation – that it does not exist.*

Morality is character, character is that which is engraved; but the sand and the sea have no character and neither has abstract intelligence, for character is really inwardness. Immorality, as energy, is also character; but to be neither moral nor immoral is merely ambiguous, and ambiguity enters into life when the qualitative distinctions are weakened by a gnawing reflection. The revolt of the passions is elemental, the dissolution brought about by ambiguity is a silent sorites that goes on night and day. The distinction between good and evil is enervated by a superficial, superior and theoretical knowledge of evil, and by a supercilious cleverness which is aware that goodness is neither appreciated nor worth while in this world, that it is tantamount to stupidity. No one is any longer carried away by the desire for the good to perform great things, no one is precipitated by evil into atrocious sins, and so there is nothing for either the good or the bad to talk about, and yet for that very reason people gossip all the more, since ambiguity is tremendously stimulating and much more verbose than rejoicing over goodness or repentance over evil.

The springs of life, which are only what they are because of the qualitative differentiating power of passion, lose their elasticity. The distance separating a thing from its opposite in quality no longer regulates the inward relation of things. All inwardness is lost, and to that extent the relation no longer exists, or else forms a colourless cohesion. The negative law is this: opposites are unable to dispense with each other and unable to hold together. The positive law is that they are able to dispense with each other and are able to hold together or, stated positively: opposites are unable to dispense with each other because of the connexion between them. But when the inward relation is wanting another takes its place: a quality is no longer related to its contrary; instead, the partners both stand and observe each other and *the state of tension thus produced is really the end of the relationship*. For example, the admirer no longer cheerfully and happily acknowledges greatness, promptly expressing his appreciation, and then rebelling against its pride and arrogance. Nor is the relationship in any sense the opposite. The admirer and the object of admiration stand like two polite equals, and observe each other. A subject no longer freely honours his king or is angered at his ambition. To be a subject has come to mean something quite different; it means to be a *third party*. The subject ceases to have a position within the relationship; he has no direct relation to the king but simply becomes an observer and deliberately works out the problem; i.e. the relation of a subject to his king. For a time committee after committee is formed, so long, that is to say, as there are still people who passionately want to be what they ought to be; but in the end the whole age becomes a committee. A father no longer curses his son in anger, using all his parental authority, nor does a son defy his father, a conflict which might end in the inwardness of forgiveness; on the contrary, their relationship is irreproachable, for it is really in process of ceasing to exist, since they are no longer related to one another within the relationship; in fact it has become a problem in which the two partners observe each other as in a game, instead of having any relation to each other, and they note down each other's remarks instead of showing a firm devotion. More and more people renounce the quiet and modest tasks of life, that are so important and pleasing to God, in order to achieve something greater; in order to think over the relationships of life in a higher relationship till in the end the whole generation has become a representation, who represent . . . it is difficult to say *who*; and who think about these relationships . . for *whose* sake it is not easy to discover. A disobedient youth is no longer in fear of his schoolmaster – the relation is rather one of indifference in which schoolmaster and pupil discuss how a good school should be run. To go to school no longer means to be in fear of the master, or merely to learn, but rather implies being interested in the problem of education. Again the differentiating relation of man to woman is never broken in an audaciously licentious manner; decency is observed in such a way that one can only describe these innocent borderline flirtations as trivial.

What in fact should one call such relationships? A tension, I think, is the best description, not, however, a tension which strains the forces to breaking-point, but rather a tension which exhausts life itself and the fire of that enthusiasm and inwardness which makes the fetters of dependence and the crown of dominion light, which makes the child's obedience and the father's authority joyful, the admiration of the subject and the exaltation of the great fearless, which gives recognized importance to the master and thus to the disciple occasion to learn, which unites woman's weakness and man's strength in the equal strength of devotion. As it is the relationships still exist but they lack the force which makes it possible for them to draw together in inwardness and unite in harmony. The relationship expresses its presence and its absence simultaneously, not completely but rather as though it were drawled out, half-awake and uninterruptedly.

Perhaps I can explain what I mean by a very simple illustration? I once knew a family who owned a grandfather clock whose works for some reason or other had got out of order. But the fault did not result in the spring suddenly unwinding, or in the chain breaking or in the hand ceasing to strike; on the contrary, it went on striking in a curiously abstract, though confusing, way. It did not strike twelve times at twelve o'clock and once at one o'clock, but struck once all through the day regular intervals. It went on striking all day long but never gave a definite time.

The same applies to a state of exhausted tension: the relationship continues; something is expressed with an abstract continuity which prevents any real break, but although it must nevertheless be described as an expression of the relationship, the relationship is not only ambiguously expressed, it is almost meaningless.

It is this deceptive lull in the relationship which continues the relation as a fact; the danger is that it favours the cunning deprivations of reflection. Against a rebellion one can use force, and an obvious counterfeit has only to wait for its punishment; but dialectical complications are difficult to root out, and it requires even better ears to track down the stealthy movement of reflection along its secret and ambiguous path.

The established order of things continues to exist, but it is its ambiguity which satisfies our reflective and passionless age. No one, for example, wishes to do away with the power of the king, but if little by little it could be transformed into something purely fictitious every one would be quite prepared to cheer him. No one, for example, wishes to bring about the downfall of the eminent, but if distinction could be shown to be purely fictitious then everyone would be quite prepared to cheer him. No one, for example, wishes to bring about the downfall of the eminent, but if distinction could be shown to be purely fictitious then everyone would be prepared to admire it. In the same way people are quite prepared to leave the Christian terminology untouched, but they can surreptitiously interpolate that it involves no decisive thought. And so they remain unrepentant, for after all they have destroyed nothing. They no more desire a powerful king than an heroic liberator or religious authority. In all innocence they want the established order to continue, but they have the more or less certain reflective knowledge that it no longer exists. Then they proudly imagine that their attitude is ironical – as though real irony were not essentially a concealed enthusiasm in a negative age (just as the hero is enthusiasm made manifest in a positive age), as though irony did not involve sacrifice, when its greatest master was put to death.

Envy

This reflective tension ultimately constitutes itself into a principle, and just as in a passionate age *enthusiasm* is the unifying principle, so in an age which is very reflective and passionless *envy* is the negative unifying principle. This must not, however, be interpreted as an ethical charge; the idea of reflection is, if one may so express it, envy, and it is therefore twofold in its action: it is selfish within the individual and it results in the selfishness of the society around him, which thus works against him.

The envy in reflection (within the individual) prevents him making a decision passionately. If, for a moment, it should seem as though an individual were about to succeed in throwing off the yoke of reflection, he is at once pulled up by the opposition of the reflection which surrounds him. The envy which springs from reflection imprisons man's will and his strength. First of all the individual has to break loose from the bonds of his own reflection, but even then he is not free. Instead he finds himself in the vast prison formed by the reflection of those around him, for because of his relation to his own reflection he also has a certain relation to the reflection around him. He can only escape from this second imprisonment through the inwardness of religion, no matter how clearly he may perceive the falseness of the situation. With every means in its power reflection prevents people from realizing that both the individual and the age are thus imprisoned, not imprisoned by tyrants or priests or nobles or the secret police, but by reflection itself, and it does so by maintaining the flattering and conceited notion that the *possibility* of reflection is far superior to a mere *decision*. A selfish envy makes such demands upon the individual that by asking too much it prevents him from doing anything. It spoils him like an indulgent mother, for the envy within him prevents the individual from devoting himself to others. Moreover, the envy which surrounds him and in which he participates by envying others, is envious in a negative and critical sense.

But the further it is carried the more clearly does the envy of reflection become a moral *ressentiment*. Just as air in a sealed space becomes poisonous, so the imprisonment of reflection develops a culpable *ressentiment* if it is not ventilated by action or incident of any kind. In reflection the state of strain (or tension as we called it) results in the neutralization of all the higher powers, and all that is low and despicable comes to the fore, its very impudence giving the spurious effect of strength, while protected by its very baseness it avoids attracting the attention of *ressentiment*.

It is a fundamental truth of human nature that man is incapable of remaining permanently on the heights, of continuing to admire anything. Human nature needs variety. Even in the most enthusiastic ages people have always liked to joke enviously about their superiors. That is perfectly in order and is entirely justifiable so long as after having laughed at the great they can once more look upon them with admiration; otherwise the game is not worth the candle. In that way *ressentiment* finds an outlet even in an enthusiastic age. And as long as an age, even though less enthusiastic, has the strength to give *ressentiment* its proper character and has made up its mind what its expression signifies, *ressentiment* has its own, though dangerous, importance. In Greece, for example, the form *ressentiment* took was ostracism, a self-defensive effort, as it were, on the part of the masses to preserve their equilibrium in face of the outstanding qualities of the eminent. The outstanding man was exiled, but everyone understood how dialectical the relationship was, ostracism being a mark of distinction. Thus, in representing a somewhat earlier period in the spirit of Aristophanes, it would be more ironical to let a completely unimportant person be ostracized than to let him become dictator, because ostracism is the negative mark of greatness. But it would be still better to let the story end with the people recalling the man whom they had ostracized because they could no longer do without him, and he would then be a complete mystery to the country of his exile, which would, of course, be quite unable to discover anything remarkable about him. In *The Knights* Aristophanes gives us a picture of the final state of corruption in which the vulgar rabble ends when – just as in Tibet they worship the Dalai Lama's excrement – they contemplate their own scum in its representatives; and that, in a democracy, is a degree of corruption comparable to auctioning the crown in a monarchy. But as long as *ressentiment* still has any character, ostracism is a negative mark of distinction. The man who told Aristides that he had voted for his exile 'because he could not endure hearing Aristides called the only just man' did not deny Aristides' eminence, but admitted something about himself. He admitted that his relation to distinction was the unhappy love of envy, instead of the happy love of admiration, but he did not try to belittle that distinction.

On the other side, the more reflection gets the upper hand and thus makes people indolent, the more dangerous *ressentiment* becomes, because it no longer has sufficient character to make it conscious of its significance. Bereft of that character reflection is cowardly and vacillating, and according to circumstances interprets the same thing in a variety of ways. It tries to treat it as a joke, and if that fails, to regard it as an insult, and when that fails, to dismiss it as nothing at all; or else it will treat the thing as a witticism, and if that fails then say that it was meant as a moral satire deserving attention, and if that does not succeed, add that it is not worth bothering about.

Thus *ressentiment* becomes the constituent principle of want of character, which from utter wretchedness tries to sneak itself a position, all the time safeguarding itself by conceding that it is less than nothing. The *ressentiment* which results from want of character can never understand that eminent distinction really is distinction. Neither does it understand itself by recognizing distinction negatively (as in the case of ostracism) but wants to drag it down, wants to belittle it so that it really ceases to be distinguished. And *ressentiment* not only defends itself against all *existing* forms of distinction but against that which is still *to come*.

Levelling

The *ressentiment* which is *establishing itself* is the process of levelling, and while a passionate age storms ahead setting up new things and tearing down old, raising and demolishing as it goes, a reflective and passionless age does exactly the contrary: it *hinders and stifles* all action; it levels. Levelling is a silent, mathematical, and abstract occupation which shuns upheavals. In a burst of momentary enthusiasm people might, in their despondency, even long for a misfortune in order to feel the powers of life, but the apathy which follows is no more helped by a disturbance than an engineer levelling a piece of land. At its most violent a rebellion is like a volcanic eruption and drowns every other sound. At its maximum the levelling process is a deathly silence in which one can hear one's heart beat, a silence which nothing can pierce, in which everything is engulfed, powerless to resist. One man can be at the head of a rebellion, but no one can be at the head of the levelling process alone, for in that case he would be the leader and would thus escape being levelled. Each individual within his own little circle can co-operate in the levelling, but it is an abstract power, and the levelling process is the victory of abstraction over the individual. The levelling process in modern times corresponds, in reflection, to fate in antiquity.

The dialectic of antiquity tended towards leadership (the great individual and the masses – the free man and the slaves); so far the dialectic of Christendom tends towards representation (the majority sees itself in its representative and is set free by the consciousness that it is the majority which is represented, in a sort of self-consciousness); the dialectic of the present age tends towards equality, and its most logical – though mistaken – fulfilment is levelling, as the negative unity of the negative reciprocity of all individuals.

It must be obvious to everyone that the profound significance of the levelling process lies in the fact that it means the predominance of the category 'generation' over the category 'individuality'. In antiquity the total number of the individuals was there to express, as it were, the value of the outstanding individual. Nowadays the standard of value has been changed so that *equally*, approximately so and so many men go to one individual, and one need only be sure of having the right number in order to have importance. In antiquity the individual in the masses had no importance whatsoever; the outstanding individual signified them all. The present age tends towards a mathematical equality in which equally in all classes approximately so and so many people go to one individual. Formerly the outstanding individual could allow himself everything and the individual in the masses nothing at all. Now everyone knows that so and so many make an individual and quite consistently people add themselves together (it is called joining together, but that is only a polite euphemism) for the most trivial purposes. Simply in order to put a passing whim into practice a few people add themselves together, and the thing is done – then they dare do it. For that reason not even a pre-eminently gifted man can free himself from reflection, because he very soon becomes conscious of himself as a fractional part in some quite trivial matter, and so fails to achieve the infinite freedom of religion. The fact that several people united together have the courage to meet death does not nowadays mean that each, individually, has the courage, for, even more than death, the individual fears the judgement and protest of reflection upon his wishing to risk something on his own. The individual no longer belongs to God, to himself, to his beloved, to his art or to his science, he is conscious of belonging in all things to an abstraction to which he is subjected by reflection, just as a serf belongs to an estate. That is why people band together in cases where it is an absolute contradiction to be more than one. The apotheosis of the positive principle of association is nowadays the devouring and demoralizing principle which in the slavery of reflection makes even virtues into *vitia splendida*. There is no other reason for this than that eternal responsibility, and the religious singling out of the individual before God, is ignored. When corruption sets in at that point people seek consolation in company, and so reflection catches the individual for life. And those who do not realize even the beginning of this crisis are engulfed without further ado in the reflective relationship.

The levelling process is not the action of an individual but the work of reflection in the hands of an abstract power. It is therefore possible to calculate the law governing it in the same way that one calculates the diagonal in a parallelogram of forces. The individual who levels down is himself engulfed in the process and so on, and while he seems to know selfishly what he is doing one can only say of people *en masse* that they know not what they do; for just as collective enthusiasm produces a surplus which does not come from the individual, there is also a surplus in this case. A demon is called up over whom no individual has any power, and though the very abstraction of levelling gives the individual a momentary, selfish kind of enjoyment, he is at the same time signing the warrant for his own doom. Enthusiasm *may* end in disaster, but levelling is *eo ipso* the destruction of the individual. No age, and therefore not the present age, can bring the scepticism of that process to a halt, for as soon as it tries to stop it, the law of the levelling process is again called into action. It can therefore only be held up by the individual attaining the religious courage which springs from his individual religious isolation.

I was once the witness of a street fight in which three men most shamefully set upon a fourth. The crowd stood and watched them with indignation; expressions of disgust began to enliven the scene; then several of the onlookers set on one of the three assailants and knocked him down and beat him. The avengers had, in fact, applied precisely the same rules as the offenders. If I may be allowed to do so, I will introduce my own unimportant self into the story and continue. I went up to one of the avengers and tried by argument to explain to him how illogical his behaviour was; but it seemed quite impossible for him to discuss the question: he could only repeat that such a rascal richly deserved to have three people against him. The humour of the situation would have been even more apparent to someone who had not seen the beginning of the brawl, and so simply heard one man saying of another (who was alone) that he was three against one, and heard the remark just when the very reverse was the case – when they were three to one against him. In the first place it was humorous because of the contradiction which it involved, as when the policeman told a man standing in the street 'to kindly disperse'. Secondly it had all the humour of self-contradiction. But what I learnt from it was that I had better give up all hope of putting a stop to that scepticism, lest it should turn upon me.

No single individual (I mean no outstanding individual – in the sense of leadership and conceived according to the dialectical category 'fate') will be able to arrest the abstract process of levelling, for it is negatively something higher, and the age of chivalry is gone. No society or association can arrest that abstract power, simply because an association is itself in the service of the levelling process. Not even the individuality of the different nationalities can arrest it, for on a higher plane the abstract process of levelling is a negative representation of *humanity pure and unalloyed*. The abstract levelling process, that self-combustion of the human race, produced by the friction which arises when the individual ceases to exist as singled out by religion, is bound to continue, like a trade wind, and consume everything. But through it each individual for himself may receive once more a religious education and, in the highest sense, will be helped by the *examen rigorosum* of the levelling process to an essentially religious attitude. For the younger men who, however strongly they personally may cling to what they admire as eminent, realize from the beginning that the levelling process is evil in both the selfish individual and in the selfish generation, but that it can also, if they desire it honestly and before God, become the starting-point for the highest life – for them it will indeed be an education to live in the age of levelling. Their age will, in the very highest sense, develop them religiously and at the same time educate them aesthetically and intellectually, because in this way the comic will receive its absolute expression. The highest form of the comic arises precisely when the individual comes directly under the infinite abstraction of 'pure humanity', without any of those intermediary qualifications which temper the humour of man's position and strengthen its pathos, without any of the concrete particulars of organization which the levelling process destroys. But that again is only another expression of the fact that man's only salvation lies in the reality of religion for each individual.

And it will add fuel to their enthusiasm to understand that it is in fact through error that the individual is given access to the highest, if he courageously desires it. But the levelling process will have to continue, and must be completed, just as the scandal had to come into the world, though woe to them by whom it comes.

It has often been said that a reformation should begin with each man reforming himself. That, however, is not what actually happened, for the reformation produced a hero who paid God dearly enough for his position as hero. By joining up with him directly people buy cheap, indeed at bargain prices, what he had paid for so dearly; but they do not buy the highest of all things. The abstract principle of levelling, on the contrary, like the biting east wind, has no personal relation to any individual but has only an abstract relationship which is the same for everyone. There, no hero suffers for others, or helps them; the taskmaster of all alike is the levelling process which itself takes on their education. And the man who learns most from the levelling and himself becomes greatest does not become an outstanding man or a hero – that would only impede the levelling process, which is rigidly consistent to the end – he himself prevents that from happening because he has understood the meaning of levelling; he becomes a man and nothing else, in the complete equalitarian sense. That is the idea of religion. But, under those conditions, the equalitarian order is severe and the profit is seemingly very small; seemingly, for unless the individual learns in the reality of religion before God to be content with himself, and learns, instead of dominating others, to dominate himself, content as priest to be his own audience, and as author his own reader, if he will not learn to be satisfied with that as the highest, because it is the expression of the equality of all men before God and of our likeness to others, then he will not escape from reflection. It may be that for one deceptive moment it will seem to him, in relation to his gifts, as though he were levelling, but in the end he will sink down beneath the levelling process. There is no good calling upon a Holger Danske or a Martin Luther; their day is over and at bottom it is only the individual's laziness which makes a man long to have them back, a worldly impatience which prefers to buy something cheap, second-hand, rather than to buy the highest of all things very dear and first-hand. It is worse than useless to found society after society, because negatively speaking there is something above them, even though the short-sighted member of the society cannot see it.

The principle of individuality in its *immediate* and beautiful formation is symbolized for the generation in the outstanding and eminent individual; it groups subordinate individualities round the representative. This principle of individuality, in its *eternal* truth, uses the abstraction and equality of the generation to level down, and in that way co-operates in developing the individual religiously into a real man. For the levelling process is as powerful where temporary things are concerned as it is impotent where eternal things are concerned. Reflection is a snare in which one is caught, but, once the 'leap' of enthusiasm has been taken, the relation is a different one and it becomes a noose which drags one into eternity. Reflection is and remains the hardest creditor in existence; hitherto it has cunningly bought up all the possible views of life, but it cannot buy the essentially religious and eternal view of life; on the other hand, it can tempt people astray with its dazzling brilliance, and dishearten them by reminding them of all the past. But, by leaping into the depths, one learns to help oneself, learns to love others as much as oneself, even though one is accused of arrogance and pride – because one will not accept help – or of selfishness because one will not cunningly deceive people by helping them, i.e. by helping them to escape their highest destiny.

Should anyone complain that what I have set forth here is known to all and could be said by anyone, then my answer is: the more the merrier – I am not asking for a position of eminence and I have nothing against everyone knowing my opinion, unless that were to mean, in a sense, that it is to be taken from me and thereby put at the disposal of a negative association. So long as I have permission to retain them, my opinions do not lose their value by being known to everyone.

Throughout many changes the tendency in modern times has remained a levelling one. These changes themselves have not, however, all of them, been levelling, for they are none of them abstract enough, each having a certain concrete reality. To some extent it is true that the levelling process goes on when one great man attacks another, so that both are weakened, or when one is neutralized by the other, or when an association of people, in themselves weak, grow stronger than the eminent. Levelling can also be accomplished by one particular caste, e.g. the clergy, the bourgeois, the peasants, by the people themselves. But all that is only the first movement of an abstract power within the concreteness of individuality.

The Public

In order that everything should be reduced to the same level, it is first of all necessary to procure a phantom, its spirit, a monstrous abstraction, an all-embracing something which is nothing, a mirage – and that phantom is *the public*. It is only in an age which is without passion, yet reflective, that such a phantom can develop itself with the help of the Press which itself becomes an abstraction. In times of passion and tumult and enthusiasm, even when a people desire to realize a fruitless idea and lay waste and destroy everything: even then there is no such thing as a public. There are parties and they are concrete. The Press, in times such as those, takes on a concrete character according to the division of parties. But just as sedentary professional people are the first to take up any fantastic illusion which comes their way, so a passionless, sedentary, reflective age, in which only the Press exhibits a vague sort of life, fosters this phantom. The public is, in fact, the real Levelling-Master rather than the actual leveller, for whenever levelling is only approximately accomplished it is done by something, but the public is a monstrous nothing. The public is a concept which could not have occurred in antiquity because the people *en masse, in corpore*, took part in any situation which arose, and were responsible for the actions of the individual, and, moreover, the individual was personally present and had to submit at once to applause or disapproval for his decision. Only when the sense of association in society is no longer strong enough to give life to concrete realities is the Press able to create that abstraction 'the public', consisting of unreal individuals who never are and never can be united in an actual situation or organization – and yet are held together as a whole.

The public is a host, more numerous than all the peoples together, but it is a body which can never be reviewed, it cannot even be represented, because it is an abstraction. Nevertheless, when the age is reflective and passionless and destroys everything concrete, the public becomes everything and is supposed to include everything. And that again shows how the individual is thrown back upon himself.

The real moment in time and the real situation being simultaneous with real people, each of whom is something: that is what helps to sustain the individual. But the existence of a public produces neither a situation nor simultaneity. The individual reader of the Press is not the public, and even though little by little a number of individuals or even all of them should read it, the simultaneity is lacking. Years might be spent gathering the public together, and still it would not be there. This abstraction, which the individuals so illogically form, quite rightly repulses the individual instead of coming to his help. The man who has no opinion of an event at the actual moment accepts the opinion of the majority, or, if he is quarrelsome, of the minority. But it must be remembered that both majority and minority are real people, and that is why the individual is assisted by adhering to them. A public, on the contrary, is an abstraction. To adopt the opinion of this or that man means that one knows that they will be subjected to the same dangers as oneself, that they will be led astray with one if the opinion leads astray. But to adopt the same opinion as the public is a deceptive consolation because the public is only there *in abstracto*. Whilst, therefore, no majority has ever been so certain of being right and victorious as the public, that is not much consolation to the individual, for a public is a phantom which forbids all personal contact. And if a man adopts public opinion today and is hissed tomorrow he is hissed by the public.

A generation, a people, an assembly of the people, a meeting or a man, are responsible for what they are and can be made ashamed if they are inconstant and unfaithful; but a public remains a public. A people, an assembly or a man can change to such an extent that one may say: they are no longer the same; a public on the other hand can become the very opposite and still be the same – a public. But it is precisely by means of this abstraction and this abstract discipline that the individual will be formed (in so far as the individual is not already formed by his inner life), if he does not succumb in the process, taught to be content, in the highest religious sense, with himself and his relation to God, to be at one with himself instead of being in agreement with a public which destroys everything that is relative, concrete and particular in life; educated to find peace within himself and with God, instead of counting hands. And the ultimate difference between the modern world and antiquity is: that 'the whole' is not concrete and is therefore unable to support the individual, or to educate him as the concrete should (though without developing him absolutely), but is an abstraction which by its abstract equality repels him and thus helps him to be educated absolutely – unless he succumbs in the process. The *taedium vitae* so constant in antiquity was due to the fact that the outstanding individual was what others *could not be*; the inspiration of modern times will be that any man who finds himself, religiously speaking, has only achieved what *everyone can achieve*.

A public is neither a nation, nor a generation, nor a community, nor a society, nor these particular men, for all these are only what they are through the concrete; no single person who belongs to the public makes a real commitment; for some hours of the day, perhaps, he belongs to the public – at moments when he is nothing else, since when he really is what he is he does not form part of the public. Made up of such individuals, of individuals at the moments when they are nothing, a public is a kind of gigantic something, an abstract and deserted void which is everything and nothing. But on this basis anyone can arrogate to himself a public, and just as the Roman Church chimerically extended its frontiers by appointing bishops *in partibus infidelium*, so a public is something which every one can claim, and even a drunken sailor exhibiting a 'peep-show' has dialectically absolutely the same right to a public as the greatest man; he has just as logical a right to put all those many noughts *in front* of his single number.

A public is everything and nothing, the most dangerous of all powers and the most insignificant: one can speak to a whole nation in the name of the public, and still the public will be less than a single real man, however unimportant. The qualification 'public' is produced by the deceptive juggling of an age of reflection, which makes it appear flattering to the individual who in this way can arrogate to himself this monster, in comparison with which concrete realities seem poor. The public is the fairy story of an age of understanding, which in imagination makes the individual into something even greater than a king above his people; but the public is also a gruesome abstraction through which the individual will receive his religious formation – or sink.

The Abstraction of the Press

The Press is an abstraction (since a paper is not a concrete part of a nation and only in an abstract sense an individual) which in conjunction with the passionless and reflective character of the age produces that abstract phantom: a public which in its turn is really the levelling power. Consequently it has an importance apart from its negative religious importance.

The fewer ideas there are at any time, the more indolent and exhausted by bursts of enthusiasm will it be; nevertheless, if we imagine the Press growing weaker and weaker because no events or ideas catch hold of the age, the more easily will the process of levelling become a harmful pleasure, a form of sensual intoxication which flames up for a moment, simply making the evil worse and the conditions of salvation more difficult and the probability of decline more certain. Although the demoralization brought about by autocracy and the decay of revolutionary periods have often been described, the decay of an age without passion is something just as harmful, though, on account of its ambiguity, it is less obvious.

It may not be without interest to consider this point. More and more individuals, owing to their bloodless indolence, will aspire to be nothing at all – in order to become the public: that abstract whole formed in the most ludicrous way, by all participants becoming third party (an onlooker). This indolent mass which understands nothing and does nothing itself, this gallery, is on the look-out for distraction and soon abandons itself to the idea that everything that anyone does is done in order to give it (the public) something to gossip about. That indolent mass sits with its legs crossed, wearing an air of superiority, and anyone who tries to work, whether king, official, school-teacher or the better type of journalist, the poet or the artist, has to struggle to drag the public along with it, while the public thinks in its own superior way that it is the horse.

A Dog with No Master

If I tried to imagine the public as a particular person (for although some better individuals momentarily belong to the public they nevertheless have something concrete about them, which holds them in its grip even if they have not attained the supreme religious attitude), I should perhaps think of one of the Roman emperors, a large well-fed figure, suffering from boredom, looking only for the sensual intoxication of laughter, since the divine gift of wit is not earthly enough. And so for a change he wanders about, indolent rather than bad, but with a negative desire to dominate. Everyone who has read the classical authors knows how many things a Caesar could try out in order to kill time. In the same way the public keeps a dog to amuse it. That dog is the scum of the literary world. If there is someone superior to the rest, perhaps even a great man, the dog is set on him and the fun begins. The dog goes for him, snapping and tearing at his coat-tails, allowing itself every possible ill-mannered familiarity – until the public tires, and says it may stop. That is an example of how the public levels. Their betters and superiors in strength are mishandled – and the dog remains a dog which even the public despises. The levelling is therefore done by a third party; a non-existent public levelling with the help of a third party which in its insignificance is less than nothing, being already more than levelled. And so the public is unrepentant, for it was after all not the public that acted but the dog; just as one says to children – the cat's mother did it. The public is unrepentant – it was not really belittling anyone; it just wanted a little amusement. For had the levelling implement been remarkably energetic, the indolent public would have been fooled because the implement itself would have been in the way; but when their betters are held down by the insignificant and the insignificant by itself, then no one is quit of anything.

The public is unrepentant, for it is not they who own the dog – they only subscribe. They neither set the dog on anyone, nor whistle it off – directly. If asked they would answer: the dog is not mine, it has no master. And if the dog had to be killed they would say: it was really a good thing that bad-tempered dog was put down, everyone wanted it killed – even the subscribers.

Perhaps someone, familiarizing himself with such a case, and inclined to fix his attention upon the outstanding individual who suffered at the hands of the public, may be of the opinion that such an ordeal is a great misfortune. I cannot at all agree with such an opinion, for anyone who really wishes to be helped to attain the highest is in fact benefited by undergoing such a misfortune, and must rather desire it even though people may be led to rebel. The really terrible thing is the thought of all the lives that are or easily may be wasted. I will not even mention those who are lost, or at any rate led completely astray: those who play the part of the dog for money, but the many who are helpless, thoughtless and sensual, who live superior lazy lives and never receive any deeper impression of existence than this meaningless grin, and all those bad people who are led into further temptation because in their stupidity they even become self-important by commiserating with the one who is attacked, without even understanding that in such a position the person attacked is always the stronger, without understanding that in this case the terrible and ironical truth applies: Weep not over him but over yourselves.

That is the levelling process at its lowest, for it always equates itself to the divisor by means of which everyone is reduced to a common denominator. Eternal life is also a sort of levelling, and yet that is not so, because the common denominator is that everyone should really and essentially be a man in a religious sense.

Hitherto I have been dealing with the dialectical categories and qualifications, and with their consequences, whether actually present at any given moment or not. I shall now abandon the dialectical analysis of the present age in order to arrive dialectically at its concrete affirmations regarding everyday life. It is here that the darker side will be seen; but although this cannot be denied, it is equally certain that just as reflection itself is not evil, so a very reflective age has its lighter side, simply because a higher degree of reflection implies greater significance than immediate passion; for when enthusiasm intervenes to gather the powers of reflection together into a decision, and because reflection confers, on the average, a greater capacity for action – then, when religion enters in, it takes command of that increased capacity for action.

Reflection is not the evil; but a reflective condition and the deadlock which it involves, by transforming the capacity for action into a means of escape from action, is both corrupt and dangerous, and leads in the end to a retrograde movement.

The present age is essentially one of understanding lacking in passion, and has therefore abolished the *principle of contradiction*. By comparison with a passionate age, an age without passion gains in *scope what it loses in intensity*. But this scope may once again become the condition of a still higher form, if a corresponding intensity assumes control of the extended field of activity which is put at its disposal. The abolition of the principle of contradiction, expressed in terms of existence, means to live in contradiction with oneself. The creative omnipotence of the differentiating power of passion, which makes the individual completely at one with himself, is transformed into the extended scope of reflective understanding: as a result of knowing and being everything possible, one is in contradiction with oneself, i.e. nothing at all. The principle of contradiction strengthens the individual's faithfulness to himself and makes him as constant as the number three spoken of so beautifully by Socrates, when he says that it would rather endure anything than become four or even a large round number, and in the same way the individual would rather suffer and be true to himself than be all manner of things in contradiction with himself.

Talkativeness

What is *talkativeness*? It is the result of doing away with the vital distinction between talking and keeping silent. Only someone who knows how to remain essentially silent can really talk – and act essentially. Silence is the essence of inwardness, of the inner life. Mere gossip anticipates real talk, and to express what is still in thought weakens action by forestalling it. But someone who can really talk, because he knows how to remain silent, will not talk about a variety of things but about one thing only, and he will know when to talk and when to remain silent. Where mere scope is concerned, talkativeness wins the day, it jabbers on incessantly about everything and nothing. When people's attention is no longer turned inwards, when they are no longer satisfied with their own inner religious lives, but turn to others and to things outside themselves, where the relation is intellectual, in search of that satisfaction, when nothing important ever happens to gather the threads of life together with the finality of a catastrophe: that is the time for talkativeness. In a passionate age great events (for they correspond to each other) give people something to talk about. Talkativeness, on the contrary, has, in quite another sense, plenty to talk about. And when the event is over, and silence follows, there is still something to remember and to think about while one remains silent. But talkativeness is afraid of the silence which reveals its emptiness.

The law governing artistic production applies, on a smaller scale, to everyone in daily life. Every man who has a real experience experiences at the same time all its possibilities in an ideal sense, including the opposite possibility. Aesthetically these possibilities are his lawful property. Not so, however, his private and personal reality. His talk and his production both rest upon his silence. The ideal perfection of his talk and of his production will correspond to his silence, and the absolute expression of that silence will be that the ideal will include the qualitatively opposite possibility. But as soon as the artist prostitutes his own reality he is no longer essentially productive. His beginning is his end, and his very first word will be a sin against the modesty of the ideal. This type of artistic production is therefore even, aesthetically speaking, a kind of private gossip. It is easily recognized because it is not balanced by its opposite; for ideality is the balance of opposites. For example, if the man who is moved to write by suffering is really initiated into the realm of ideals, he will reproduce the happiness as well as the suffering of his experience with the same affection. The condition of his attaining this ideal is the silence with which he shuts off his own real personality. Otherwise, in spite of all precautions, such as changing the scene to Africa, his one-sided predilection will be privately recognizable. For an author, like anyone else, must have his own private personality, but it must be his own 'Holy of Holies'; and just as the entrance to a house is barred by the crossed bayonets of the guards, the approach to a man's personality is barred by the dialectical cross of qualitative opposites in an ideal equilibrium.

What is true of the greater relationship and is very clear in the above circumstances, which is why they were instanced, is also true in a lesser degree of the smaller ones; and, once again, silence is the *conditio sine qua non* of all educated social intercourse. The more thoroughly a man grasps the ideal and the idea – in silence – the more capable will he be of reproducing man's daily life so that it seems as though he only talked of particular things at a certain distance. The less ideal, the more superficial his talk, and his conversation will become a meaningless repetition of names, of 'absolutely reliable' private information of what this and that person – mentioning all their names – had said, &c. &c., and conversation in general will take on a talkative confidential note about what one is doing or going to do, what one would have said on a certain occasion, which particular girl one is making love to, why nevertheless one does not want to marry. The introspection of silence is the condition of all educated social intercourse; the exteriorized caricature of inwardness is vulgarity and talkativeness.

One finds excellent examples of the kind of talkativeness I am referring to in the novel. It consists entirely of trivialities, people's names are always mentioned and they are people whose trivial way of life is interesting because of their names. People who are talkative certainly chatter away about something and, indeed, their one wish is to have an excuse for more gossip, but the subject is non-existent from the ideal point of view. It always consists of some trivial fact such as that Mr. Madsen is engaged and has given his fiancée a Persian shawl; that Petersen, the poet, is going to write some new poems, or that Marcussen, the actor, mispronounced a certain word last night. If we could suppose for a moment that there was a law which did not forbid people talking, but simply ordered that everything which was spoken about should be treated as though it had happened fifty years ago, the gossips would be done for, they would be in despair. On the other hand, it would not really interfere with any one who could really talk. That an actor should have mispronounced a word could only be interesting if there was something interesting in the mispronunciation itself, in which case the fifty years makes no difference – but Miss Gusta, for example, would be in despair, she who had been at the theatre that very evening, in a box with Alderman Waller's wife; for was it not *she* who noticed the slip and even noticed a member of the chorus smiling, &c. &c. It really would be a shame and cruelty to all those silly gossiping people who must all the same be allowed to live – and so the law is only posited.

With gossip, therefore, the vital distinction between what is private and what is public is obliterated, and everything is reduced to a kind of private-public gossip which corresponds more or less to the public of which it forms part. The public is public opinion which interests itself in the most private concerns. Something that nobody would dare to tell to a gathering, that nobody could *talk* about, and which even the gossips would not like to admit to having gossiped about, can perfectly well be written for the public and, as a member of the public, people may know all about it.

'On Principle'

What is *formlessness*? It is the result of doing away with the vital distinction between form and content. Formlessness may, therefore, unlike madness or stupidity, have a content that is true, but the truth it contains can never be essentially true. It will be capable of being extended so as to include everything or touch upon everything, whereas a real content is clearly, and, if one likes, miserably limited because of its intensity and self-absorption.

The universality of formlessness in a passionless but reflective age is expressed, moreover, not only by the fact that the most varied ideas are found dallying in the same company but by the diametrically opposite fact that people find a paramount longing for and pleasure in 'acting on principle'. A principle, as the word indicates, is what comes first, i.e. the substance, the idea in the undeveloped form of feeling and of enthusiasm which drives on the individual by its own inner power. That is entirely wanting in a passionless individual. To him a principle is something purely external for the sake of which he does one thing as willingly as another, and the opposite of both into the bargain. The life of an individual without passion is not the development of a self-revealing principle. On the contrary, his inner life is something hurrying along, always on the move and always hurrying to do something 'on principle'. A principle, in that sense, becomes a monstrous something or other, an abstraction, just like the public. And while the public is something or other so monstrous that not all the nations of the world and all the souls in eternity put together are as numerous, everyone, even a drunken sailor, can have a public, and the same is true of 'a principle'. It is something immense which even the most insignificant man can add to the most insignificant action, and thus become tremendously self-important. When an honest insignificant man suddenly becomes a hero for the sake of a principle, the result is quite as comic as though fashion decreed that everyone was to wear a cap with a peak thirty feet long. If a man had a little button sewn on the inner pocket of his coat 'on principle' his otherwise unimportant and quite serviceable action would become charged with importance – it is not improbable that it would result in the formation of a society.

It is acting 'on principle' which does away with the vital distinction which constitutes decency. For decency is immediate (whether the immediateness is original or acquired). It has its seat in feeling and in the impulse and consistency of an inner enthusiasm. 'On principle' one can do anything and what one does is, fundamentally, a matter of indifference, just as a man's life remains insignificant even though 'on principle' he gives his support to all the 'needs of the times', even when, by virtue of being a mute and in that capacity as 'the organ of public opinion' he is as well known as the figures on a barrel-organ that can move forward and bow, plate in hand. 'On principle' a man can do anything, take part in anything and himself remain inhuman and indeterminate. 'On principle' a man may interest himself in the founding of a brothel (there are plenty of social studies on the subject written by the health authorities), and the same man can 'on principle' assist in the publication of a new Hymn Book because it is supposed to be the great need of the times. But it would be as unjustifiable to conclude from the first fact that he was debauched as it would, perhaps, be to conclude from the second that he read or sang hymns. In this way everything becomes permissible if done 'on principle'. The police can go to certain places on 'official duty' to which no one else can go, but as a result one cannot deduce anything from their presence. In the same way one can do anything 'on principle' and avoid all personal responsibility. People pull to pieces 'on principle' what they admire personally, which is nonsensical, for while it is true that everything creative is latently polemical, since it has to make room for the new which it is bringing into the world, a purely destructive process is nothing and its principle is emptiness – so what does it need space for? But modesty, repentance and responsibility cannot easily strike root in ground where everything is done 'on principle'.

Superficiality

What is *superficiality* and the desire to show off? Superficiality is the result of doing away with the vital distinction between concealment and manifestation. It is the manifestation of emptiness, but where mere scope is concerned it wins, because it has the advantage of dazzling people with its brilliant shams. Real manifestation is homogeneous, because it is really profound, whereas superficiality has a varied and *omnium gatherum* appearance. Its love of showing off is the self-admiration of conceit in reflection. The concealment and reserve of inwardness is not given time in which to conceive an essential mystery, which can then be made manifest, but is disturbed long before that time comes and so, as a reward, reflection attracts the gaze of egotism upon its varied shams whenever possible.

Flirtation

What is *flirtation*? It is the result of doing away with the vital distinction between real love and real debauchery. Neither the real lover nor the real debauchee are guilty of flirting. A flirtation only toys with the possibility and is therefore a form of indulgence which dares to touch evil and fails to realize the good. To act 'on principle' is also a kind of flirtation, because it reduces moral action to an abstraction. But in mere scope flirtation has all the advantages, for one can flirt with anything, but one can only really love *one* girl. From the point of view of love, properly understood, any addition is really a subtraction (even though in a confused age a capricious man may be blinded by pleasure), and the more one adds the more one takes away.

Reasoning

What is *reasoning*? It is the result of doing away with the vital distinction which separates subjectivity and objectivity. As a form of abstract thought reasoning is not profoundly dialectical enough; as an opinion and a conviction it lacks full-blooded individuality. But where mere scope is concerned, reasoning has all the apparent advantage; for a thinker can encompass his science, a man can have an opinion upon a particular subject and a conviction as a result of a certain view of life, but one can reason about anything.

Anonymity

In our own day anonymity has acquired a far more pregnant significance than is perhaps realized: it has an almost epigrammatic significance. People not only write anonymously, they sign their anonymous works: they even talk anonymously. The very soul of a writer should go into his style, and a man puts his whole personality into the style of his conversation, though limited by the exception which Matthias Claudius noted when he said that if anyone conjured a book its *esprit* should appear – unless there was no *esprit* in it. Nowadays one can talk with anyone, and it must be admitted that people's opinions are exceedingly sensible, yet the conversation leaves one with the impression of having talked to an anonymity. The same person will say the most contradictory things and, with the utmost calm, make a remark, which coming from him is a bitter satire on his own life. The remark itself may be sensible enough, and of the kind that sounds well at a meeting, and may serve in a discussion preliminary to coming to a decision, in much the same way that paper is made out of rags. But all these opinions put together do not make one human, personal opinion such as you may hear from quite a simple man who talks about very little but really does talk. People's remarks are so objective, so all-inclusive, that it is a matter of complete indifference who expresses them, and where human speech is concerned that is the same as acting 'on principle'. And so our talk becomes like the public, a pure abstraction. There is no longer anyone who knows how to talk, and instead, objective thought produces an atmosphere, an abstract sound, which makes human speech superfluous, just as machinery makes man superfluous. In Germany they even have phrase-books for the use of lovers, and it will end with lovers sitting together talking anonymously. In fact there are hand-books for everything, and very soon education, all the world over, will consist in learning a greater or lesser number of comments by heart, and people will excel according to their capacity for singling out the various facts like a printer singling out the letters, but completely ignorant of the meaning of anything.

Thus our own age is essentially one of understanding, and on the average, perhaps, more knowledgeable than any former generation, but it is without passion. Everyone knows a great deal, we all know which way we ought to go and all the different ways we can go, but nobody is willing to move. If at last someone were to overcome the reflection within him and happened to act, then immediately thousands of reflections would form an outward obstacle. Only a proposal to reconsider a plan is greeted with enthusiasm; action is met by indolence. Some of the superior and self-satisfied find the enthusiasm of the man who tried to act ridiculous, others are envious because he made a beginning when, after all, they *knew* just as well as he did what should be done – but did not do it. Still others use the fact that someone has acted in order to produce numerous critical observations and give vent to a store of arguments, demonstrating how much more sensibly the thing could have been done; others again, busy themselves guessing the outcome and, if possible, influencing events a little so as to favour their own hypothesis.

Two English Noblemen

It is said that two English noblemen were once riding along a road when they met a man whose horse had run away with him and who, being in danger of falling off, shouted for help. One of the Englishmen turned to the other and said, 'A hundred guineas he falls off.' 'Taken,' said the other: With that they spurred their horses to a gallop and hurried on ahead to open the toll-gates and to prevent anything from getting in the way of the runaway horse. In the same way, though without that heroic and millionaire-like spleen, our own reflective and sensible age is like a curious, critical and worldly-wise person who, at the most, has vitality enough to lay a wager.

Life's existential tasks have lost the interest of reality; illusion cannot build a sanctuary for the divine growth of inwardness which ripens to decisions. One man is curious about another, everyone is undecided, and their way of escape is to say that someone must come who will do something – and then they will bet on him.

It is quite impossible for the community or the idea of association to save our age. On the contrary, association is the scepticism, which is necessary in order that the development of individuality may proceed uniformly, so that the individual will either be lost, or disciplined by such abstractions, will find himself religiously. Nowadays the principle of association (which at the most is only valid where material interests are concerned) is not positive but negative; it is an escape, a distraction and an illusion. Dialectically the position is this: the principle of association, by stregthening the individual, enervates him; it strengthens numerically, but ethically that is a weakening. It is only after the individual has acquired an ethical outlook, in face of the whole world, that there can be any suggestion of really joining together. Otherwise the association of individuals who are in themselves weak, is just as disgusting and as harmful as the marriage of children.

Formerly the sovereign and the great each had their opinion and the rest were satisfied and decided enough to realize that they dared not or could not have an opinion. Now everyone can have an opinion; but they have to band together numerically in order to have one. Twenty-five signatures make the most frightful stupidity into an opinion, and the considered opinion of a first-class mind is only a paradox. But when the context is meaningless it is useless to take a broad survey. The best that can be done is to consider each part of speech by itself. And if only nonsense comes out of a man's mouth it is useless to try and make a coherent speech, and it is better to take each word separately – and so with individuals.

Recognizable or Unrecognizable

The change which will come about is this. In the old order (which sprang from the relation between the individual and the generation) the officers, generals, heroes (i.e. the man of distinction, the leader within his own sphere) were *recognizable*, and everyone (in proportion to his authority, with his little detachment, fitted picturesquely and organically into the whole, both supporting and supported by the whole. From now on the great man, the leader (according to his position) will be without authority because he will have divinely understood the diabolical principle of the levelling process; he will be *unrecognizable*; he will keep his distinction hidden like a plain-clothes policeman, and his support will only be negative, i.e. repelling people, whereas the infinite indifference of abstraction judges every individual and examines him in his isolation. This order is dialectically the very opposite of that of the Prophets and Judges, and just as the danger for them lay in their authority not being recognized, so nowadays the unrecognizable is in danger of being recognized, and of being persuaded to accept recognition and importance as an authority, which could only hinder the highest development. For they are unrecognizable and go about their work like secret agents, not because of any private instruction from God! – for that is the case of Prophets and Judges – but are unrecognizable (without authority) because they have understood the universal in equality before God, and, because they realize this and their own responsibility every moment, are thus prevented from being guilty of thoughtlessly realizing in an inconsistent form this consistent perception. This order is dialectically the opposite of the organizing order symbolized in the outstanding personality, which makes the generation into a support for the individual, whereas now, like an abstraction, the generation is negatively supported by the unrecognizable, and turns polemically against the individual – in order to save every single individual religiously.

And so when the generation, which itself desired to level and to be emancipated, to destroy authority and at the same time itself, has, through the scepticism of the principle association, started the hopeless forest fire of abstraction; when as a result of levelling with this scepticism, the generation has rid itself of the individual and of everything organic and concrete, and put in its place 'humanity' and the numerical equality of man and man: when the generation has, for a moment, delighted in this unlimited panorama of abstract infinity, unrelieved by even the smallest eminence, undisturbed by even the slightest interest, a sea of desert; then the time has come for work to begin, for every individual must work for himself, each for himself. No longer can the individual, as in former times, turn to the great for help when he grows confused. That is past; he is either lost in the dizziness of unending abstraction or saved for ever in the reality of religion. Perhaps very many will cry out in despair, but it will not help them – already it is too late. If it is true that in former times authorities and powers were misused and brought upon themselves the nemesis of revolution, it was weakness and impotence which, desiring to stand alone, brought this final nemesis upon them. Nor shall any of the unrecognizable presume to help directly or to speak directly or to teach directly at the head of the masses, in order to direct their decisions, instead of giving his negative support and so helping the individual to make the decision which he himself has reached; any other course would be the end of him, because he would be indulging in the short-sighted compassion of man, instead of obeying the order of divinity, of an angry, yet so merciful, divinity. For the development is, in spite of everything, a progress because all the individuals who are saved will receive the specific weight of religion, its essence at first hand, from God himself. Then it will be said: 'behold, all is in readiness, see how the cruelty of abstraction makes the true form of worldliness only too evident, the abyss of eternity opens before you, the sharp scythe of the leveller makes it possible for everyone individually to leap over the blade – and behold, it is God who waits. Leap, then, into the arms of God.' But the 'unrecognizable' neither can nor dares help man, not even his most faithful disciple, his mother, or the girl for whom he would gladly give his life: they must make the leap themselves, for God's love is not a second-hand gift. And yet the 'unrecognizable' (according to his degree) will have a double work compared with the 'outstanding' man (of the same degree), because he will not only have to work continuously, but at the same time labour to conceal his work.

But the desolate abstraction of the levelling process will always be continued by its servants, lest it should end with a return of the old order. The servants of the levelling process are the servants of the powers of evil, for levelling itself does not come from divinity and all good men will at times grieve over its desolation, but divinity allows it and desires to bring the highest into relation with the individual, i.e. with each and every man. The servants of the levelling process are known to him who is 'unrecognizable', but he dare not use either power or authority against them, for that would be to reverse the development, since it would become immediately apparent to a third person that the 'unrecognizable' was an authority, and in that way the third man would be prevented from attaining to the highest.

Only by suffering can the 'unrecognizable' dare to help on the levelling process and, by the same suffering action, judge the instruments. He dare not overcome the levelling process directly, that would be his end, for it would be the same as acting with authority. But he will overcome it in suffering, and in that way express once more the law of his existence, which is not to dominate, to guide, to lead, but to serve in suffering and help indirectly. Those who have not made the leap will look upon his unrecognizable action, his suffering as failure; those who have made the leap will suspect that it was victory, but they can have no certainty, for they could only be made certain by him, and if he gave that certainty to a single person it would be the end of him, because he would have been unfaithful to the divinity in desiring to play at being authority: that would mean that he had failed; not only by being unfaithful to God in trying to use authority, but because he did not obey God and teach men to love one another by compelling himself, so that even though they begged him to do so he should not have deceived them by exerting authority.

But I break off. All this is only fooling, for if it is true that every man must work for his own salvation, then all the prophecies about the future of the world are only valuable and allowable as a recreation, or a joke, like playing bowls or cards.

But it must always be remembered that reflection is not in itself something harmful, that, on the contrary, it is necessary to work through it in order that one's actions should be more intensive. The stages of all actions which are performed with enthusiasm are as follows: first of all comes immediate enthusiasm, then follows the stage of cleverness which, because immediate enthusiasm does not calculate, assumes with a calculating cleverness the appearance of being the higher; and finally comes the highest and most intensive enthusiasm which follows the stage of cleverness, and is therefore able to see the shrewdest plan of action but disdain it, and thereby receive the intensity of an eternal enthusiasm. For the time being, however, and for some time to come, this really intensive enthusiasm will remain completely misunderstood, and the question is whether it can ever become popular, i.e. whether one may presume upon such a degree of cleverness in the average man that cleverness will no longer seduce and enchant him, and may presume that he will be able to dominate it by having attained the highest form of enthusiasm, but as it were squander it – for an enthusiastic action, being always the opposite of shrewd, is never obvious. The enthusiasm of Socrates was not immediate. On the contrary, he was clever enough to see what he had to do in order to escape, although he disdained to act according to that opinion, just as he refused the proffered speech. That is why there is nothing obvious about his heroic death, and even in death he remained ironical by putting to the shrewd and the clever the question whether he could really have been clever, since he did the reverse. That is the point at which cleverness is left hanging in mid-air, hoist with its own reflective judgement and that of the world about it, afraid that an action performed in the teeth of cleverness may be confused with an action performed without cleverness. An immediate enthusiasm does not know such a danger, and therefore requires the *impetus* of the most intense enthusiasm in order to get through life. Such an enthusiasm is not mere rhetorical twaddle about 'high seriousness', a still 'higher seriousness' and an 'all highest seriousness'. It can be known from its category: that it acts against understanding. Neither does immediate goodness know the danger of reflection – where goodness and weakness are mistaken and confused; and it is precisely for that reason that, after reflection, it requires a religious *impetus* to set goodness afloat again.

In our times, when so little is done, an extraordinary number of prophecies, apocalypses, glances at and studies of the future appear, and there is nothing to do but to join in and be one with the rest. Yet I have the advantage over the many who bear a heavy responsibility when they prophesy and give warnings, because I can be perfectly certain that no one would think of believing me. So I do not ask that anyone should make a cross in their calendar or otherwise bother to see whether my words are fulfilled. If they are fulfilled, then people will have something else to think about than my accidental being and if they are not fulfilled, well, then I shall simply be a prophet in the modern sense of the word – for a prophet nowadays means to prognosticate and nothing more. In a certain sense a prophet cannot do anything else. It was providence that fulfilled the words of the older prophets, so perhaps we modern prophets, lacking the addition coming from providence, might say with Thales: what we predict will either happen or not; for to us too has God granted the gift of prophecy.

6. Scheherazade

It is terrible when I think, even for a single moment, over the dark background which, from the very earliest time, was part of my life. The dread with which my father filled my soul, his own frightful melancholy, and all the things in this connection which I do not even note down. I felt a dread of Christianity and yet felt myself so strongly drawn towards it.

And later on what I suffered through Peter, when he became morbidly religious.

As I have said, it is terrible to think, at moments, of the life I led in the hidden centre of my heart, of course literally never a word breathed to anyone, not even daring to note down the least thing about it – and that I was able to clothe that life with an outwardly lively and cheerful existence.

How true are the words I have so often said of myself, that as Scheherazade saved her life by telling fairy stories I save my life, or keep myself alive by writing.

7. I am again myself

When Regine Olsen got engaged to Fritz Schegel in June 1843, she wrecked the subtle dialectical intentions of Repetition, *in which 'repetition' was held out as a possi-*

bility. Now there was no such possibility. Kierkegaard was so irate that he went straight to the printers and pulled out the last ten pages of the work, and substituted an ad hoc, *adventitious conclusion to the book. That is why the book cannot, finally, be interpreted* coherently, *since the original design was destroyed by the writer. The various warring terms in the text are deprived of a context.*

What the Young Man feels, though, in this dramatic moment is reflected variously in the last letters of the book: relief, to be rid of the problem; contempt, to be treated so cavalierly; infuriation, that so much literary planning (on Fear and Trembling *as well as* Repetition*) had been rendered otiose by the actions of a wounded and headstrong girl.*

Yet, in spite of all the recrimination and the heart-ache, the dominant feeling is sheer relief. Abraham and the Knight of infinite resignation, they had both, then, after all, made the right choice. Now the writer was free to serve his calling. For this freedom, it was necessary to leave behind the temporal cares of the ethical man, the married man, and the world of human love. Wild with relief to be free of the human, Kierkegaard steps, like his own 'Antigone', into the silence and loneliness of the tomb.

MY SILENT CONFIDANT:

She is married – to whom I do not know, for when I read it in the paper it was as though I had a touch of apoplexy, and I lost the notice and have not had patience to make a closer inspection. I am again myself, here I have the repetition, I understand everything, and existence seems to me more beautiful than ever. It came as a thunderstorm after all, though I owe its occurrence to her magnanimity. Whomever she has chosen (I will not even say 'preferred,' for as a husband every man is preferable to me), she has at any rate showed magnanimity toward me. Though he were the most beautiful man in the world, a paragon of amiability, capable of enchanting every girl, and though she may have brought the whole sex to despair by giving him her 'Yes,' she nevertheless has acted magnanimously toward me – if in no other respect, at least by forgetting me completely. What is so beautiful as feminine magnanimity! Let the earthly queen of beauty fade, let the luster of her eyes be dimmed, let her erect figure be bent by the weight of years, let her curls lose their fascinating power when they are hidden by the humble coif, let her royal glance which swayed the world now embrace and watch over with motherly love the family circle she protects – a girl who has been so magnanimous never grows old. Let existence reward her as it has, let it give her what she loved more – it gave me also what I loved more . . . myself, and gave it through her magnanimity.

I am again myself. This self which another would not pick up from the road I possess again. The discord in my nature is resolved, I am again unified. The terrors which found support and nourishment in my pride no longer enter in to distract and separate.

Is there not then a repetition? Did I not get everything doubly restored? Did I not get myself again, precisely in such a way that I must doubly feel its significance? And what is a repetition of earthly goods which are of no consequence to the spirit – what are they in comparison with such a repetition? Only his children Job did not receive again double, because a human life is not a thing that can be duplicated. In that case only spiritual repetition is possible, although in the temporal life it is never so perfect as in eternity, which is the true repetition.

I am again myself, the machinery has been set in motion. The snares in which I was entangled have been hewn asunder, the magic spell which bewitched me so that I could not return to myself has now been broken. There is no one any more who lifts up her hands against me, my liberation is assured, I am born to myself, for so long as Ilithia folds her hands one who is in travail cannot bring to birth.

It is over, my yawl is afloat, the next minute I am where my soul's yearning was, where the ideas foam with elemental rage, where thoughts arise boisterously like the nations in migration, where at another season there is a stillness like the profound silence of the South Sea, so that one can hear oneself speak even though the movement goes on in one's own interior – there where one every instant stakes one's life, every instant loses it, and wins it again.

I belong to the idea. When that beckons me I follow, when it appoints a tryst I await it day and night, no one calls me at midday, no one awaits me at supper. When the idea calls I forsake everything, or rather I have nothing to forsake, I deceive nobody, I grieve nobody by being faithful to the idea, my spirit is not grieved by having to grieve another. When I return home no one reads in my looks, no one deciphers in my countenance, no one extorts from my being an explanation which not even I can give to another, as to whether I am blissful in gladness or despondent in distress, as to whether I have gained life or have lost it.

The chalice of inebriation is again held out to me, already I inhale its fragrance, already I am sensible of its foaming music – but first a libation to her who saved a soul which sat in the solitude of despair. Hail to feminine magnanimity! Long life to the high flight of thought, to moral danger in the service of the idea! Hail to the danger of battle! Hail to the solemn exultation of victory! Hail to the dance in the vortex of the infinite! Hail to the breaking wave which covers me in the abyss! Hail to the breaking wave which hurls me up above the stars!

8. The laughter is on my side

Something wonderful has happened to me. I was caught up into the seventh heaven. There sat all the gods in assembly. By special grace I was granted the privilege of making a wish. 'Wilt thou,' said Mercury, 'have youth or beauty or power or a long life or the most beautiful maiden or any of the other glories we have in the chest? Choose, but only one thing.' For a moment I was at a loss. Then I addressed myself to the gods as follows: 'Most honorable contemporaries, I choose this one thing, that I may always have the laugh on my side.' Not one of the gods said a word; on the contrary, they all began to laugh. From that I concluded that my wish was granted, and found that the gods knew how to express themselves with taste; for it would hardly have been suitable for them to have answered gravely: 'Thy wish is granted.'

LIST OF SOURCES

PART ONE

Epigraph: 'I have just returned...', from *The Journals of   Kierkegaard 1834-1854,* translated and edited by Alexander   Dru (Oxford University Press, 1938), p.27. Reprinted by   permission.

1. 'It is now about four years ago...', from *Concluding Unscientific Postscript,* translated by David Swenson & Walter Lowrie (Princeton, Princeton University Press, 1941), pp.164-6.

2. 'A walk on the heath...', from *Søren Kierkegaard's Journals and Papers,* edited and translated by Howard V. Hong and Edna H. Hong (Bloomington, Indiana University Press, 1967-78), Vol. II, p.259.

3. 'A man should never lose his courage...', from *Either/Or,* translated by D.F. & L.M. Swenson (New York, Doubleday Anchor Books, 1959), Vol. I, pp.26-7.

4. 'July 29. As one goes...', from *The Journals of Kierkegaard, 1834-1854,* pp.12-13.

5. 'Without letting anybody know...', from *Repetition, An Essay in Experimental Psychology*, translated by Walter Lowrie (New York, Harper Torchbooks, 1964), pp.54-7

6. 'Letters home...', from *Kierkegaard: Letters and Documents,* translated by Henrik Rosenmeier (in *Kierkegaard's Writings*, Vol. XXV) (Princeton, Princeton University Press, 1978), pp.98-100, 100-1.

7. '*The Talisman* was to be performed...', from *Repetition*, p.73-7.

8. 'Dear Reader: I wonder if...', from *Either/Or*, Vol. I, pp.3-7.

9. 'Starting from a principle...', ibid., pp.281-96.

10. 'One ought to be a mystery...', ibid., p.26.

11. 'One must be very naïve...', ibid., p.32.

12. 'As a humorist exists...', from *Concluding Unscientific Postscript*, pp.402-3.

13. 'These two familiar strains...', from *Either/Or*, Vol. I, pp.29-30.

14. 'If we apply this explanation...', ibid., pp.118-19.

15. 'If you marry...', ibid., pp.37-39.

16. 'The demonaical is *shut-up-ness*...', from *The Concept of Dread*, translated by Walter Lowrie (Princeton University Press, 1944, 1957), pp.110-12, 114-15;
    and
    'The demonaical is the sudden...', ibid., pp.115-18.

17.   'Every child knows...', from *Stages on Life's Way*, translated by Walter Lowrie (London, Oxford University Press, 1945), pp.181-5.

18.   'Dear Jette, *Above all*...', from *Kierkegaard, Letters and Documents*, pp.214-15.

19.   'Dear *Conferentsraad*...', ibid., pp.252-5.

20.   'All this fear of Germany...', from *The Journals of Kierkegaard 1834-1854*, p.230.

21.   'It is a miserable existence...', ibid., pp.282-3;
       and
       'The second time I talked ...', ibid., pp.283-6;
       and
       'The third time I visited him ...', ibid., pp.286-9.

22.   'That is the old story...', ibid., p.379.

Part Two

Epigraph: 'I do not maintain...', from *The Journals of   Kierkegaard 1834-1854*, pp.334-5.

1.   'In Gribs Forest...', from *Stages on Life's Way*, pp.60-7.

2.   'Constantine spoke as follows...', ibid., pp.60-7.

3.   'Hardly had Victor finished...', ibid., pp.76-80.

4.   'Thereupon Johannes the Seducer...', ibid., pp.81-8.

5.   'They rose from the table...', ibid., pp.88-92.

6.   'May 19. Half past ten...', from *The Journals of Kierkegaard 1834-54*, p.59.

7.   'Yes, my good wise man...', from *Either/Or*, Vol. II, pp.313-15.

8.   'I suppose that when...', from *Crisis in the Life of an Actress*, translated by Stephen Crites (London, Collins, 1967), pp.67-91.

Part Three

Epigraph: 'Do you not know...', from *Either/Or*, Vol. II, p.164.

1.   'It is extraordinary...', from *The Journals of Kierkegaard 1834-1854*, pp. 117-118
      and
      'The way of tribulation...', ibid., p.215.

2.   'Why was I not born...', from *Either/Or*, Vol. I, p.39.

3.   'As I tried to show...', from *The Journals of Kierkegaard 1834-1854*, pp.15-20.

4.   'Once upon a time...', from *Fear and Trembling*, translated by Walter Lowrie (New York, Doubleday/Anchor Books 1954), pp.26-9.

5. 'Problem I: Is there such a thing...', ibid., pp.64-5, 66-7, 69-73, 76-7.

6. 'But now as for Abraham...', ibid., pp.121-9.

7. 'I candidly admit...', ibid., pp.49-56.

8. 'But back to Socrates...', from *Concluding Unscientific Postcript*, p.222, pp.250-1.

9. 'My life has been brought to an impasse ...', from *Repetition*, pp.104-8;
    and
    'Job! Job! Job! Job! ...', ibid., pp.101-3.

PART FOUR

Epigraph: 'What I do lack...', from *The Corsair Affair*, translated by Howard V. Hong and Edna H. Hong (in *Kierkegaard's Writings*, Vol. XIII) (Princeton University Press, 1982), p.226.

1. 'Perhaps I may venture to offer...', from *Concluding Unscientific Postscript*, p. 174-5.

2. 'Almost everything that flourishes...', from *The Journals of Kierkegaard 1834-1854*, pp.181-4.

3. 'There is no use at all...', ibid., pp.185-6.

4. 'As I was walking down the street...', from *Kierkegaard, Letters and Documents*, pp.259-64;
    and
    'First a little story...', ibid., pp.267-71;
    and
    'It was indeed a remarkable year...', ibid., pp.299-301.

5. 'Our age is essentially one...', from *The Present Age*, translated and edited by Alexander Dru and W. Lowrie (London, Collins, Fontana Library, 1962), pp.33-99. (First published by Oxford University Press, 1944; reprinted with permission.)

6. 'It is terrible when I think...', from *The Journals of Kierkegaard 1834-1854*, p.274.

7. My silent confidant. She is married...', from *Repetition*, pp.125-7.

8. "Something wonderful...', from *Either/Or*, Vol.I, pp.41-2.